Child Therapy in the Great Outdoors

RELATIONAL PERSPECTIVES BOOK SERIES

Volume 29

RELATIONAL PERSPECTIVES BOOK SERIES

LEWIS ARON AND ADRIENNE HARRIS
Series Editors

Child Therapy in
The Great Outdoors

A Relational View

Sebastiano Santostefano

THE ANALYTIC PRESS

2004   Hillsdale, NJ   London

Published by
The Analytic Press, Inc., Publishers
Editorial Offices:
101 West Street
Hillsdale, NJ 07642

www.analyticpress.com

Design, typesetting, photographs* by
Christopher Jaworski, Bloomfield, NJ
qualitext@verizon.net

*Mount Desert Island, Maine (p. i), Brookdale Park, Essex County, New Jersey
(p. iii), Niagara Parks Botanical Gardens, Ontario, Canada (pp. v, vii, 1, etc.).
Copyright © 1991, 2002, 1992, respectively, by Christopher Jaworski.

Typefaces: 11/13 Hoefler, Arial

Index by Leonard S. Rosenbaum,
Indexing and Abstracting Services
Washington, DC

Library of Congress Cataloging-in-Publication Data

Santostefano, Sebastiano, 1929–
    Child therapy in the great outdoors : a relational view /
    Sebastiano Santostefano
      p. cm. (Relational perspectives book series ; v. 29)
    Includes bibliographical references and index
    ISBN 0–88163–426–3
    1. Child psychotherapy. 2. Psychotherapist and patient.
    3. Nature, Healing power of. I. Title

    RJ504.S254 2004
    618.92'8914—dc22

                                                          2004057871

Printed in the United States of America
10 9 8 7 6 5 4 3 2 1

Contents

Acknowledgments

Gratitude and appreciation go to my wife, Susan, who joined me, after I stepped down from my position at McLean Hospital and Harvard University Medical School, in organizing, launching, and directing the clinical, training, and research programs of the Institute for Child and Adolescent Development (ICAD). I am grateful, too, to the Board of Directors of the Institute for their guidance and commitment to ICAD's mission: Patricia Burke, Ph.D., Janet Cantalupo, Jim Dow, Julia Ganson, M.S.W., Peter Randolph, M.D., Douglas Reed, of ASLA. I also express my appreciation and thanks to Bridget O'Connell and Lindsay MacAuley for their devoted and skillful participation in the research projects we have conducted in various community-based sites, including our collaboration with Dr. Maria Angeles Quiroga Estevez, who is supervising psychological services provided to children living in Children's Villages in Spain because they were abandoned or their parents were unable to provide them with adequate care. In addition, I owe Lindsay and Bridget many thanks for their assistance in the preparation of this volume. I am also especially grateful to the parents of Vera and Ernest for giving me permission to describe how their children participated in treatment, descriptions that I believe bring alive the concepts and techniques I describe. Last, I am grateful to the many colleagues from whom I have learned as I have tried to contribute to their training and development, notably Dr. Patricia Burke, Dr. J. Scott Creighton, Dr. Asimina Panayoutou, and Dr. John Calicchia and Cabriella Martinez Fontz, who composed the drawings depicting enactments by Ernest and Vera that make up the figures in chapters 2 and 3.

I conclude by acknowledging La Famiglia, which over the years has continued to grow within in spite of storms without: Damon, Natalie, Stephanie, Jessica, and Cristiano. And to our Sebbie, whose brilliant flight continues in another world.

Introduction

Concepts that are being increasingly emphasized by psychoanalytic-relational theorists have had a nonverbal, visceral influence on me for decades. In the 1950s, when I attended a graduate school program in clinical psychology, the students were assigned undergraduates who had applied for treatment. One of my cases, a member of the varsity wrestling team, asked from time to time if we could walk around outside while discussing his concerns. I agreed to participate with him in this way and noticed that the thoughts and feelings he experienced and expressed when interacting with me while we walked were different from those he expressed while we sat in the office. My supervisor, representing a view still maintained in many quarters that therapy should take place in an office, advised me to analyze within myself why I had agreed to go outdoors with this student.

After receiving my doctorate, I participated in a two-year postdoctoral fellowship in clinical child psychology at the University of Colorado Medical Center. I soon began twice weekly sessions with a seven-year-old boy within the psychoanalytic tradition, to which I had made a commitment. As treatment got underway, I noticed that his affect was very flat, and a robotic-like quality characterized the way he interacted with me. I wondered to myself if, in spite of the excellent care he had been receiving from an aunt, what I observed was related in some way to his mother's dying during the third year of his life.

In the late 1950s, the psychoanalytic camp was paying little attention to the significance of interactive experiences that occur during the first years of life; psychoanalysis was, instead, focusing on how children resolve their oedipal conflicts. Instead of making interpretations, however, I invited this boy to play games with me outdoors. We played hide-and-seek, each of us taking turns searching for the other, and we played Simon Says, each of us taking turns imitating the movements and gestures of the other.

When I reviewed these sessions with my supervisor, who was an excellent psychoanalyst, he repeated a comment he made whenever I described such sessions with other children. "As I told you, I do not know what you are doing, but I do know that what you are doing is not psychotherapy." My supervisor and I had not yet come across London's (1964) proposal that therapy that integrates action and insight might be more effective than an approach that emphasizes only one of these modalities.

After completing my postdoctoral training, I was offered a faculty appointment at the University of Colorado Medical Center, where a group of psychoanalysts, among them Rene Spitz, John Benjamin, and Gaston Blom, had organized child clinical and research programs. I was invited to participate in a study of monozygotic twins in which I was able to express my early interest in embodied meanings and the issue of enacting embodied metaphors. One assessment method I devised involved asking each twin (with the other absent) to stand on one of two wooden boxes that were identical except that one box was half the height of the other. With each pair of twins, I found that one twin stood on the taller box and the other on the shorter box. Significantly, this behavior correlated with observations made independently by other members of the research team who were conducting observational play sessions with each pair of twins. The twin who was observed during these play sessions to be more dominant and assertive when interacting and playing with his or her sibling stood on the taller box.

Several years later, I moved to Massachusetts to begin psychoanalytic training at the Boston Psychoanalytic Institute. I simultaneously joined the faculty at Clark University, where I had the benefit of becoming familiar with Heinz Werner and his organismic developmental theory. Following this experience, I accepted a faculty position at the Boston University Medical Center, where, in addition to conducting my own research, I participated in Louis

Sander's psychoanalytically oriented investigation of the interacting and negotiating that takes place between infant and caregiver, a model described in this volume.

The initial integration of my psychoanalytic training and developmentally oriented research resulted in, for example, studies investigating ways to assess how unconscious meanings are expressed in actions (e.g., Santostefano, 1965a, b, 1970; Santostefano and Wilson, 1968) and studies of the developmental relations among the modalities of taking action, fantasizing, and verbalizing (e.g., Santostefano, 1977). Those experiences influenced my proposal that principles of infant development can provide an heuristic guide for conducting child psychotherapy (Santostefano and Berkowitz, 1976).

Subsequently at Boston University Medical Center and during the two decades I devoted to directing a child and adolescent program at McLean Hospital while serving on the faculty of the Harvard University Medical School, my research activities continued to be integrated with my clinical work. For example, I reported a review of the free association method within the context of the concept of developmental levels for expressing meanings (Santostefano, 1976); a study of how children and adolescents who did or did not injure themselves or attempt to commit suicide differed in the ways in which they organized and expressed movement in fantasies (Santostefano, Rieder, and Berk, 1984); studies related to metaphor (Santostefano, 1985), and how the concepts of relational psychoanalysis served in the treatment of hospitalized, aggressive children (Santostefano and Calicchia, 1992).

While I was completing my adult and child psychoanalytic training in the early 1970s, these various research experiences also influenced how I participated during treatment sessions. For instance, one of my analytic cases, a very successful businessman, arrived for each session with a piece of paper on which he had written a list of items he wanted to discuss. For weeks the many and various interpretations I made were not successful in helping him put his paper to one side and free-associate. In one session, because I felt that we had developed a solid alliance, I spontaneously introduced an "active technique." I asked him to get off the couch and, using a ruler, carefully line up each of the window shades hanging from the five windows in my office so that the bottom of each shade was the same distance from the window sill as all the others. He chuckled and complied, joking, "You're crazy, Seb, but I trust you know what you're doing." After lining up the shades, he returned to the couch, took out his sheet of paper, and continued discussing his agenda as usual.

I included the "window shade" technique for the next seven or eight sessions. Then in one session, after he had lined up the window shades, I asked him to do something else before he returned to the couch. I demonstrated, pulling the shade down a few inches and then releasing it, which resulted in the shade's quickly snapping and rolling upward. He complied and did the same with the remaining shades. I noticed that he was much more anxious than was typical during the moment just before he took hold of the shade and snapped it up.

That night he was awakened by a "nightmare" that he reported the next day. He dreamt that he was falling through black space and throwing his arms about in a desperate attempt to find something to clutch and stop his fall. From this session on, the doors that had been tightly shut, sealing off his inner world, were thrown open. In the next weeks we interacted and analyzed issues related to trauma he had endured as a child. Of course, when I presented this case at a seminar, many eyebrows were raised. Fortunately, however, a few psychoanalysts supported what I was trying to do because they also had a relational orientation.

Given the opinions about child therapy and development that were developing within me, illustrated by these clinical and research anecdotes, you will understand why I was very pleased when the viewpoint of relational psychoanalysis gained momentum, as reflected, for example, by Mitchell's (1988) volume and by the launching of The Analytic Press's Relational Perspectives Book Series. The emerging school of relational psychoanalysis has championed the ideas of interaction, participation, negotiation, mutuality, and enactment, concepts defining therapeutic technique in ways that provided me with tools to articulate my views of how child psychotherapy should be conducted and understood.

I hope this volume contributes to elaborating the psychoanalytic-relational viewpoint as it applies to child psychotherapy. I propose that children who are participating in treatment sessions be invited to make use of various locations, including the outdoors. They should be allowed to engage the therapist in a wide range of interactions that eventually give rise to the child's enacting embodied meanings representing the conflict with which he or she is struggling. Accordingly, I describe how a therapist can participate in

these enactments in authentic ways and conceptualize the relationship that child and therapist construct to include the physical locations in which they interact and the meanings they assign to these
locations.

Although I frame my proposal from the conceptual viewpoint of
relational psychoanalysis, I am obliged to address how it relates to
the schools of environmental psychology and ecopsychology, both of
which emphasize the importance of location. While it is likely that
most psychoanalytically oriented child psychotherapists are not familiar with how environmental psychology and ecopsychology conceptualize environments, it is my impression that many are also not
aware of the shift occurring within psychoanalysis toward a relational
viewpoint, an opinion expressed by others: "With few exceptions the
child's psychoanalytic world was, until recently . . . seemingly unaffected by the relational turn in the literature" (Altman et al., 2002).
My goal here is to cultivate interest in the contributions that psychoanalytic-relational psychology can make to guide technique in child
psychotherapy, including a conceptualization of the role played by
environments in the therapeutic relationship.

The emphasis I give to locations in which child and therapist interact, and the meanings they give to these experiences, corresponds
to research and theoretical models proposing that all meanings given
to both nonstressful and stressful interactions are constructed during childhood from experiences with one's body and from interactions between one's body and the bodies of others, as well as with
animate and inanimate environments. That embodied meanings
form a critical part of the foundation of psychological development,
then, draws attention to and converges with the importance of the
location in which therapy takes place. A typical playroom, with its
games and toys, offers a narrow range of textures, temperatures,
sounds, contours, elevations, movements, emotional tones, and smells,
as well as a narrow range of ways in which child and therapist can participate when interacting.

In contrast, the outdoors, hallways, and stairwells make available
a wider range of attributes with which the child can interact and onto
which a child can project meanings that he or she and the therapist
can negotiate. Multiple environments provide the child with more
opportunities to relive and master stressful events than does the
landscape of an office or a playroom. In short, the mission of this
volume is to demonstrate that environments in which child and

therapist interact and participate, plus the relationship they develop and the embodied meanings they enact together, provide *the path that leads to the pathway of change*.

I recognize that proposing that treatment take place outdoors and in hallways, as well as in an office, may very likely strike most mainstream psychoanalytically oriented child therapists as peculiar, if not ridiculous. After all, psychoanalytic child psychotherapists have long held the view that the playroom is a holy temple in which therapy should take place, and interpretations of a child's play make up the holy grail that produces change. I believe these therapists will discover in what follows that core ingredients of the process of psychotherapy are expanded when enactments of embodied meanings, expressed during interactions with various environments, are integrated within the therapeutic process.

Inasmuch as I am especially interested in engaging psychoanalytically oriented child therapists, a piece of history might prevent them from walking away before considering what I have to say. Sigmund Freud treated the composer Gustav Mahler during walks they took together, and he provided a single psychoanalytic session to another person while they hiked over a mountain trail (Gay, 1998). Of course, inasmuch as therapists following the viewpoints of ecopsychotherapy already believe in the healing power of nature, they might take my proposal for granted and also look no further. I hope they discover in what follows that many important issues are not considered in the current views of nature-guided therapies.

Another issue raised by my proposing that treatment take place in various environments applies to child therapists of all persuasions. Conducting psychotherapy in locations that include the outdoors invites children to enact meanings by expressing vigorous, physical activity and intense emotions in ways that do not typically occur in a playroom or office. A therapist would be required, therefore, to participate in ways that are not typical, certainly for mainstream psychodynamically oriented therapists. For therapists interested in how and why enacting embodied meanings with children in various environments promotes significant change, this volume makes available material I believe should be considered.

In chapter 1, I discuss several topics related to why enacting embodied life-metaphors during treatment with children, instead of engaging in verbal discussions, has the most power to resolve the impact of trauma and promote change. I conceptualize a child's self to include the meanings the child has given to experiences with human and nonhuman environments with which the child has interacted. I discuss how traumatic experiences disrupt this self and interfere with further development. I also describe why enacting embodied meanings instead of interpretation is necessary to resolve at the embodied level the impact that is interfering with the child's development.

In chapters 2 and 3, I illustrate my proposal by describing the treatment of two children, Ernest and Vera, each presenting with major behavioral and emotional difficulties. Having been made aware that they could make use of my office, the hallways, and a Therapeutic Garden, in addition to a playroom, these children differed significantly in when and how they ventured outside the playroom. Ernest immediately engaged a cavelike area outdoors and other locations. In contrast, Vera made use of the playroom, my office, and hallways for more than a year before she ventured outdoors. Accordingly, each child enacted in ways that highlight the significance of locations used during treatment.

I am aware that, when reviewing these treatment cases, many child psychoanalysts and psychodynamically oriented child therapists may view as "nonanalytic" my participation in the enactments that Ernest and Vera performed. Here a comment by Freud (1912) is relevant. He noted, "This technique is the only one suited to my individuality; I do not venture to deny that a physician quite differently constituted might find himself driven to adopt a different attitude to his patients and to the task before him" (p. 111). As Greenberg (1995) points out, unfortunately Freud "rarely told us what it was about himself that shaped his technique" (p. 2), except for one detail cited most often in the literature; namely, Freud preferred that patients lie on a couch because he disliked being stared at and because he could better reflect on his own thoughts and feelings as the patient free-associated. As to how the technique I am advocating is suited to my individuality, I have reported elsewhere (Santostefano, 1998a) aspects of my makeup and life experiences that influenced a program of developmental research related to the form of child psychotherapy I propose, which requires very active participation by the therapist.

How these children interacted with me and the relationships we formed when outdoors or in the playroom, office, and hallways raise a number of questions. Does the geography in which treatment takes place play a role in the relationship that child and therapist construct, how they participate, and the meanings they negotiate? Is the sequence of locations in which a child participates during the course of treatment of any significance? Does physical interaction between child and therapist promote less or more change than do discussions and interpretations? And, when a child engages the therapist in physical interactions in various locations, does the child symbolize conflicts and meanings at a developmental level that differs from that which prevails when the child and therapist use toys and discuss issues in a playroom?

In response to these questions, after describing how these children participated in treatment, in chapter 4 I summarize two schools of thought: environmental psychology, which emphasizes the person-in-the-environment as the unit of study, and the emerging field of ecopsychology, with its nature-guided therapies. Then, from the viewpoints of environmental psychology and ecopsychology, I examine the treatment process each child constructed and ask psychoanalytic-relational psychology to critique these formulations from its point of view. With this critique, I attempt to show that, while environmental psychology and ecopsychology contribute to an understanding of the importance of place and the use of the outdoors in psychotherapy, they leave unanswered important questions about the treatment process that relational psychoanalysis could address. In chapter 5, I describe a psychoanalytic-relational model to guide child psychotherapy, and in chapter 6 I discuss several important topics this model brings into focus.

A Tour of the Therapeutic Garden

My presentation of treatment cases described in this volume emphasizes when and how each child made use of particular locations in the clinic's facility and in a Therapeutic Garden. This garden has been used by many children and the staff of the Institute for Child and Adolescent Development (ICAD) during treatment sessions over the course of more than 10 years. ICAD is a nonprofit diagnostic and treatment center founded to serve children and adolescents who suffer from a variety of emotional, cognitive, and behavioral difficulties resulting from stressful or traumatic experiences. The construction of the Therapeutic Garden, depicted in a topographic, schematic drawing in Figure 1, was funded by Judith Pillsbury and Henry

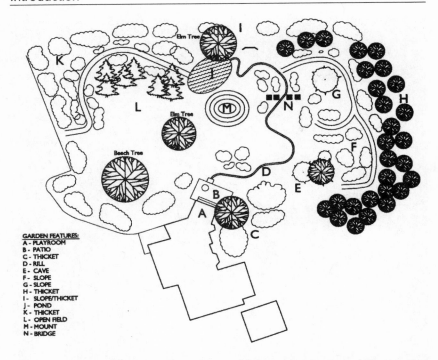

FIGURE 1   Schematic drawing of the Therapeutic Garden at the Institute for Child and Adolescent Development. By Stefano Ventresca.

Pillsbury through the Pillsbury United Communities (Minneapolis Foundation) to whom I express my gratitude. The garden was designed by Douglas Reed, a member of the American Society of Landscape Architects (ASLA), with whom I have discussed the psychological significance of environments for several years, discussions I very much appreciate. In designing the garden, the goal was to make available a range of natural features that could result in experiences that might help a child enact embodied meanings and emotions, especially those the child may not be able to express verbally. ASLA issued the 1997 President's Award of Excellence to the ICAD Therapeutic Garden (Dunwell, 1997).

Our tour begins in the playroom (Figure 1, area A; Figure 2), which is bordered by large windows on two walls and large glass doors on a third wall that lead into the garden. From the playroom the garden is always in view, and a child decides whether or not and when he or she leaves the playroom to enter the garden. On entering the garden, the child steps onto a stone-and-lawn terrace (Figure 1, area B;

FIGURE 2   Playroom leading to the Therapeutic Garden.

Figure 3) and comes upon a granite basin with water bubbling over its sides. The water travels underneath the terrace in stainless steel pipes, emerges on the other side of a fieldstone wall that borders the terrace, and, pouring into a rill that winds through the garden, eventually flows into a pond (Figure 4). This rill, the main organizing

FIGURE 3   Stone-and-lawn terrace with fountain at entrance of the Therapeutic
Garden.

element of the garden, is intended to encourage children to follow it
and explore the landscape. On its way to the pond, the rill passes a
cave formed by a deep indentation in the side of a hill and by a canopy
of large hew bushes (Figure 1, area E). If a person is sitting in the cave,
the rill and other areas of the garden can be seen through the
branches of the bushes (Figure 5). Between the terrace and the pond
is a mount about 10 feet in height (Figure 6).

The outer edge of one side of the garden that borders the cave
area and the pond consists of an elevated slope approximately 20 feet
at its highest point from ground level (Figure 1, areas F, G, H, and I).
Along the upper edge of this slope, pathways travel through trees and
thick bushes (Figure 7). The other half of the garden consists of a
large open glade (Figure 1, area L) with a large beech tree and oak tree
in the center and evergreen trees and bushes surrounding the periphery. Pathways also run through this area (Figure 1, area K; Figure 8).
As described by Dunwell (1997), "the plants, the preexisting trees,
and the various landforms are masterfully layered in such a way that
the entire garden is never revealed from any single vantage point.
The design encourages children to discover the garden's magic . . . by
emerging themselves in the landscape" (p. 47).

FIGURE 4   Rill winding through the Therapeutic Garden.

FIGURE 5   View of the Therapeutic Garden from the cave.

FIGURE 6   View of the mount from the terrace.

FIGURE 7   Pathway through the upper slope (areas F and G).

The rippling rill, pond, elevations, and many plants allow for a wide range of visual, olfactory, tactile, kinesthetic, and auditory experiences. I realize that child therapists typically do not have access to a therapeutic garden adjoining the building in which their offices are located. Nonetheless I urge them to make every effort to determine if a nearby park, street, alleyway, or open field is accessible, making available various locations in which a child can interact and experience a range of embodied metaphors, experiences that this volume demonstrates hold the power to resolve a child's difficulties at the embodied level.

FIGURE 8   Pathway through periphery of open glade (area L).

1 Interacting and Enacting with a Therapist and Environments

The Path to the Pathway of Change

The mission of this volume is to encourage child psychotherapists to consider and accept a position, framed within the viewpoint of relational psychoanalysis, that mutually negotiating and enacting embodied life-metaphors, which represent a child's conflicts, has more power to promote change than do discussing and interpreting these conflicts. To set the stage, in this chapter I begin with a historical sketch to point out that, when child psychotherapy was launched, it inherited the view from classical psychoanalysis that children overcome their conflicts when they can express in words the thoughts, meanings, and emotions representing these difficulties. I discuss how this position is contradicted by developmental research demonstrating that, during the first years of life, as a child negotiates developmental needs and issues, the meanings the child gives to these experiences are constructed and expressed, not with words but, rather, with nonverbal language that includes rhythms of gestures, facial expressions, tactile and kinesthetic perceptions, actions, postures, and emotional tones experienced by the child while interacting with others.

Relying on several developmental models, I describe how, as a child engages in dialectical interactions with others and with nonhuman environments within which they are interacting, the meanings the child constructs from these experiences are integrated to form the child's unique *matrix of embodied life-metaphors,* which, in turn, becomes an integral part of the child's self and represents how developmental issues and needs have been negotiated with human and nonhuman environments. I compare my constructivistic definition of nonhuman environments with that offered by others which follows the positivistic assumption that nonhuman environments inherently contain stimulation independent of the person interacting with it. I also describe how this matrix of embodied life-metaphors remains in the child's mind from the first years of life and spirals throughout development, prescribing how a child interprets ongoing interactions and, at the same time, undergoing revisions based on these experiences. Along the same lines, I discuss how traumatic experiences affect a child's matrix of embodied life-metaphors, disrupt the ability of the self to experience and see the possibilities for positive experiences that are available, and guide the child to seek interactions with human and nonhuman environments that provide opportunities to reexperience stimulation and emotions associated with past trauma.

Since embodied meanings remain in the mind, I argue that all the difficulties a child brings to treatment have roots in embodied life-metaphors. Accordingly, I propose that, to help a child overcome these difficulties, a therapist should use body language when enacting traumatic meanings with a child, as well as when enacting solutions to the quandaries they present. These several considerations converge into the school of relational psychoanalysis, a point of view emphasizing that a person is motivated by meanings given to interactions rather than biological drives and that the treatment process should involve both patient and therapist, mutually participating, negotiating, and interacting and providing the patient with new experiences and the opportunity to revise meanings that guide how she or he participates in relationships.

Since the First Days of Child Psychotherapy, Words Have Been Viewed as the Language Necessary to Express Meaning and Promote Change

The focus on verbalizing as the vehicle for promoting change during psychotherapy is rooted in the origin of classical psychoanalysis formulated by Freud. These roots appear to have influenced all the schools of psychotherapy that emerged years later.[1] In brief, as most of you are aware, with classical psychoanalytic treatment of adults, the patient lies on a couch and expresses in words whatever thoughts and feelings come to mind. Gradually the patient experiences fantasies, wishes, urges, and emotions that are projected onto the person of the analyst. The analyst remains out of view and anonymous, as much as possible, so as to facilitate the development of these transference experiences. The analyst also offers interpretations, pointing out how these previously unconscious conflicted feelings, fantasies, and motivations the patient is experiencing toward the analyst stem from experiences with other people in the past, and how they influence the patient's interactions in the present. It is assumed that the knowledge generated by these interpretations provides the patient the ability to regulate behavior and emotions in more constructive and growth-fostering ways.

Of special relevance to my proposal is that within this model Freud (1900), relying on the reflex-arc as it was understood at the time, conceptualized a sharp distinction between words and actions (see also Renik, 1993). From this viewpoint, impulses are channeled along one of two pathways: the efferent pathway, which leads to motor activity and action, or the afferent pathway, which leads to stimulation of the sensory systems and results in thoughts and fantasies. A person, therefore, either acts or thinks. Accordingly, Freud viewed particular actions by the patient in everyday life or in treatment sessions as helping the patient to avoid discussing memories, fantasies, and emotions, and also as interfering with the patient's gaining the power provided by knowledge. Therefore, "to get people to analyze their impulses, [Freud proposed that] the analyst first has to get them to stop acting on these impulses" (Aron, 1996, p. 192).

Soon after Freud launched his concepts and techniques, the approach gave rise to the treatment of children. Even in this application, emphasis was given to the importance of expressing fantasies, emotions, and motivations in words. Beginning in 1913, just one year after Freud (1912) published his seminal papers describing technical

---

[1]Excellent discussions of classical psychoanalysis and recent changes in concepts and techniques can be found in Aron (1996), Frank (1999), Greenberg (1995), and Mitchell (1991, 1994).

recommendations for practicing psychoanalysis, Hermine Hug-Hellmuth, the originator of play therapy, invited children to free-associate not on the couch but on the floor while playing (Benveniste, 1998). During the decades that followed, although playing with toys continued to be the method used in treatment, the importance of children's expressing their fantasies and feelings in words also continued to be emphasized. For example, Anna Freud (1965) proposed that a child "gains its victories and advances whenever [conflicts] are grasped and put into thoughts or words" (p. 32). Similarly, Erik Erikson (1964) noted, "Children . . . need to be induced by systematic interpretation to reconsider, on a more verbal level, the constellations that have overwhelmed them in the past" (p. 265).

The emphasis on verbalizing conflicts and interpretations continued for years, whether authors described traditional psychodynamic approaches to child therapy (e.g., Coppolillo, 1987) or interpersonal approaches (e.g., Spiegel, 1989). For example, Coppolillo (1987), echoing Anna Freud and Erik Erickson, noted, "The therapist has a powerful tool in tackling the task of inducing the child to express conflicts in verbal terms" (p. 245). Similarly, after discussing the treatment of a child to illustrate how play and enactments serve to express thoughts and feelings, Van Waning (1991) states that a child therapist "must seek to learn how to bring about a shift from expressions in direct action to expressions in thought and words. . . . The ability to verbalize may give [the child] the opportunity to exercise some control over his actions and to understand his motivations better" (p. 548).

Cognitive-behavioral therapies appear to have inherited the view that change is promoted primarily with words. For instance, Knell (1995) proposes an integration of cognitive-behavioral methods and play to treat children. Although noting that "therapy must be more experiential than verbal" and "the child should be allowed to interact without the need for complicated language skills" (p. 28), Knell highlights the importance of language, which bears the stamp of classical child psychoanalysis:

Therapeutic intervention [involves] encouraging . . . the child's language to describe experiences and emotions . . . teaching youngsters . . . how to say it in words instead of behavior may be a beginning in helping them deal with their feelings. . . . Labeling the aggression . . . can offer the child some other, more adaptive way of dealing with his frustration and anger [pp. 28–29].

Similarly in horticultural therapy (e.g., Stamm and Barber, 1978) and ecopsychotherapy (Burns, 1998), which emphasize that contact with outdoor environments facilitates a shift from personal turmoil to pleasurable experiences, patients are encouraged to describe to their therapists, or to think about privately, the particular features of nature that bring pleasure.

For classical psychoanalytic therapy, then, verbalizing was and continues to be viewed by many as the main vehicle for expressing thoughts and feelings, resolving conflict, and promoting change. As Greenberg (1995) points out, although Freud's emphasis on free-associating and interpreting may well have been valid in his time and place, nonetheless, it has traveled "across oceans and decades to contemporary practice" (p. 2). I have already sketched how, in my view, Freud's emphasis on verbalizing meanings given to experiences has also landed on the shores of psychoanalytic child therapy and cognitive-behavioral and nature-guided therapies. Yet, when we consider how meanings are given to experiences and expressed during the first years of life, we are reminded that words typically play no role at all. Before we consider how infants and children construct and express meanings, let us review the process of meaning-making.

How Meaning Is Given to an Experience: The Triad of Experiencing, Knowing, and Representing

For decades investigators have proposed that all activity involves the construction of meanings in addition to the acquisition of information (Overton, 1994b). To give meaning to an event, a person experiences the event according to the properties that belong to something else (Billow, 1977; Ortony, 1979). In this process, the meaning a person experiences is termed the referent; how the meaning gains expression is termed the vehicle (Smith, 1979). Once a meaning is constructed, it can be expressed by any one of three modalities or by a combination: physical actions and gestures, images and fantasies, and spoken words. When constructed, a meaning synthesizes a person's present and past experiences with the objects in question. Consider, for example, a 20-month-old watching mother place a hat on her head and leave the house, saying, "See you later, sweetie." Sitting in a highchair with a nanny nearby, the child places a napkin on her head as mother has done many times in a play ritual. This behavior integrates the vehicles of action and imaging to synthesize properties of past experiences with mother and napkins, and present experiences with mother and her hat, as well as tactile sensations caused by the napkin on the child's head. Here the toddler is experiencing and representing in action the meaning, "Although my mother is absent, I can maintain her presence on me and in me with this hat."

That anecdote illustrates that having an experience is connected simultaneously with knowing about and giving meaning to the experience. The triad of experiencing, knowing, and symbolizing is holistic, contextual, and embodied, integrating patterns of sights, smells, sounds, actions, tactile and kinesthetic perceptions, and spoken words. From this sketch of how experiences are symbolized, we come to a question of central importance in child psychotherapy. How are meanings constructed in the first years of life, and what types of meanings do infants and toddlers construct? The answers to these questions become especially important if we accept the developmental principle that early meanings are not replaced by later meanings but become integrated within them (Werner and Kaplan, 1963; Johnson, 1987; Aron and Anderson, 1998). The meanings a child experiences and expresses during treatment, therefore, have their roots in the first years of life.

The Body in the Mind: How Meanings Are Constructed During the First Years of Life

The first model defining the meanings that a child gives to experiences during the first years of life, and the circumstances that allow these meanings to influence later development, was proposed by Freud (1916, 1923, 1933). We are familiar with his model defining stages in the construction of meanings in terms of experiences children have with the body zone, which Freud conceptualized as the vehicle symbolizing experiences during particular ages: oral stage, anal stage, and phallic stage. Fast (1992) notes that, by proposing that mental functioning originated in bodily experiences, Freud was successful in rejecting the segregation of mind and body that had plagued European thought from the time of the classical Greek philosophers. But his view that infants are oblivious to the environment, and sensitive only to stimulation from the body, has been dismissed by the results of infant research (Piaget, 1952; Sander, 1964, 1987, 1989; Stern, 1985).

These investigators have articulated a view of how meanings given to experiences are constructed during the first years of life much more complex than that presented by Freud's psychosexual stages. Collectively, the findings of these investigators demonstrate that, in addition to infants' body sensations, their interactions and negotiations with the bodies of other persons, physical objects, and locations also make major contributions. Moreover, these investigators offer to child psychotherapy a way of conceptualizing how interacting with various locations and the body and person of the therapist become extensions of the first embodied meanings.

Jean Piaget's Model: How Cognition Copies and Symbolizes Body Experiences

In his pioneering research, Piaget (1952; Flavell, 1963) drew attention to how infants construct knowledge, give meaning to experiences, and develop an understanding of environments. Piaget's well-known model conceptualized that infants engage in cycles of activity he termed circular reactions that become elaborated during the first two years of life (Table 1–1).

During the first month, the infant's activity results in a variety of bodily sensations (e.g., sucking, tongue movements, tactile perceptions, sounds, smells) when contacting his or her own body, the bodies of others, and things in the environment. Although these cycles of activity are initially uncoordinated, they result in the beginnings of mental representations of bodily experiences. From the second to the fourth month, the infant's cycles of activity begin to coordinate meanings involving two or more modalities. The infant sucks her or his thumb not because of chance contact but by coordinating hand and mouth; the baby relies on mental schemas that derived from previous experiences with each of these body parts. From five to eight months, the infant's activity is focused on provoking responses from others to make interesting experiences last, as Piaget put it,

TABLE 1–1

How Meanings Are Constructed in the First Years of Life: The Body in the Mind

Mo.	*Piaget— Cognitive Development*	Mo.	*Stern— Self-Development*	Mo.	*Sander—Infant (I) and Mother (M) Negotiations*
0–1	*Acquired adaptation.* Cycles of activity result in a variety of bodily sensations and the beginnings of mental representations.	0–2	*Emergent self.* Bodily experiences and emotions interrelate when interacting with caregiver and things.	0–3	*Initial adaptation.* I's cues and M's responses to them become coordinated.
2–4	*Primary circular reactions.* Rhythmic cycles of activity coordinating schemas of experiences with different senses and body parts.	3–7	*Core self.* Summarizing and conserving representations of interactions that are repeated with others (RIGs); experiencing oneself as separate from others.	4–6	*Reciprocal exchange.* I and M take turns being active and passive during emotional-behavioral exchanges.
5–8	*Secondary circular reactions.* Provoking responses from others to make interesting experiences last; registering intentions in one's self and others.	8–14	*Subjective self and intersubjective relatedness.* Defining oneself and others in terms of actions and emotions that are shared; understanding motives that guide actions.	7–9	*Early directed activity.* I initiates interactions and anticipates a response; M accommodates.
				10–15	*Focalization.* I directs M in more differentiated ways to meet needs, including M's unconditional availability.

Age	Description
9–12	*Coordinate secondary circular reactions.* Coordinating activities to deal with new solutions; imitate actions of others with behaviors that are analogous.
13–18	*Tertiary circular reactions.* Performing actions that become play rituals; discovering new ways of accomplishing goals.
19–24	*Experimenting with mental representations of things.* Imitating persons that are absent—deferred imitation.
15–24	*Verbal self.* Infant and caregiver share personal knowledge with verbal language as well as action symbols they coauthored.
24–36	*Narrative self.* Sharing, conveying and discussing with others the content of one's private representational world with action and language symbols.
12–20	*Self-assertion.* As I individuates, I asserts self in opposition to M; M gives permission and sets limits.
18–24	*Testing aggression.* I's assertions become explicitly aggressive behaviors; M punishes, permits, and provides alternatives.
24–36	*Modifying aggressive intentions.* I develops various ways for expressing assertiveness and accepts alternative goals.
12–36	*Inventing shared symbolic behaviors.* By inventing and sharing symbols, I and M solidify their relationship and participate in mutual regulation.
0–36	*Consolidate body image.* I develops perceptions of body sensations and a body image.

Adapted from Santostefano (1998).

and begins to be oriented beyond the body-self. For example, the infant deliberately imitates a sound or movement performed by another so that the other person will continue interacting with the infant by making that sound or movement. In a related way, the infant begins to show that he or she experiences intentions in herself or himself and in others. Toward the end of the first year of life (9 to 12 months), cycles of activity are coordinated to deal with new situations and imitate actions of others with behaviors that are analogous rather than identical. For example, when Piaget opened and closed his eyes, the infant first opened and closed his hand and then his mouth.

During the first half of the second year of life, the infant's cycles of activity are intended to establish play rituals and to discover new ways of accomplishing a goal; and during the second half, the toddler's cycles of activity now rely more on mental experimentation than on trial-and-error actions. Another development that is a hallmark of this stage involves the capacity for what Piaget termed deferred imitation. When an important person or thing is absent, the toddler reproduces the person or thing in some way, showing that she or he is capable of symbolizing by transferring properties from one object to another. The toddler I mentioned earlier, who placed a napkin on her head when mother put on a hat and left, is an example.

Daniel Stern's Model: Developing a Sense of Self

The model proposed by Daniel Stern (1985) centers on the role of emotions and interpersonal interactions in constructing meanings and in an infant's developing a sense of self (see Table 1–1). To illustrate this proposal, it might be interesting to consider one of Piaget's observations of his two-month-old child, an example he offered to illustrate the characteristics of primary circular reactions.

> [The infant] scratches and tries to grasp, lets go [repeatedly] observed [only] during feeding time when the infant gently scratches his mother's bare shoulder—[also] the infant scratches the [bed] sheet, then grasps it and holds it a moment, then lets it go . . . and repeats the cycle without interruption. This play lasts a quarter of an hour at a time, several times during the day [cited in Flavell, 1963, pp. 93–94].

With this observation, Stern would focus on the relation between the infant's rhythmic scratching of mother's shoulder and bed sheet, emotions he experienced during these moments, and how meanings constructed during these interactions with human and nonhuman environments give rise to a sense of self and others.[2] Stern also proposed that, if a child interacting with others and things repeatedly experiences constellations of sensations, perceptions, emotions, and actions that differ in only minor ways, he or she gradually constructs a generalized memory of these experiences that prescribes what to expect and how to interact. Stern conceptualized this accumulation of meanings of similar experiences as representations of interactions (that have) generalized (RIGs).

What happens when an interaction occurs that is similar in many respects to a RIG that has already been constructed but, at the same time, differs in particular ingredients? The ongoing experience activates the related RIG, which is compared with ingredients unique to the ongoing interaction, a process Stern called the "evoked companion." Evoked companions, always operating during interactions with others, enable the child to determine whether a given interaction is going as expected or whether a major ingredient has changed. As an example, consider a mother who has played peekaboo many times with her child, but today, depressed, is playing peekaboo in a different way. In response, the infant compares the already established RIG, representing previous peekaboo episodes with mother, with the way mother is now playing peekaboo and experiences a salient difference in mother's emotional tone and body movements. If this particular interaction is repeated a number of times, the infant constructs a new RIG representing mother's depressed tone and sluggish motions, which collides with the other representation of mother's emotional tone and movements, possibly resulting in the child experiencing conflict.

Evoked companions also operate when the child is alone. Consider a toddler who when alone stacks blocks and then bursts with exuberance. The child's exuberance stems from an evoked memory

---

[2]Later in his career, Piaget (1973) suggested that he had come to the same view, that early cognitive development is embedded in interpersonal experiences. "I also suggested . . . that the first object endowed with permanence was another person, and not an indifferent inanimate object" (p. 260).

of stacking blocks as an enthusiastic caregiver cheered. You may notice that the concept of evoked companion is similar to Piaget's (1952) concept of "deferred imitation," which, Piaget proposed, emerges at about 18 months. Stern (1985) argues that the process emerges at three months. Last, in Stern's model, the process of constructing RIGs and using evoked companions to evaluate experiences plays a major role in the infant's developing, during the first three years of life, five "senses of self," each building on the previous one and organizing experiences in a new way.

Emergent self (0 to 2 months). The first global sense of self emerges during the first two months of life as the infant interrelates bodily experiences and emotions that occur within his or her body and when interacting with caregivers and things.

Core self (3 to 7 months). The infant summarizes and conserves repeated interactions with others involving constellations of actions, sensations, and emotions (RIGs). These representations enable the infant to anticipate what should be expected in interactions with others and to determine whether an ongoing experience is the same as or different from previous ones. In addition, the infant begins to sense that she or he and the caregiver are physically separate, each having unique emotional experiences.

Subjective self and intersubjective relatedness (8 to 14 months). The infant defines himself or herself and other persons in terms of physical actions, emotions, and mental states they do and do not share. In addition, the infant begins to understand the motives that lie behind and guide interactions.

Verbal self (15 to 24 months). Interactions between infant and caregiver include personal knowledge of each other that is expressed and shared with verbal symbols, in addition to action symbols, which the infant and caregiver construct together.

Narrative self (24 to 36 months). Equipped with both action and verbal symbols constructed during interactions with others, the toddler enacts, shares, and discusses the contents of his or her private, representational world.

Louis Sander's Model:
Issues Mother and Infant Negotiate

The model proposed by Louis Sander (1962, 1964, 1987, 1989) elabo-rates in significant ways the proposals of Piaget and Stern. Sander's model conceptualizes the interpersonal issues that infant and care-giver negotiate that contribute to the meanings an infant constructs, representing interactions, and influence how an infant moves physi-cally; expresses emotions; and seeks, engages, and avoids interac-tions with others. The success that mother and infant achieve in negotiating one issue influences the success with which the next is-sue is negotiated. Although Sander defined these negotiations as tak-ing place between infant and mother, other persons who are involved in the infant's care are also viewed as partners in these negotiations (see Table 1–1).

Initial adaptation (o to 3 months). During the first three months, the infant enacts cues about his or her physical and emotional state at the moment (e.g., various cries, fussing, being content). In response, mother coordinates, for example, the way she holds, feeds, and baths the infant. If this first issue is successfully negotiated, the infant devel-ops a predictable rhythm of sleeping and wakefulness and begins to re-spond to mother in discriminating ways, quieting for her more readily than for others. On mother's side of the coin, success with negotiating this issue is reflected in her developing a sense that she "knows" her child and distinguishing between what is unique about her child and her projections of what she would prefer the child to be.

Reciprocal exchange (4 to 6 months). Mother and infant negotiate taking turns being active and passive; for instance, mother smiles and pauses, allowing the baby to respond; then she moves her smiling face closer, adding a touch and new sounds. In response, the baby adds new giggles and movements. The rhythmicity with which mother and child respond to each other, and the emotional crescen-dos they share during feeding, bathing, and changing, define the suc-cess with which this issue is negotiated.

Early directed behavior (7 to 9 months). To this point interactions between mother and infant have been initiated for the most part by mother. Now the baby, anticipating a particular response, begins to use smiles and gestures to initiate and direct interactions with mother. In addition, the baby shows preferences for certain types of stimulation by actively trying to control or avoid particular stimulation. To contribute to a successful negotiation of this issue, mother should remain more passive than she was during the previous periods and, at the same time, honor the infant's directions for particular experiences. Notice that negotiating this issue is much like Piaget's (1952) third stage, in which the infant provokes responses from the environment in order to make interesting experiences last.

Focalization (10 to 15 months). The child becomes physically more mobile, exploring larger spaces and sending more differentiated cues to mother that concern the need to explore the unknown and to be protected from stressful stimulation. In response, mother may sometimes contact the child physically and at other times give only her complete attention. In short, the infant is negotiating that mother be unconditionally available, an important prerequisite for developing autonomy. If mother provides an optimal degree of focalization, while maintaining the reciprocity negotiated earlier, the child, beginning to explore increasingly larger geographies with competence, individuates and asserts himself or herself against mother and the larger environment, a process that is the focus of the next period.

Self-assertion (12 to 20 months). Negotiating self-assertion emerges gradually midway through the previous phase as the toddler, who is now just beginning to walk, cultivates the beginning of a sense of autonomy and shows more negativism, possessiveness, and exhibitionism. In response, mother attempts to set limits and also gives permission both physically and with emotional reactions. Mother's responses may vary in consistency and the imagination she uses in suggesting alternatives (e.g., if the child refuses to wear a particular hat, mother offers a suitable alternative). To negotiate self-assertion successfully, and to make further gains in autonomy, the child should experience that at least some of his or her victories in being self-assertive are accepted.

Testing aggression (18 to 24 months). While negotiating self-assertion, the child gradually becomes explicitly aggressive toward persons and things. For example, expressing a sense of achievement with an emotional exclamation or body posture, the child attempts to destroy a toy or pushes her plate of food off the high chair to the floor. At the same time, the child may attempt to "make up" with mother by initiating an activity that pleases her or by undoing the aggressive act. During negotiations, mother should distinguish among aggressive intentions the child displays (e.g., biting in play versus in anger), coordinate her responses accordingly, and allow alternative aggressive behaviors (e.g., the toddler bangs a toy hammer against the refrigerator; mother sets an old pan nearby and invites the child to hammer it instead). Mother should also provide the child with opportunities to make up by repairing or witnessing the repairing of some damaged object, responses that set the stage for negotiating the modification of aggressive intentions.

Modifying aggressive intentions (24 to 36 months). If a flexible range of opportunities for aggressing has been opened, the child's aggressive intentions and behaviors are gradually modified. The child develops multiple ways to express assertiveness, accepts alternative goals as satisfying a particular aggressive intention, internalizes parental standards for aggressing, renders more realistic his or her sense of omnipotence, and begins to test these standards with other people. If the toddler's aggressive intentions are effectively negotiated, the child does not surrender ambition and assertiveness, attributes that facilitate future participation in relationships.

Inventing symbolic behaviors during interactions (12 to 36 months). While toddler and caregiver are negotiating self-assertion, testing aggression, and modifying aggressive intentions, they are developing ways of communicating through symbolic behaviors (body postures, gestures, facial expressions, emotional tones, verbal metaphors), negotiating whether and how they coauthor symbols during interactions and play. If this negotiating is successful, the child internalizes action and verbal symbols that have been invented in interactions with mother. By coauthoring symbols they share, child and mother solidify their relationship and increase their understanding of the other's intentions and of the alternatives they can use to participate in mutual exchanges.

Consolidating a body image (0 to 36 months). Throughout the first three years of life, the child negotiates and constructs a body image, expresses curiosity in his or her body and the bodies of others, and engages in assertive, exhibitionistic, seductive, and autostimulating behaviors. Parents respond with interest, stimulation, and prohibitions, engaging in play and discussions about the body and body parts. Throughout these transactions the child develops perceptions of body sensations, cognitive schemas representing body parts, and a body image.

Beebe and Lachmann's Three Developmental Principles

Beebe and Lachmann (2002) postulate three principles that operate during interactions between an infant and a caregiver that establish the foundation of how an infant gives meanings to experiences.

The principle of ongoing regulation. Ongoing regulation consists of two interrelated systems: self-regulation by the infant and mutual regulation by infant and caregiver. With self-regulation, infants gradually construct mental schemas representing interactions that guide what they expect in their interactions with caregivers. Stern's (1985) concept of RIGs and Piaget's (1952) concept of sensorimotor schemas are examples. With mutual regulation, an infant and a caregiver develop expectations that regulate their interactions and guide how each is affected by and affects the other. Sander's (1962, 1964) concept of the issues that infant and caregiver negotiate and Stern's (1985) concept of evoked companion are examples of mutual regulation. Ongoing regulation also involves a dialectic between self-regulation and mutual regulation. During face-to-face, playful interactions between infants and their mothers, investigators observed that, at the moment before looking away, the infants' heart rates increased sharply, suggesting that they were stressed by the level of stimulation taking place. After the infants looked away, their mothers lowered stimulation, and the infants' heart rates decreased. The same behavior, then, with which the infants regulated their arousal (i.e., looking away) served to regulate the interaction with their mothers.

The principle of disruption and repair. Some interactions fail to fulfill what an infant expects from mother. Beebe and Lachmann report studies showing that as early as the second month of life, infants and mothers match their behaviors (e.g., facial expressions, body movements) only about 30 percent of the time, whether they are interacting in real-life situations or in experimentally designed conditions. However, when mothers and infants enter a state of disruption, they return to mutual regulation within two seconds about 70 percent of the time. Infants as young as two months of age have been observed using such behaviors as smiling and head turning to repair disruptions created by a nonresponsive mother. Infants who had many opportunities to successfully repair disruptions during the first months of life showed more secure attachments with others and a greater sense of competence at one year of age than did infants who had not had many opportunities.

The principle of heightened affective moments. Some supercharged emotional interactions can influence in unique ways the representation of a particular interaction, an issue that relates to trauma. An adult patient, for example, remembered a physical sensation that he termed a "stick in the tushie." Later it was learned that this sensation referred to a lumbar puncture the person had experienced at the age of six months. Beebe and Lachmann propose that a highly emotionally charged interaction can shape a representation because the experience cannot be averaged with other, similar experiences.

The three principles, bodily experiences, and internalization. Consistent with the conceptions of Piaget (1952), Stern (1985), and Sander (1962, 1964), Beebe and Lachmann emphasize that the body is involved in everyday interactions between infant or toddler and caregiver, and that representations of these interactions influence how interactions are represented later in life, a position consistent with embodiment theory to which we turn next.

Mark Johnson's Model: The Body in the Mind

Mark Johnson (1987; Lakoff and Johnson, 1999) also proposes that "body image schemas" are constructed during the first years of life and represent bodily experiences and interactions with others. Johnson suggests that these early body-based meanings are "metaphorically projected," influencing meanings we give to experiences later in life. Accordingly, the body remains in the mind; it forms the foundation of all meanings experienced and expressed later. To illustrate this idea, a child negotiated individuation and self-assertiveness with a play ritual that involved running to the top of a flight of stairs leading to a doorway, stopping, and then bursting into laughter. Each time he was yanked back by anxious parents and sometimes slapped. Now, as a teenager in treatment sessions, when describing his experiences before a school exam, he clutched the arms of his chair and felt "very much on the edge," a linguistic metaphor he eventually connected to his early bodily experiences at the top of the stairs. Discussing how all linguistic symbols derive from bodily experiences, Benveniste (1998) reminds us of the many conventional statements that demonstrate this notion—for example, "This relationship is suffocating" and "He bit off more than he could chew."[3]

Enacting Embodied Life-Metaphors: How a Child Expresses and Negotiates Developmental Issues and Needs

We have so far considered how bodily experiences and interactions with persons and things contribute to an infant's or toddler's constructing the first meanings, and how later in development these body-based meanings spiral into what a child does, fantasizes, and verbalizes. To conceptualize these embodied meanings in ways that serve child psychotherapy, I have proposed the concept of enacting "embodied life-metaphors" (Santostefano, 1988, 1994, 1995, 1998a). Although you may be familiar with the concept of metaphor, I believe we should pause for a moment to consider the purpose served

---

[3]Aron and Anderson (1998) elaborate the significance of bodily experiences and expressions for psychotherapy.

by expressing a metaphor and the particular vehicle used to express it, because this matter relates to my proposal that enacting metaphors is the major language child and therapist should use.

Typically, the purpose served by metaphors has been considered from the vantage point of meanings expressed with the vehicle of words. Aristotle (cited in Ortony, 1979), for example, proposed that metaphors are ornamental, making verbal exchanges less dull. While agreeing with Aristotle, others argued later that these ornaments distort meaning, that language should convey only facts. In sharp contrast, Ortony (1979) proposed that metaphors are "necessary" rather than "nice" and serve several important functions: they condense information, reconstruct experiences, and lie closer to a person's bodily experiences than do words. Of the vehicles used to express metaphors, a spoken sentence is typically assumed to be the exclusive mode (Ortony, Reynolds, and Arter, 1978), a position seen in writings on the use of metaphor in psychotherapy (e.g., Witzum, van der Hart, and Friedman, 1988). Disagreeing with this position, Billow (1977) underscores the need to study metaphor construction in the process of play and imaging and wondered if metaphor construction is an example of imaged thinking. Along the same lines, Verbrugge and McCarrel (1977) have proposed that metaphors invite pretending and imaging and "may be basic to all growth and understanding, whether in the playroom, the psychotherapeutic setting, the scientific laboratory, or the theater" (p. 495), a position with which I agree.

Referring to the models of development discussed earlier, I consider sensorimotor schemas, RIGs, negotiating issues, and embodied image schemas as integrated in the process of constructing the first nonverbal editions of embodied life-metaphors. I propose that, when child and therapist enact pathological, embodied life-metaphors, they "become" and "live" the meaning of an embodied life-metaphor. Thus, they make use of a powerful tool to resolve the embodied impact of early traumatic experiences.

A Definition of Embodied Life-Metaphors: Embodied Plans for Action

Phenomenologically, an embodied life-metaphor is an organized constellation of bodily and touch sensations, actions, rhythms of

gestures and dialogue, facial expressions, images, and emotions that
represent past interactive experiences with human and nonhuman
environments constructed while particular interactive/intrapersonal
issues and needs are being negotiated—for example, attachment/
trust/love, loss/detachment, separation-individuation, dependence–
autonomy, safety–risk taking, initiating–reciprocating, deferring–
dominating, asserting/competing, self-love–idealizing others.

The Origins of Embodied Life-Metaphors

The first edition of an embodied life-metaphor emerges beginning at
about 8 to 12 months, when a child organizes and repeats nonverbal
play rituals that serve to negotiate developmental issues. For a play
ritual to give rise to an embodied life-metaphor, the infant should
have achieved the following developmental landmarks: reached Piaget's (1952) fifth stage of cognitive development during which ter-
tiary circular reactions uncover new ways of accomplishing goals and
become play rituals; constructed the beginnings of Stern's (1985) subjective self within which the infant comes to understand the motives
of others and is able to share meanings; negotiated Sander's (1962,
1964) issues of reciprocal exchange and directed activity and become
involved in negotiating focalization, and self-assertiveness, conveying more differentiated directions to caregivers; and distinguished
whether the disruption of a negotiation was repaired or allowed to
remain ruptured. The first edition of an embodied life-metaphor un-
dergoes a series of revisions throughout childhood. With each revision, the child negotiates a series of interrelated meanings at the levels
of action, fantasy, and language, each building on previous editions.
This process of representing, enacting, and revising a revolving series
of representations of interpersonal interactions spirals throughout
childhood and adolescence (Overton, 1994a; Santostefano, 1994, 1998a).

An Illustration of the Development of
Embodied Life-Metaphors

To illustrate the development of embodied life-metaphors in a relatively normal context, and how each edition builds on previous
ones, consider these observations. At 18 months, a child repeated

the following play ritual for a number of weeks. He sat on father's lap and directed him to button and then unbutton his shirt around the boy's body. Then the toddler slipped off father's lap and scampered away, while father played at searching for him. Enacted at the dawn of symbolic functioning, the first edition of an embodied life-metaphor was being constructed and negotiated: attachment (at one with father's body) and separation-individuation (running off while father searched for him).

About a year later the child initiated another play ritual that elaborated the meaning of attachment–separation to include allegiance. Now the child insisted he sit immediately next to father at mealtime and gradually extended this seating arrangement to the family car, restaurants, and the homes of relatives.

During the first months of his third year, the child introduced another edition, now including negotiating self-assertion while retaining a positive identification with father. The child requested that during mealtimes he use a glass identical to father's and that the amount of water or milk poured into each glass be exactly the same. After drinking, child and father placed the glasses side by side and carefully judged which glass contained "bigger" or "smaller" amounts.

Relying on the previously negotiated issues, the child engaged father a few years later in playing checkers; he negotiated competition against the idealized parent. And still later he engaged father in debates over the relative merits of the hometown professional basketball team versus those of a team located in a state where father had spent his childhood.

That anecdote illustrates Overton's (1994a) "arrow of time," describing interrelated changes that take place in the construction and expression of embodied meanings. Applied to our example, each new cycle of activity did not return to the original starting point but spiraled, moving the system of child and father toward greater complexity and resulting in new patterns of interacting that reflected increased differentiation, integration, and flexibility—for example, from "I am in you and also separate from you" to "I am by your side" to "Who is bigger or smaller?" to "Who is the greatest?"

As illustrated by this anecdote, the concept of embodied life-metaphors also includes the sequence in which modalities participate in the construction and expression of embodied meanings. Initially, the vehicles a child uses to construct and share a meaning entail primarily bodily sensations, movements, perceptions, and gestures (e.g., the "shirt" game). Gradually, fantasy differentiates as a modality and assimilates actions and gestures (e.g., the glasses in the fantasized drinking game represented the persons of the boy and father). And, still later, linguistic metaphors emerge as a modality assimilating fantasy and action (e.g., the debate over the merits of two basketball teams, each representing child and father). With this example I turn now to discuss how I integrate the process of a child's enacting and negotiating embodied life-metaphors into the process of how the child constructs his or her psychological self and defines environments.

A Child's Self: The I-Self and the Me-Self and the Matrix of Embodied Life-Metaphors

As Wolfe (2003) notes, although the concept of self has become "one of the hottest topics in psychology and psychotherapy, there is still a lack of clarity regarding what the term means" (p. 84). Of the many theories that have been presented to conceptualize the self, I rely on William James's (1890) proposal that it is important to distinguish between two intimately intertwined aspects of a person's sense of self—namely, the "I-Self" and the "Me-Self," a concept that has had a major impact on discussions of the self (Harter, 1999). The I-Self is a person's sense of initiating, perceiving, knowing, and interpreting what is going on within and around himself or herself. The Me-Self consists of a person's experiences with his or her body and with human and nonhuman environments to which the I-Self gives meaning.

James (1890) suggested that components of the I-Self include the sense of being the author of one's thoughts and actions and understanding one's experiences; an appreciation of one's needs, thoughts, and emotions; and the sense that one remains the same person over time. Components of the Me-Self include a person's emotional, tactile, and kinesthetic experiences with his or her body, other persons, social roles, and material things. Of particular significance for my model, James's conceptualization that experiences with one's body and the bodies of others form the foundation of a hierarchy of experiences that constitute the Me-Self converges with the research-based models of infant development discussed earlier.

Aron (1998b) conceptualizes a dialectical relationship between the I-Self and the Me-Self termed self-reflexive functioning, which holds that, in the absence of intense, emotionally upsetting experiences, the self that experiences and the self that gives meaning to experiences continuously and reflexively communicate with and define each other. With this elaboration, Aron has made available a way of understanding how traumatic experiences affect a person's self, a topic to which I return at a later point.

Relying on James's concept as elaborated by Aron, I define a child's self as consisting of two interrelated components. One consists of the dialectical process that takes place between a child's I-Self and the Me-Self, which constructs meanings given to experiences, resulting in embodied life-metaphors defined earlier. The other consists of the content, interrelationships, and organization of these meanings, which form what I term a child's *matrix of embodied life-metaphors*. This matrix, unique to each child, simultaneously represents past experiences with human and nonhuman environments, construes the environments with which the child is currently interacting, and prescribes behaviors and emotions that define what to search for and expect and how to continue negotiating developmental issues and needs.[4]

Fast (1992) takes a similar position when discussing the embodied mind from the perspective of psychoanalytic-relational psychology:

> We propose that the basic units of experience are bodily interactions between self and other (human or nonhuman) . . . called . . . events. An event includes all aspects of a particular activity. In the infant's experience, for example, a nursing event might include the infant's own vigorous sucking, the smell of milk, the feel of mother's body . . . the creak and motion of the rocker and the movement of the light overhead [p. 397].

---

[4]By conceptualizing this matrix, I focus on the meanings a child has given to past experiences with humans, nature, and inanimate objects (Kobayashi, 1993; Bergman and Lefcourt, 1994), unique rhythms of nonverbal and verbal dialogue (Jaffe et al., 2001), and unique styles of touching and gesturing (Acredolo and Goodwyn, 1998; Blackwell, 2000).

In summary, to conceptualize a child's self, which I term the psychological landscape, Me-Self–I-Self, I integrate the models of Piaget, Stern, and Sander; the dialectical process between a child's I-Self and the Me-Self, which process constructs embodied life-metaphors; the notion that these meanings are interrelated and organized to form a unique matrix; and the view that these body-based meanings contribute to determining how the child construes environments and participates in interactions and what the child expects from experiences.[5]

The Dialectical Relationships Between a Child's Psychological Landscape/Self and Environments

In a discussion of psychoanalytic theories from the perspective of development, Fonagy and Target (2003) note, "Although psychoanalytic accounts vary in terms of the relative emphasis given to the environment, they share a certain lack of sophistication in considering its influence" (p. 11). Along the same line, Spitzform (2000) has pointed out that psychoanalytic developmental theory lacks a framework for understanding the role played by a person's interactions with "nonhuman" environments in the development of the person's "human" sense of self. What follows is my effort to conceptualize, in a way that serves conducting child psychotherapy, the relationship between a child's self, as defined earlier, and human and nonhuman environments.

My model differentiates three environments into which a child's I-Self projects meanings from his or her matrix of embodied life-metaphors to negotiate developmental issues; within that matrix the Me-Self gains experiences that the I-Self interprets (Figure 1–1). The landscape that is most proximal to the child's psychological landscape or self contains the unique body builds, tempos, style of touching and gesturing, rhythms of nonverbal and verbal dialogue, sensory

---

[5]One source of support for the concept of a matrix of embodied life-metaphors consisting of meanings that integrate experiences with human and nonhuman environments is to be found in Wells (1998). When asked to discuss their experiences with gardening, adults reported that plants triggered early memories of interactions with loved ones.

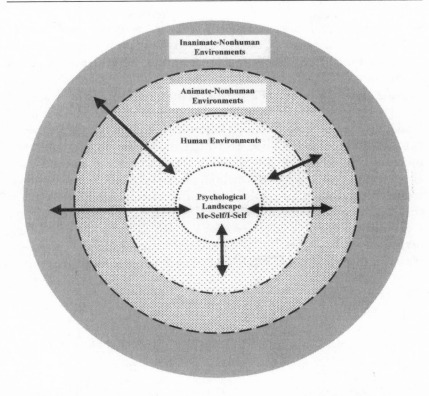

FIGURE 1–1   Dialectical relationships between a child's psychological landscape/ self and environments that form the child's matrix of embodied life-metaphors.

thresholds, sounds, and smells of persons with whom the child inter- acts. The next, more distal landscape contains animate-nonhuman attributes located within the child's home environment and also within, for example, the alleyway or open field that borders the house or apartment building in which the child lives (e.g., animals, trees, bushes, elevations, flowers, plants, running water). The most distal landscape contains significant inanimate-nonhuman objects (e.g., a blanket mother wrapped around the child when holding him; a toy rabbit grandfather gave the child for her birthday). As noted earlier, the integration and organization of meanings representing interac- tions within each of these landscapes forms a child's matrix of embodied life-metaphors.

In my model, a dialectical relationship exists between a child's psychological landscape/self and each of these environments, so that the particular landscape into which the I-Self projects a meaning for the Me-Self to experience contributes to the organization the meaning of that experience achieves. To illustrate, I ask you to recall my discussion of Piaget's (1952) observations of an infant who, while nursing, repeatedly grasped and scratched mother's bare shoulder and a bed sheet. According to my model, that infant's psychological landscape/Me-Self experienced vigorously sucking mother's breast and smelling mother's milk, to which the I-Self had assigned the meaning of attachment/trust/love. At the same time, the infant's self also projected this embodied meaning into the available human environment (grasping and scratching mother's bare shoulder) and into the available inanimate-nonhuman environment (grasping and scratching the bed sheet) where the Me-Self gathered additional experiences to which the I-Self assigned the same meaning (Figure 1–2). Now imagine that mother, without conscious awareness, frequently

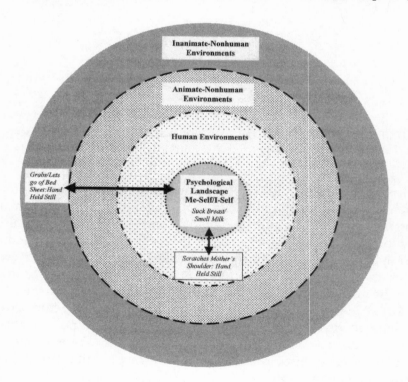

FIGURE 1–2   Dialectical interaction between the psychological landscape/self of a two-month-old infant and human and nonhuman environments.

held the baby's hand still whenever he scratched her bare shoulder or grabbed and let go of the bed sheet because subtle, touch sensations and wrinkled sheets annoyed her. The infant's experience in these particular environments would contribute an embodied meaning of constraint to the negotiation of attachment/trust/love.

For another example, recall the toddler described earlier who repeated a play ritual of sitting on father's lap, having father button and unbutton his shirt around the boy's body, following which the boy playfully scampered away while father searched for him. As I noted, with this ritual the toddler was negotiating the embodied life-metaphor, "I am in you and also separate from you" by projecting this meaning into the available human environment (father's body) and inanimate-nonhuman environment (father's shirt, buttons, and furniture the boy hid behind). Now let us imagine a different scenario. After participating reluctantly in the shirt game a number of times, father, who is somewhat obsessive, does not want to wrinkle his shirt and asks the boy to sit on his lap without having the shirt buttoned around him. The boy complies, and they repeat the play ritual for several days. Thereafter, whenever the boy initiates this ritual, father either indicates he is "busy" or participates without buttoning his shirt around the boy. In this hypothetical situation, unique attributes of the human and nonhuman environments with which the boy interacted contributed the following ingredient to the embodied life-metaphor the boy is negotiating: "Sometimes I am in you, but most of the time I am not. Who are you? And who am I?"

Comparing My Definition of Nonhuman Environments with Others

To clarify my view, compare my definition of nonhuman environments with Spitzform's (2000). Spitzform considered interactions with nature, and the concept of an ecological self, in the context of relational psychoanalysis. She expressed an opinion with which my earlier discussion agrees: "There is a sense of self which emerges within an ecological context and is maintained into adulthood by relationships with a wide range of nonhuman others" (p. 265). When considering how this sense of self emerges, however, Spitzform follows the positivistic assumptions of Harold Searles (1960), who postulated that experiences with nonhuman environments contain stimulation independent of the person experiencing it that fosters the development of a human sense of self. He proposed, for example, that the stability of a kitchen table provides the infant or toddler with a sense of emotional stability that is "quite different from the fluid world of interpersonal relatedness. . . . The nonhuman environment, Searles believed, offers relief from certain kinds of tensions, and can be a source of solace and companionship at times of loneliness or anxiety" (Spitzform, 2000, p. 278).

As one illustration of her concept of ecological self that follows this assumption of positivism, Spitzform shared a clinical anecdote concerning a single woman who was struggling with feeling that she was unattractive to men. During treatment sessions this patient discussed "her delight in . . . her visits to Glacier National Park, where she felt exhilarated and restored by her experience of hiking. . . . Gardening or hiking engaged her in a relatedness where social norms of attractiveness were not applicable" (p. 279).

Rather than assuming that gardening and hiking inherently contain ingredients that exhilarated and restored this woman, my model holds that her psychological landscape/self projected the embodied meaning of being attractive into gardening and hiking and, at the same time, projected the embodied meaning of being unattractive into the human environment of adult males. Imagine that early in her life, because of the way she was held, touched, and responded to by an uncle, she experienced her body-self as attractive. At the same time, because of the way she was held, touched, and responded to by father, she also experienced herself as unattractive. These cycles of interactions resulted in Spitzform's patient's developing two opposing embodied meanings within her psychological landscape/self and matrix of embodied life-metaphors: men experience me as attractive and also as unattractive. With the second assumption, particular experiences in the early years of this woman's life resulted in her extending the meaning that she was attractive into available animate-nonhuman landscapes. For example, during visits with her uncle, she sat near him as he gardened and toddled alongside him as he walked into nearby woods. As a result, although the embodied meaning that she was attractive was withheld from human environments containing males, it was projected into and negotiated within animate-nonhuman environment (gardening and hiking).

To illustrate further the dialectical relationship between a person's self and nonhuman environments in the construction of embodied meanings, consider the childhood experiences Burns (1998) shared in the preface of his book devoted to ecopsychotherapy:

> A special part of my own childhood living place was a tree house built by my father in an old eucalyptus tree that domi-nated our back yard.... It was to here that I would retreat.... I quickly forgot ... the scolding I'd had from my mother.... If I wanted to feel happier or calmer, I would climb into the gen-tle motion of the tree's branches, listen to the soft song of its leaves in the breeze [p. xiii].

My model would ask several questions about this experience. Did climbing up to the tree house located in a tree that "dominated" the backyard enable Burns to project and reexperience the meaning of "up," power and competence that had roots in a play ritual that took place between Burns and his father? For example, with exuberance father playfully tossed him up in the air many times. By projecting this embodied meaning of ascendance and power into his experience while in the tree house father had built, Burns enabled himself to for-get the scolding he had received from mother. Along the same lines, did climbing into the "gentle motion of the tree's branches [and] lis-ten[ing] to the soft song of its leaves in the breeze" derive from Burns's projecting from his psychological landscape/self the embod-ied meaning of security and happiness that had its roots in mother's rocking him while singing softly? Only Burns can answer these questions.

A final example: psychoanalytically oriented therapists in partic-ular may be interested in childhood memories shared by Freud as re-ported by Gay (1998). When Freud's father was 40 years old, he married the 20-year-old, attractive woman who was to be Sigmund's mother. One year after his parents married, Freud was born in Freiberg. He was three years old when the family moved to Leipzig and then to Vienna. According to Gay, "Freud found his first years in Vienna unworthy of recall. He was in mourning for Freiberg, espe-cially for the lovely countryside in which it was embedded" (p. 9). When Freud was 43 years old, he wrote, "I never felt really comfort-able in the city. I now think that I never got over the longing for the beautiful woods of my home, in which (as a memory remaining from those days attests) scarcely able to walk, I used to run off from my father" (p. 9).

Years later, in a letter thanking the mayor when a bronze tablet was unveiled at his birthplace, "Freud . . . singled out one secure relic from his distant past [and shared the following]: 'Deep within me . . . there still lives that happy child from Freiberg, the firstborn son of a youthful mother, who had received the first indelible impressions from this air, from this soil'" (p. 9). Gay proposes that the "rhythmic rhetoric" of Freud's words "'from this air, from this soil' . . . carries its own validation . . . bespeaking his never-quenched thirst for the days when he loved his young, beautiful mother and ran away from his old father" (p. 9). Gay also notes that Freud typically took long walks in the countryside when on vacation. For the concept I am illustrating, we could assume that, when he was taking these walks, Freud's psychological landscape/self extended the following embodied meaning into the surrounding human and nonhuman environments, a meaning initially constructed during the third year of his life when he repeatedly scampered away from his father into the "beautiful woods": "If I can get away from this old man, I will have the beautiful queen all to myself." Here, too, only Freud could answer this question.

The Impact of Trauma on a Child's Matrix of Embodied Life-Metaphors and Its Relationships with Human and Nonhuman Environments

What happens to the dialectical relationships between a child's matrix of embodied life-metaphors and human and nonhuman environments when a child experiences traumatic events? To address this question, I rely on Aron's (1998b) discussion of how trauma interferes with a person's self-reflexive functioning. Aron reviews descriptions of the inability of traumatized adult patients to experience and express feelings and share how they interpreted some event. For example, one report describes patients "who appear detached, flat in their affect, and mechanical, robotic . . . in their presentation" (p. 12). This presentation, as Aron points out, results from trauma's having broken the link between the experiencing Me-Self and the observing I-Self. Thus, these persons are left "anesthetized, out of touch with their feelings and emotions" (p. 15). "Unable to utilize their body sensations, . . . traumatized patients are unable to reflect on their traumatic experiences, self-reflexive functioning fails" (p. 25).

My model also integrates Aron's view with Steven Stern's (2002) discussion of how trauma disrupts the process of a child's identifying with others. Stern reminds readers that, as relational models replaced the structural model of classical psychoanalysis, the role that identification plays in development became obscured, if not lost: "I argue that identification remains as central to psychological life as Freud thought" (p. 723). To formulate his discussion, Stern relied on the infant investigators we discussed earlier who proposed that an infant's experiences with various needs do not become psychologically real until the infant identifies with and internalizes the responses of significant others toward these needs. Stern emphasizes that developing a sense of self by identifying with others is so critical for psychological development that it is "something analogous to our need for oxygen. . . . I view identification as fundamental to psychological life" (p. 725). Stern also considers situations in which a child identifies with and internalizes traumatic responses of others and notes that, when internalizing both positive and traumatic responses of others, the child develops a segregated self.

Integrating Aron's (1998b) view that traumatic experiences disrupt the dialectical link between a child's I-Self and Me-Self with Stern's (2002) emphasis on the importance of identification, my model proposes that responses by others that abused the child's attempts to negotiate embodied life-metaphors, and that the child internalized, form a major part of the child's matrix of embodied life-metaphors and eclipse positive interactions the child may also have internalized. In addition, given that the dialectical relationship between the I-Self and the Me-Self has been broken, the I-Self fails to make use of meanings of available nontraumatic, interactive experiences that could revise the original traumatic, interactive meaning. Accordingly, the child's matrix of embodied life-metaphors becomes dominated by an organization of pathological meanings that leads the child to repeat actions and expect responses from relationships that satisfy what the original traumatic experiences prescribe.[6]

---

[6]The notion that a person's matrix of embodied life-metaphors searches for toxic oxygen to satisfy internalized traumatic meanings given to past experiences relates to and elaborates Wachtel's (1987) concept of "cyclical psychodynamics."

Traumatic experiences also disrupt the dialectical relationship between a child's matrix of embodied life-metaphors and available human and nonhuman environments in any of three ways. With the first, a child's psychological landscape/self becomes constricted, extending meanings into only narrow, selected aspects of human and nonhuman environments so as to continue reliving the meanings of the traumatic responses that have been internalized. Ernest, whose treatment we consider in the next chapter, provides an example. He spent months placing his hands against pine needles, screaming in pain, and running in fear from the spray of water he construed as poison; he was thus reliving the responses of pain and danger he had internalized during hospitalizations he had experienced early in life.

With the second type of disruption, the child's matrix of embodied life-metaphors projects meanings into only one of the available environments. Vera, whose treatment we consider in chapter 3, is an example. For many months during treatment, her matrix projected meanings only into the inanimate-nonhuman environment where she lined up and slowly moved toy animals.

With the third type of disruption, the child's matrix struggles at all costs to avoid projecting meanings into any of the three environments. We will learn later that Ernest is a vivid example here, too. By the age of four years, he had detached himself from human and nonhuman environments to such a degree that he was experienced by others as autistic.

Enacting Embodied Life-Metaphors: The Language with the Most Power to Resolve the Impact of Trauma

There has been a surge of interest in revising the view that verbalizing meanings has the most power to promote change. This surge comes from the school of relational psychoanalysis, discussed in more detail later. Here I address one of its proposals: that interacting and enacting, rather than discussing and interpreting, are the main vehicles of change (Frank, 1999). In a radical departure from the position of classical psychoanalysis, Aron (1996) states, "In interpersonal psychoanalytic work, the focus is on what the patient does with the analyst, how the patient is being with the analyst, rather than predominantly on what the patient is saying to the analyst" (p. 75). My model for conducting child psychotherapy includes this focus but also gives attention to the other side of the coin; it is equally important to focus on what the therapist does with the child and how the therapist acts with the child, rather than what the therapist is saying to the child.

If we accept the idea that the mind is embodied, and if we accept as well the proposals that we reviewed by Piaget, Stern, and Sander that the language of action is our original "mother tongue," how should a therapist speak when trying to help a troubled child? And if the mind is relational, involving experiences with one's body and physical interactions with others, what should the role of a therapist be? My response to these questions is that enactments should promote change in children; enactments are not inversely related to verbalizing; instead, they are "continuously interpenetrating each other" (Mitchell, 1994, p. 99).

What Is an Enactment?

Many definitions of an enactment have been proposed for therapy with adults. These definitions assume a wide range of conscious and unconscious behaviors that occur during interactions (e.g., a sigh, a chuckle, a gasp). Verbalizing, however, remains the vehicle through which these nonverbal expressions occur (Chused, 1991; McLaughin, 1991; Ellman and Moskowitz, 1998; Maroda, 1998; Frank, 1999, 2002; Hirsch, 2000). In contrast, as I use the term in child psychotherapy, an enactment is devoid of, or at least minimizes, discussing thoughts and feelings. An enactment consists of a constellation of physical actions, gestures, rhythms of movements and dialogue, facial expressions, touch perceptions, images, fantasies, and emotions that the child repeats with the intention of introducing into the intersubjective world that child and therapist share a particular embodied life-metaphor that creates conflict for the child and poses a problem to be solved. Using this definition, I recommend that a therapist respond to a child's enactment by enacting in the same action language with the intention of elaborating the meaning the child expressed, providing a solution for the problem it poses, or both.

At first glance this definition might imply that just about anything a child does, or anything a therapist does, qualifies as an enactment. Most children, if permitted to be themselves in a treatment situation, continually express a wide range of actions; for example, a child may play a board game, draw a picture and tear it up, and walk a toy animal across the floor. Should each of these actions be considered an enactment to which the therapist responds with an enactment? I say no. A therapist responds with an enactment only after child and therapist have become sufficiently familiar with the matrix of embodied life-metaphors of the other and have adequately negotiated and constructed a shared interactive language that enables the therapist to register and understand the meaning the child is expressing and what the meaning requires.

Constructing and Participating in an Enactment Requires Negotiating

The word negotiate is typically linked to two persons or organizations who oppose each other. In his discussion of psychoanalysis and negotiation, Goldberg (1987) proposes that negotiation is defined not by a context of opposing forces but as a "communication" that is expressed to settle some matter and as a "sharing of meanings" (p. 109), a definition that coincides with the negotiating that takes place between infant or toddler and caregiver as conceptualized by Sander (1962, 1964).

Similarly, I define negotiating as interactions between child and therapist during which each attempts to share a meaning with the intention that the meaning will be understood, accepted, or modified to better fit the world they are coconstructing. During this process, then, child and therapist, attempting to understand the matrix of embodied life-metaphors and the interactive language of the other, participate in preliminary cycles of negotiations (defined in detail in chapter 5). Briefly, these negotiations address the proposition that, in the beginning of any therapeutic relationship, a child's and a therapist's matrix of embodied life-metaphors, and the interactive language between the child and the therapist, is foreign to the other. Accordingly, the negotiations that take place between therapist and child are intended to construct an understanding of each other's interactive language so that enactments eventually represent a shared meaning permitting a child to enact his or her embodied conflicts and the therapist to enact solutions.

Anecdotes from Child Psychotherapy to Clarify My Definition of Enactment

My definition of enactment is, I think, clarified by a vignette reported by Coppolillo (1987). It concerns a boy who, for a number of sessions, was "guarded, reluctant to reveal anything about himself and showed little inclination to explore the significance of anything he said" (p. 215). This boy, then, was not expressing meanings in the language mode. In one session, the boy began to play a game of solitaire with a deck of cards he had brought with him. The therapist verbally interpreted this behavior: "Do you suppose that by playing solitaire, you're showing me how it feels to be ignored? The boy replied, 'No solitaire. Just sit here and talk to this old shit-head, son-of-a-bitch.' With this, the boy walked away and handled some items in a disinterested way" (p. 215).

That boy enacted an embodied life-metaphor in the action mode (playing solitaire), but the therapist responded in the language mode. The boy's response to the therapist's interpretation makes clear that he experienced its meaning outside the therapist–patient dialectical relationship and angrily rejected it. How else might the therapist have responded? First, it seems likely that by playing solitaire the boy was enacting the guarded behavior he had been displaying over a number of sessions. When the boy first began playing solitaire, the therapist could have expressed himself in the interactive language the boy was using; he could have, for example, taken out a deck of cards, sat at the far end of the room, and preoccupied himself with a game of solitaire. By so doing he would have been saying, in the nonverbal, interactive vocabulary of the moment, "I hear what you're saying. I know what it feels like to be ignored." The child would very likely have responded by expressing other enactments in the nonverbal language he preferred, elaborating the embodied meaning and conflict with which he was grappling.

A second vignette, described by Spiegel (1989), also helps to clarify my view of enactment and the negotiating required. Daniel, a 10-year-old, was being seen because of encopresis. One day, when the boy walked into the playroom, Spiegel smelled feces and said, "It smells like you had an accident in school today" (p. 32). Daniel replied that he had not had an accident, continued to play with a car he had constructed that was propelled by an inflated balloon expelling air, and was extremely careful to ensure that the car was well balanced by balls of clay. Spiegel thought to himself that, "at some level, the propulsion by air from the balloon could have represented flatulence or the expelling of feces" (p. 33). While playing with the car, Daniel performed what I define as an enactment. He took a small chunk of clay and placed it on the end of his nose. At this moment, Spiegel understood the meaning of Daniel's enactment as a metaphor: "on a hunch and with no danger of injury to his self-esteem [Spiegel commented to Daniel], 'You look like Pinocchio. Pinocchio lied to Gipetto about school. Sometimes telling the truth is just too difficult and embarrassing'" (p. 33). When Daniel ignored this comment and continued to play, Spiegel thought to himself, "I pursued the matter no further. . . . I do not know for certain that when Daniel placed clay on his nose, he consciously or even unconsciously was aware of his wish to convey to me that he had, in fact, lied. . . . it is conceivable that his behavior had another meaning" (pp. 33–34).

Rather than responding in the interactive language Daniel was using (an action symbol), Spiegel used a linguistic metaphor for Daniel's having lied. By placing clay on the end of his nose, Daniel was, I suggest, enacting any of several meanings (which Spiegel essentially acknowledges). I suggest also that the therapist should have set out with Daniel to discover which meaning the boy was experiencing and expressing. To mention only a few possible meanings, the clay could have symbolized feces on the end of the therapist's nose as a retaliation for commenting about the odor in the first place ("Take that!"), or it could have symbolized Daniel's acknowledging that he smelled, or that Daniel believed the therapist thought Daniel "stinks" as a person.

How might Spiegel have responded to learn with Daniel the meaning he was expressing? Again, I propose that the therapist speak as much as possible with action symbols, even when fantasy or language modes participate in the child's expression. From this point of view, for example, Spiegel could have become very involved with Daniel in locating pieces of clay in the car he was constructing to ensure that it was "perfectly balanced." Or Spiegel could have placed a piece of clay on the end of his own nose by way of saying," I hear you, tell me more."

The Need for Child Psychotherapy to Catch Up to the Insights of Sándor Ferenczi: The Emerging View of Relational Psychoanalysis

If a child therapist is to minimize verbally labeling and interpreting thoughts, emotions, fantasies, and wishes, then what is a therapist to do? As I noted in my discussion of embodied life-metaphors and clinical anecdotes, I propose that the therapist speak as much as possible using the vocabulary of action metaphors while "being" or enacting a meaning that responds to the predicament the child is enacting. Emphasizing enactments as the focus of therapy with children is consistent with the opinions of a growing number of psychoanalytic therapists who have criticized the emphasis given to verbal interpretation and who urge that we pay more attention to interactions (e.g., Mitchell, 1988; Gill, 1995; Frank, 1999; Holinger, 1999). When working with the children presented in this volume, I attempted as much as possible to get to know the interactive language of each child and help that child to get to know mine. Whenever the child repeated a constellation of behaviors, expressing an embodied metaphor representing some aspect of a traumatic experience the child endured, I responded by enacting roles that enabled me to experience what the child was experiencing as well as to express solutions to the quandary the child presented.

The view that change is promoted by patient and therapist enacting embodied meanings was advanced decades ago by psychoanalysts who remained eclipsed until recently. One of these clinicians, Sándor Ferenczi, a controversial figure in the early years of classical psychoanalysis, published a number of clinical "experiments" that played a major role in the origin of relational psychoanalysis. Aron (1996) points out that Ferenczi's contribution to the early history of the psychoanalytic movement was second only to that of Freud and, "sixty years after his clinical experiments . . . we return to his work 'to find new veins of gold in temporarily abandoned workings'" (pp. 160–161). "Not only did he anticipate our contemporary views (i.e., those of relational psychoanalysis), but we may still have to catch up with his insights" (p. 169).

An Overview of Relational Psychoanalysis

Discussions during the past three decades within psychoanalytic psychology have challenged the classical view of a person as a self-contained system and have given rise to several schools of thought.[7] While each differs in the emphasis given to some aspect of psychoanalytic

---

[7]For excellent reviews of these alternative schools, see Mitchell (1988), Aron (1996), and Frank (1999).

theory, all are in favor of shifting from a one-person psychology to a two-person psychology. From among these alternative schools, relational psychoanalysis is viewed by many as having had the greatest impact, resulting in a "conceptual and technical revolution" (Aron, 1996, p. 208). In broadest terms, the relational approach places at its theoretical center relationships and the meanings given to them, rather than the two drives (libido and aggression) proposed by classical psychoanalysis. Aron notes that various statements, such as the following by the late Emanuel Ghent, form the foundation on which a relational model is constructed.

> Relational theorists have in common an interest in the intrapsychic as well as the interpersonal, but the intrapsychic is seen as constituted largely by the internalization of interpersonal experiences. . . . Due weight is given to what the individual brings to interactions: temperament; bodily events; distinctive patterns of regulation; and sensitivity. . . . Relational theorists do not minimize the importance of the body or of sexuality in human development . . . [and] . . . continue to be interested in conflict . . . seen as taking place between opposing relational configurations rather than between drive and defense [quoted by Aron, 1996, p. 16].

Several concepts together form the foundation of psychoanalytic-relational psychology.

Constructivism. According to the assumptions of constructivism, psychoanalytic-relational psychology accepts the position that what a patient perceives, experiences, and understands about his or her therapist and what a therapist perceives, experiences, and understands about the patient are "constructions" based on each of their histories, unique style of relating, and expressing emotions (Hoffman, 1992).

The embodied mind. Relational theory relies on embodiment theory, which, as discussed earlier, conceives of the mind as emerging from, and developing within, a person's embodied experiences and practices. Echoing observations by infant investigators, Aron and Anderson (1998) stated, "In infancy, our bodily sensations are greatly affected by the qualities of the 'holding' and 'handling' that we receive from caretakers . . . [therefore] our self is first and foremost a body-as-experienced-being-handled-and-held-by-other self " (p. 20). As we discussed earlier, the embodied mind develops from infancy into adulthood during interactions with other persons in a dialectical process within which each person influences the other and each contributes to the construction of meanings given to experiences (see also Aron, 1998a; Mueller and Overton, 1998; Overton, 2004).

Motivation. Relational psychoanalysis opposes the classical position that reduces motivation to the two biologically based drives, libido and aggression; it proposes instead that a person is motivated by meanings given to interactions with others (interpersonal configurations) and by how the person construes the matrix of relationships in which she or he participates and has participated (intrapsychic configurations). Conceptualizations of motivation offered by relational psychoanalysts have been influenced by studies of interactions between infants or toddlers and caregivers. For example, Lichtenberg (1989) proposes five motivational systems constructed during the many transactions that take place between infants or toddlers and caregivers: (1) the need to regulate one's demands with those of another; (2) the need to experience attachment and affiliation; (3) the need to explore and to assert; (4) the need to withdraw from or to oppose another person; and (5) the need for sensual enjoyment. His formulation converges with Sander's (1962, 1964) model, emphasizing that infants and caregivers negotiate a number of issues during their interactions.

Psychological conflict. Conflict a person experiences among his or her desires and fantasies, and between these desires and environmental opportunities and prohibitions, is not seen as occurring "in the person" but, as in the case of motivation, within two interrelated domains: one concerns the interactions in which a person participates (interpersonal configurations); the other involves the different ways in which a person construes the matrix of relationships in which he or she has participated (intrapsychic configurations).

The relational process in treatment: Participating, negotiating, and interacting. In sharp contrast to the classical view that, while the therapist remains neutral, the "patient is expected to stop acting and instead speak about his conflictual feelings and thoughts" (Mitchell,

1994, p. 98), relational psychoanalysis proposes that "the analyst influences the patient and the patient influences the analyst. . . . it is presumed that the analyst is different with different people and in different relationships . . . one can legitimately claim that the very essence of who the patient and analyst are with each other is negotiated" (Aron, 1996, p. 140).

Relational psychoanalysis, then, takes the position that the process of psychotherapy consists primarily of dialectical negotiations, interactions, and enactments between patient and therapist that promote change. I have located within this position my concept of enacting embodied life-metaphors in the treatment process, a technique elaborated in chapter 5. Along the same lines, Mitchell (1994) proposed that enactments by patient and therapist "are not departures from the psychodynamic [treatment] process but the very stuff of analyzing" (p. 99). Change is seen as emerging primarily from patient and therapist participating in interactions as they gradually construct new ways of being with each other. "[Relational therapists] . . . generally believe that what is most important is that the patient have a new experience rooted in a new relationship" (Aron, 1996, p. 214) and that interactions could serve as interpretations by conveying meaning.

Transference. The fantasies and conflicts a patient reveals in her or his associations are not remnants of the past projected onto the therapist but relational issues the patient is struggling to manage during interactions with personal characteristics unique to the therapist. "The analyst's personality affects . . . the so-called real relationship, but also the nature of the transference itself" (Aron, 1996, p. 50). In this sense, as Gill (1984) put it, the transference is coauthored by the patient and the therapist.

Authenticity and spontaneity. When participating and negotiating with a patient, it is important that the therapist remain authentic and spontaneous, sharing his or her personal thoughts and feelings whenever they facilitate the treatment process.

Projective identification and enactments. The patient recruits the therapist into enacting a role that relates to and serves negotiating an issue the patient is struggling to resolve. The therapist is encouraged to assume the role, whenever indicated, in order to participate in resolving the issue in question. As I noted earlier, in the treatment of adults, enactment refers to the subtle ways in which patient and therapist act toward one another while engaged in verbal interactions (e.g., gestures, postures, tone of voice). When applying the concept of enactment in child psychotherapy, elaborated in chapter 5, I propose that enactments primarily involve symbolic, physical activity and interactive participation and avoid verbally describing a thought or feeling. My position is consistent with that of developmentally oriented psychoanalysts who have pointed out that "something more" than interpretation and discussion promotes change in psychoanalytic therapy—namely, the relationship that child and therapist construct and the interacting and the negotiating they share (Stern et al., 1998).

A Summary of Proposals Concerning Therapeutic Technique with Children in Relational Psychoanalysis

Because Ferenczi, as well as many other authors, focused on treatment with adults, I have shaped the following statements so that they relate to the form of psychotherapy with children I am proposing here.[8]

- Because the roots of pathology lay in early relationships and experiences, a phase of experiencing must precede the customary phase of understanding in order for a cure to occur.
- Repeating behaviors indicates that the child is reexperiencing a meaning from the past.
- The child is viewed as recruiting the therapist to play roles in the service of entering a phase of experiencing that precedes understanding.
- While the therapist is enacting roles, his or her task is to help a child relive, during interactions with the therapist, meanings the child gave to early traumatic experiences as well as meanings related to negotiating developmental issues.

---

[8]The outline that follows draws on Aron's (1996) review of Ferenczi's contributions as well as on selected writings by Ferenczi (1931, 1932; see also Rachman, 1997).

- To facilitate the child's reliving early traumas, the therapist should exhibit spontaneity, accessibility, and emotional honesty. As Ferenczi (1932) noted,

> Patients cannot believe that an event really took place . . . if the analyst, as the sole witness of the event, persists in his cool, unemotional . . . purely intellectual attitude, while the events are of the kind that must evoke, in any-one present, emotions of revulsion, anxiety, terror, vengeance, grief and the urge to render immediate help, to remove or destroy the cause or person responsible [p. 24].

- As the therapist plays roles directed by the child, the child experiences and internalizes how the therapist participates and enacts solutions.
- By the child's reexperiencing and resolving meanings of past traumas, a new present is created that includes a new self, a new other, and new possibilities for what can occur in interactions with others.

Concluding Comments

I have discussed several issues, elaborated in chapters 5 and 6, to frame my main position—namely, that the technique of negotiating and enacting embodied life-metaphors representing a child's conflicts is more effective than discussing and interpreting these conflicts. I reminded us that child psychoanalytic psychotherapy, as well as the cognitive-behavioral therapies, inherited the distinction classical psychoanalysis maintained between words and action, as well as its position that a therapist must encourage a child to stop expressing feelings, motives, and conflicts in action and instead express them with words. I brought to our attention, however, that developmental research supports the view that, from the first years of life, when a child gives meaning to experiences with human and nonhuman environments, words play a relatively small role—or no role at all—in symbolizing the experience. We learned that a child's experiences negotiating developmental issues and needs are symbolized at the embodied level, represented by an integration of patterns of sights, sounds, tactile and kinesthetic perceptions, actions, facial expressions, postures, and emotional tones.

Moreover, we considered how, as the child continues negotiating developmental needs and issues into adolescence, these first editions of embodied meanings spiral throughout development, influencing the meanings the child gives to interactions while, at the same time, undergoing revisions based on what the child experiences.

With this foundation, I conceptualized that meanings given to experiences during dialectical interactions between a child and human and nonhuman environments become integrated to form the child's unique matrix of embodied life-metaphors, a matrix that becomes a core part of the child's self; it guides the types of stimulation the child seeks and how experiences with human and nonhuman environments are interpreted. I also emphasized the difference between my definition of nonhuman environments as extensions of a child's embodied self and the definition offered by others that views nonhuman environments as inherently containing stimulation independent of the child experiencing it. I then considered how traumatic experiences affect a child's matrix of embodied life-metaphors as well as the relationship between this matrix and human and nonhuman environments in which the child is participating, with the result that the child seeks interactions that enable the child to reexperience traumatic meanings with his or her emotions.

Integrating these several considerations, I proposed that, to resolve a child's emotional conflicts at the embodied level, a therapist must join the child in enacting the matrix of traumatic embodied metaphors the child expresses, as well as enact solutions to the conflicts represented by these metaphors. I provided an operational definition of enacting and emphasized that negotiations between child and therapist are critical before enacting can be effective. I proposed that, by internalizing the responses the therapist enacts, the child revises his or her matrix of embodied life-metaphors, thus making it possible for the child to assume a growth-fostering developmental pathway. I concluded with a review of the main concepts of relational psychoanalysis that form a scaffold within which the various topics we considered can be configured and interrelated.

With the several issues we discussed in this chapter, I aim to clarify what I had in mind when participating and enacting during the treatment of two children presented in the next chapters as illustrations of the relational model I am advocating. When reviewing these cases, notice that, while each child interacted with me and various indoor and outdoor environments, both children also enacted a series of embodied life-metaphors symbolizing meanings related to the trauma they had endured. I participated in each relationship in an effort to help each child relive these representations and to enact solutions the child could internalize.

Notice also that, after the enactment of a series of life-metaphors, the embodied roots of the difficulties with which each child had been struggling were destroyed. From this achievement, each child eventually evolved a new self and matrix of embodied life-metaphors that made available possibilities for interacting in new ways with others. Last, I hope the issues we have considered serve you in evaluating whether or not the availability of outdoor and indoor environments, in addition to a playroom, made a significant contribution to each child's resolving conflicts and forging a new beginning.

2   Ernest

I Detached My Embodied Self from Relationships Because of the Pain and Emotional Deprivation I Experienced

Ernest was referred for an evaluation at the age of four years, two months. Interacting with me and with nature during treatment sessions contributed significantly to his overcoming what initially appeared to be a major barrier to his psychological development.

My Interview with Ernest's Parents

Ernest's parents, who clearly seemed devoted to helping him overcome his difficulties, began by sharing with me the results of their conference with Ernest's teacher a few weeks after the preschool program had begun. The teacher reported that he was not participating in classroom activities and did not seem to understand instructions given to the children or those directed specifically to him. For instance, at the end of a free period, when the children routinely returned their play materials to the appropriate bins, Ernest wandered around in a detached, dreamy state, sometimes flapping his arms and slowly turning his body. In an effort to help Ernest connect with the other children, the teacher addressed him in a reassuring tone, reminding him to join the others and help pick things up, but he failed to respond. On several occasions, the teacher placed a wooden cube in his hand, led him to a large box where the wooden cutouts were stored, and helped him release the cube into the box. She then urged him to look about for other wooden cutouts and return them to the box, but Ernest continued to wander about the room. The teacher also reported that, in addition to his inattentiveness and lack of involvement, Ernest rarely made eye contact with her or his classmates and seemed unaware of the presence of other children unless they took a toy located near him. He typically spent much of his time playing alone on the floor usually arranging and rearranging the position of cars of a toy train set. When spoken to, he frequently echoed what was said to him, rarely using language interactively.

The parents shared the teacher's concerns with their pediatrician, with whom they had discussed their own concerns. He reminded them that in spite of medical problems Ernest had experienced during his first two years of life, recent examinations did not reveal possible physical causes for his current difficulties at school. The pediatrician wondered if Ernest was developing an autistic disorder, or selective mutism, or Asperger's syndrome. To address this question the parents and the pediatrician scheduled several evaluations.

A speech-and-language evaluation was conducted first during two one-hour sessions. The examiner attempted to administer several standardized tests and reported that Ernest had difficulty understanding directions so that only a few valid results were obtained. Ernest was able to identify common sounds (e.g., animal sounds, a siren) and could correctly express single words on a picture vocabulary test. In terms of receptive language, however, he had difficulty deriving meaning from spoken language. The examiner concluded that Ernest's hypersensitivity to auditory stimuli, and his confusion with spoken language, appeared to result at times in his "shutting down." Although his expressive language skills seemed stronger, his spontaneous verbal output contained a considerable amount of echolalic speech and sometimes was unintelligible. Of special note, the examiner found that Ernest's ability to understand her verbal instructions improved whenever she deliberately accompanied her comments with gestures. A program of speech and language therapy was recommended.

The occupational therapist worked with Ernest during a single hour-and-a-half session to administer standardized tests of fine- and gross-motor movement. This examiner also reported that Ernest had difficulty following instructions, so much so that many of the test items could not be administered. The occupational therapist observed that Ernest occasionally flapped his arms, as reported by the teacher, and that he did not make eye contact or initiate conversation. Also, most of his verbal responses were echolalic. On the basis of the limited data available, Ernest's fine- and gross-motor development appeared to be delayed by at least one year and a program of physical therapy was recommended.

After discussing the reports of those evaluations, the parents reviewed with me Ernest's early history and the difficulties they had been struggling to manage. Ernest was born four weeks prematurely. During his first 18 months, he was hospitalized on three occasions, each for a duration of about three weeks, because of intestinal difficulties. In addition, when he was two months old, mother required a brief hospitalization because of medical difficulties and also experienced postpartum depression during most of Ernest's first year. When Ernest reached his second birthday, mother gave birth to a stillborn infant. Needless to say, this tragedy added considerable stress to the emotional climate of their home. Mother acknowledged that, as a result of her physical and emotional difficulties, as well as her pregnancy, she did not respond adequately to Ernest's needs. The parents hired an au pair shortly after Ernest's birth to aid in his care, but she resigned after a few months. They hired another au pair who caused the parents concern. Shortly after Ernest turned two years old, they noticed that from time to time he slapped himself on the legs, chest, or face. Wondering if the au pair occasionally spanked Ernest, they asked her, but she denied using physical force. This au pair left when Ernest was three years old, and another, Nancy, was recruited. She was still in their employ.

The parents spontaneously offered that, in spite of their efforts to provide Ernest with the best possible care, they had been overwhelmed by the medical complications surrounding his first months of life, by mother's medical problems and depression, and by the stillbirth of their second child. As a result, they frequently argued intensely, sometimes in Ernest's presence. "He witnessed more than his share," mother commented.

As for developmental milestones, Ernest did not walk until 16 months of age and spoke only in single words until he was about three years old. At the same time, he sometimes spontaneously repeated a long phrase that he had heard on a TV commercial and accurately echoed sentences when one of his parents read a story to him. But he had difficulty using language interactively. Typically, he did not respond to the parents or the au pair and instead occupied himself by slowly moving toy cars along the floor or placing them in a row and repeatedly changing their positions. Ernest was toilet trained at the age of three and a half years and could dress and undress himself. At the time of the evaluation, however, he was wearing diapers to bed because of frequent accidents. Because of the difficulties they were experiencing in their relationship, the parents began participating in couples therapy after the tragic death of their second child; they terminated this program just a few months before my evaluation. They wondered if psychological treatment could help Ernest, as it had them. They also noted that, like the pediatrician, they wondered if Ernest was developing an autistic disorder.

My Psychological Evaluation of Ernest

When I entered the waiting room for my first meeting with Ernest, his mother was there, seated in a chair alongside a curved couch set against one corner of the waiting room. But Ernest was not seated. Nor was he anywhere to be seen. I greeted mother and asked, "Where is Ernest? I was looking forward to meeting him." In response, while casting several glances at the curved couch, mother replied that Ernest had, in fact, accompanied her but did not want to see anyone. I surmised that Ernest was crouching behind the couch in the corner of the room. Continuing to chat with mother, I commented that I was disappointed because I had hoped Ernest and I could meet each other today and get to know each other. Then I excused myself, telling mother I would be right back. I went to the playroom, picked up a piece of clothesline about four feet long, and returned to the playroom.

I sat on the curved couch with my back to the corner. Holding one end of the rope, draping it over my shoulder and behind the couch, I knew that it was surely dangling next to Ernest. I hoped the rope would provide him with a way of connecting with me. I chatted with mother once again. I discussed the weather, inquired about the traffic she had run into while driving to the clinic, and commented that I was sure that when Ernest was ready for us to meet he would let me know. I winked at mother and made several facial expressions, trying to help her understand what I was doing. Mother gestured in response, indicating that she understood. As mother and I continued chatting, my hope that Ernest would tug on the rope, signaling the beginning of a connection, was, regrettably, not fulfilled. When the hour passed, I asked mother to come again with Ernest and noted that I was sure he would let me know when he was ready to meet me.

Later I telephoned the parents, who shared that, on entering the waiting room, Ernest had immediately climbed behind the couch. He demanded, "No people." Mother thought he was referring to the speech and occupational therapy evaluations he had undergone during the previous weeks. I acknowledged that as a possibility and reviewed an issue I had discussed with them during the intake interview in an effort to help them understand the approach I would be using to engage Ernest. I reminded them that the previous evaluations had taken place during either one or two sessions and that both examiners had noted that they were not as successful as they had hoped in helping Ernest complete test items. I also reminded the parents that, if we were to obtain data that could answer their questions, and given that Ernest had shut out the world, he needed to be given time to enter our world in his own way. I asked the parents to consider bringing Ernest to at least three or four more sessions, providing me the opportunity to explore whether or not he and I could establish a connection. The parents accepted my recommendation.

The second meeting turned out to be much like the first. When I entered the waiting room, Ernest was not visible. Again I sat on the couch with the rope draped over my shoulder and the back of the couch and chatted with mother. And again I received no response from Ernest. The third meeting aroused my hope for some success. About five minutes before the meeting was to come to a close, I felt the rope over my shoulder become slightly taut. Clearly Ernest had taken the other end in his hand. As I continued chatting with mother, I pulled ever so slightly (so I thought) on my end of the rope. But he let go immediately. Looking back at this moment, I decided that because of my eagerness to make a connection with Ernest, I had pulled the rope too soon and too hard, at least for his tone and

body tempo. Referring to the infant-research–derived concepts discussed in the previous chapter, I thought I had behaved like one of
those mothers discussed by Beebe and Lachmann (2002), who "chased"
their infants and caused the infants to look away and tune out. I vowed
to try to regulate the intensity of my wanting to connect with Ernest.

The fourth meeting went much as the others but with a few additional developments. This time I felt Ernest's hand on the other end
of the rope about 10 minutes after the session had begun rather than
near the end of the hour. Influenced by my reflections on the issue of
mutual regulation, instead of immediately tugging my end of the
rope, I waited for a few minutes and then tugged my end of the rope
ever so slightly. I was delighted that he held on to his end throughout
this long moment. Hoping that he would respond by tugging his end,
I gave my end another slight tug; he let go. Discouraged but committed to continuing to communicate with Ernest using this enactment,
I continued chatting with mother. About 15 minutes after my last tug
and his release, I felt that he had taken the rope in hand again. This
time, while chatting with mother, I waited at least five minutes before pulling slightly on my end of the rope. When I did, he continued
holding on to his end for several minutes before letting go. I was encouraged once again. At the end of this session, I telephoned the parents and described what had happened. I asked them to consider my
having two or three more sessions with Ernest before we decided
whether or not it was possible for me to conduct an evaluation.

A major development occurred during the fifth meeting. About
10 minutes into the session, I felt Ernest holding his end of the rope,
and again I waited several minutes before pulling slightly on my end.
When I did, Ernest held on for several minutes while I continued to
chat with mother. Then I felt a slight tug! A few seconds later, he relaxed his grip. I waited four or five minutes and then tugged on my
end. Again he held on and, after several minutes, he tugged ever so
slightly on his end. This "interacting" continued throughout the
hour with Ernest and me exchanging slight tugs with the rope.

I finally saw Ernest at the sixth meeting. As had been the case in
the previous session, we continued exchanging tugs on the rope every five minutes. Then it happened! Near the end of the hour, when,
responding to a tug by him, I pulled slightly on my end of the rope,
Ernest not only held on but gradually stood up, his eyes peering over
the back of the couch. I turned my head and said, "Hi." He responded, "Hi." Still holding the rope, he again crouched behind the

couch. Turning to mother, I commented that I really enjoyed meeting Ernest and could not wait until I saw him again at our next meeting.

When I entered the waiting room for our seventh meeting, rope in hand, Ernest was, as usual, crouched behind the couch. After we exchanged tugs on the rope for about 15 minutes, he stood up after I had tugged on the rope, much as he had at the close of the previous meeting. This time, however, instead of peering over the back of the couch, he climbed out from behind the couch and stood near mother. He was a handsome boy with thick hair and sparkling brown eyes. I handed him one end of the rope, which he took with both hands. I asked him if he wanted to "look over this place" with me. He did not respond verbally. But as I leaned forward, slowly taking a step, he began to walk behind me, rope in hand. Holding my end of the rope, I continued walking slowly out of the waiting room, and Ernest followed, holding the other end. As we walked down the corridor, I made a few comments about the pictures on the walls.

When we entered the playroom, Ernest looked about but said nothing. I commented that I would like us to do some things when he felt ready. He walked over to a cupboard (I followed him, rope in hand) and stared for a long moment at toy trucks located on a shelf. Still holding one end of the rope while I held the other, he placed a toy truck on the floor and rolled it back and forth. I took another toy truck, sat on the floor near him, and rolled my truck back and forth. I called my truck "Joe" and his truck "Tom" and made comments such as "Hey, Tom, let's go over here." Ernest echoed the names and my comments and sometimes moved his truck in the direction of mine. His speech seemed immature, but I was able to understand him. At other times I followed his truck with mine and commented, "Hey, Tom, wait for me. Here I come." On those occasions it seemed to me that sometimes Ernest paused with his truck, waiting for me to push my truck alongside his. I thought our trucks interacted during these moments. Yet, if I remained still and watched him slowly roll his truck about, I saw him as being in another world.

As had been the case when we were in the waiting room, during this activity I wondered if my eagerness to enter his subjective world was causing my emotional tone and rhythm of movements to be too intense, given Ernest's body tempo and emotional tone. Was I exaggerating my emotional expressions when my truck interacted with his? Was I imagining that he sometimes waited for me to push my truck alongside his? Was he, in fact, totally submerged in his own world, oblivious to my presence? Throughout this "play," however, I was pleased to notice that he continued to hold one end of the rope while I held the other. We, indeed, seemed to be maintaining some connection.

At one point, he left his truck on the floor, stood up, walked over to an inflated tire tube located in one corner of the playroom, and sat in it. Holding my end of the rope since he was still clutching his, I walked over with him. Given my deliberations of a few moments earlier, I decided that I was being too eager and assertive in my efforts to engage him. Therefore, I sat on the floor next to the tire tube, held on to my end of the rope, and waited. After sitting for two or three minutes in silence, Ernest stood up and stepped into and out of the tube several times. I chuckled, said quietly, "Wow. That's great," and asked if I could try it. He did not respond verbally but stood still in the tube for a number of minutes. I thought that meant his response was no. Then he stepped out of and to one side of the tube, which seemed to be an invitation. I stepped in and out of the tube several times in slow motion, dramatizing that I might slip and fall, and mumbling expressions of exuberance. On a few occasions he smiled quietly in a way that I saw as an expression of his own humor rather than an imitation of mine.

Then he walked over and surveyed the large rug that covered one end of the floor of the playroom. The background of the rug was dark blue over which were gold medallions. I stepped on a medallion as if I were hopping onto something in slow motion. Ernest spontaneously imitated me by stepping on another medallion in slow motion while still holding on to our rope. I was thrilled to observe this behavior for it signaled the presence of several developmental achievements that expatiated the meaning of Ernest's holding on to the rope. In Piaget's (1952) model, Ernest was coordinating circular reactions, showing that he was capable of imitating the body movements of another. In Stern's (1985) model, Ernest appeared to have developed aspects of a subjective self, sensing and understanding the intentions of another. And, following the model of Sander (1962, 1964), Ernest seemed capable of participating in negotiating reciprocity.

After stepping on and off the medallions a couple of times, I placed my hand on one and asked, "What's this?" He responded, "Stone." Then I placed my hand on the blue background and asked, "What's this?" He responded, "Water." I continued in slow motion, gingerly stepping from one medallion to another and commenting,

"Careful, don't fall in the water." Ernest grinned and again imitated me by stepping from one medallion to another in slow motion. At this point, because it was time to conclude the session, I noted that there would be more things to do when he returned. Holding the rope in tandem, we walked back to the waiting room.

In the next six sessions, I administered several psychological tests. Ernest held one end of the rope while I held the other during most of these meetings. Between and during procedures, I interrupted the testing whenever I thought he needed a break or whenever he initiated an activity. Most often he returned to the rug and slowly stepped from one medallion to another. I joined him. Imitating me, he chuckled as we enacted being careful not to fall in the water. At other times, he walked away from the table where we were working and rolled a car on the floor or slowly walked on the edge of the rug instead of stepping on the medallions, and I imitated him. These activities gave me the impression, as in Sander's model, that Ernest was controlling stimulation and anticipating some response from me.

Because the details of results of the psychological tests fall outside our focus here, allow me to mention a few examples. My main interest was in obtaining data, in addition to clinical observations, about his cognitive functioning and capacity to symbolize that could assist me in formulating an opinion about whether or not intensive treatment would be helpful. During the evaluation, Ernest coped with most of the test items and responded appropriately, although sometimes he echoed my instructions. Assessments of color perception and laterality indicated no difficulties. On an intelligence scale, Ernest successfully completed 9 of the 13 items required of children between the ages of 48 and 53 months (he was 51 months old), and his time scores with several items received credit at the age range of 54 to 59 months. His performance with one of the subtests reflected adequate receptive and expressive language skills and an understanding of the outside world. The following are examples of Ernest's responses to my questions: *What runs?* "Dog." *What cries?* "Baby." *What sleeps?* "Mom." *What scratches?* "Pin." *What blows?* "Wind." Ernest gave correct responses to 16 of the 20 questions. The four questions he failed clearly relate to how he construed experiences involving aggression and injury (*What bites? What shoots? What stings? What aches?*) To these he mumbled responses that I could not understand. I thought his response to the question "What sleeps?" suggested he was symbolizing his interactions with mother during her phase of depression.

Ernest's performance with the personality tests showed age-adequate ability to symbolize and no signs of major distortions of reality. Several of his responses to the Rorschach inkblot test, (e.g., "butterfly," "bat") depicted images that are frequently produced by others. In addition, the content of one image represented a meaning suggesting that Ernest was motivated unconsciously to step into the outside world and continue growing. When examining a particular inkblot, he responded, "Tree; got leaves on it; blooms."

I also administered a series of normed cognitive tests (Santostefano, 1978, 1988, 1998b). The results obtained played a major role in my deciding if Ernest had the cognitive tools to benefit from experiencing and perceiving his experiences when interacting. In one test, the child is asked to visually scan pictures printed randomly on each of four sheets of paper. The examiner asks the child to mark with a pencil as many items as he can within the time limit (30 seconds). On the first sheet are pictures of geometric shapes; on the second, everyday objects (e.g., telephone, shoe); on the third, food-related items (e.g., spoon, bottle of milk); and, on the fourth, weapons (e.g., sword, rifle). A comparison of a child's performance on the first trial with each of the others provides data regarding whether or not the child's scanning is compromised by anxiety related to emotions and fantasies. Ernest's performance when scanning pictures of geometric shapes was age-adequate. He scanned the pictures of everyday objects, but his performance fell below age expectation. When surveying pictures of food-related items, he scribbled on the test form, walked away, and appeared detached. The fourth trial, therefore, was not administered.

Another test assesses the manner in which a child holds information in memory over time, while managing neutral and emotionally evocative test stimuli, and compares that information with perceptions of present information. In keeping with age expectations, Ernest was able to detect changes that occurred in a series of pictures depicting a toy wagon. But with pictures of a house and of two persons greeting each other he walked away after surveying only a few displays and slipped into a detached state. With another procedure, he constructed appropriate groups of black and white geometric cutouts but could not form groups with everyday items (e.g., cup, spoon, candle, key). Overall, Ernest's performance with the cognitive tests suggested that, with neutral stimuli, the cognitive functions assessed operated adequately for his age, but he withdrew into his private world when stimulation evoked emotions and fantasies associated with human or nonhuman stimulation.

When discussing the results of the evaluation with the parents, I shared my opinion that, while Ernest appeared autistic-like, I believed his detachment from relationships was a strategy that helped him avoid experiencing the fear and anxiety evoked by the outside world because of physical and emotional trauma he had endured early in life. I also expressed my opinion that the person residing in that inner world showed evidence that he wanted to enter the outside world and grow. The test data supporting this opinion included, for example, the image he constructed of a tree starting to bloom, as well as the finding that Ernest's cognitive functions operated adequately if the information he was managing did not evoke emotions and fantasies. Clinical observations also supported this opinion. For example, Ernest eventually did take hold of one end of the rope, enter my world, and cope with the demands of tests I administered. I recommended psychoanalytic-relational psychotherapy, two sessions a week for at least four months, to determine if the process was effective in helping Ernest to establish a relationship and participate with me. We could determine later if we should meet more frequently. The parents agreed.

The Pathway and Course of Ernest's Treatment

While participating in treatment sessions with Ernest, and in keeping with the developmental issues discussed in chapter 1, I recognized that our respective interactive languages were especially foreign to each other, given Ernest's detached tone and my tendency to be physically active and animated. I tried to keep in mind, therefore, that I should regulate my rhythms of nonverbal and verbal dialogue in ways that could help us negotiate mutual regulation. Although he and I achieved some success during the evaluation and he was able to complete test items, we were embarking on a different journey. The goal now was to help Ernest free himself from his autistic withdrawal by reliving his trauma and constructing a new self. To achieve this goal, following the issues discussed in chapter 1, I thought it was important to repeat my participation in a play ritual in exactly the same way as I had before as much as possible, providing Ernest with opportunities to construct representations of interactions. Ernest's treatment can be organized in phases, each defined by the embodied life-metaphor he experienced, expressed, and negotiated with me. Whenever he made use of some part of the Therapeutic Garden, I suggest you see Figure 1 in the Introduction.

Phase I

Metaphor   The outside world is dangerous and can hurt you. Approach with caution. But safe places can be found.
Period   May to early September.
Age   4 years, 4 months to 4 years, 8 months.
School   Completed preschool. Did not attend school programs during summer.

Overview

Ernest spent each session in the Therapeutic Garden. His interactions and enactments with me and features of landscape vividly represented how he construed the outer world and why he had remained withdrawn and detached at home and in school. For Ernest, the outer environment was dangerous and inflicted pain, but he accepted that we two could find safe locations. He also joined me in negotiating early developmental issues, such as reciprocating, and in constructing the beginnings of a shared subjective world. Parenthetically, at the start of each session in this phase, Ernest repeated the enactment of crouching behind the couch in the waiting room. And I continued to sit on the couch, lowered the rope over my shoulder, and wondered where he was. Each time Ernest immediately took the rope in hand, crawled over the couch, and walked with me to the playroom.

Summary of the Sessions

When I entered the waiting room for our first treatment session, Ernest was hiding behind the couch, and Nancy, the au pair, was sitting nearby. I had with me the piece of rope I had used during the evaluation. I sat down and lowered the rope over my shoulder, and within seconds he took hold of it, stood up, and climbed over the couch. We walked to the playroom, each of us holding one end of the rope. On entering the playroom, I commented, "We finished my things. What do you want to do?" After echoing "Want to do," Ernest paused before each of the windows of the playroom, scanned the surroundings, and commented, "Trees."

I mentioned that we could go outside anytime he wanted. He echoed, "Go outside," slowly walked through the open doors onto the terrace, and paused to stare at the water bubbling from the fountain. Then he walked alongside the rill to the pond, each of us still holding on to the rope. Scanning the surrounding landscape, he circled the mount and stopped before a cluster of very large yews that hung over the cave area (area E, Figure 1, Introduction). He entered the cave and sat down on a large stone, and I sat next to him. He remained silent for the rest of the hour, his head bowed and the rope in hand. On occasion, it seemed to me that he raised his head and peered through the branches of the yew. During these moments I imitated him peering straight ahead while pushing a branch to one side. On two occasions, in an effort to stimulate him to share the meaning he was giving to this experience, I commented, "Hey, what's out there?" Ernest responded by lowering his head. Because of his response, I reminded myself that I again was "chasing" him and needed to pay attention to regulating myself according to his rhythm. When I mentioned that our session was over and we would meet again in a few days, he did not respond with a gesture or facial expression but followed me into the building. He seemed more detached than he had been during our evaluation sessions, but each of us still held an end of the rope.

In the next session, Ernest walked directly to the cave, sat still for a number of minutes, and occasionally peered through the branches. I imitated him but this time did not comment. At one point, he draped our rope over a limb above us and held on to the two ends of the rope for several minutes. Then he slowly pulled down on the rope, lowering the branch so it almost touched our heads, and then released the tension on the rope, which caused the branch to swing up to its natural position. He repeated this action three or four times. In between, he sat in silence for several minutes and peered through the branches. I wondered to myself if I should say or do something to facilitate cultivating the meaning of what we were experiencing. I considered, for example, pretending that I was the bush and playfully exclaiming, "Hey you! What are you doing to my arm?" I also considered asking if I could have a turn pulling on the rope. But, recalling that during the previous session he stopped peering through the branches when I made a comment, I reminded myself that Ernest and I had not yet adequately negotiated a shared interactive language (see chapter 5). Accordingly, noticing that he was sitting very still between those moments when he slowly pulled on the rope, I tried to match his emotional tone and sat still with my hands folded.

At one point when he slowly pulled the rope down, I whispered, in a long, soft, singsong voice, "aaah." The next time he pulled the rope I again sang, "aaah." Then, to my pleasant surprise, when he again lowered the branch, he joined me in vocalizing the same sound. I noticed that he was smiling. Ernest and I repeated this activity many times. I felt that our participating in "singing this song" indicated that we were beginning to negotiate our self-expressions, achieving some success in regulating ourselves to fit the other's emotional tone.

In the next session, Ernest introduced a significant elaboration. During one of our "aaah" arias, when he released the tension of the rope so that the branch snapped back up to its original position, he spontaneously sang out, "choo!" and laughed. He repeated this sound many times during the session, and I joined him singing "aaah" while he lowered the branch and "choo" when he released the rope and the branch snapped up (Figure 2–1). During the next several sessions, Ernest and I either quietly sat in the cave while peering out into the Garden, or we played the "aaah-choo" game. Gradually, the crescendo of our singing "aaah-choo" increased, and each song concluded with our bursting into laughter. The first interactive words he spoke spontaneously, "Like it," occurred in one of these sessions, and he uttered "mountain" in another, as he peered through the branches at the mount before us. He also began looking into my face and eyes more often.

Our relationship was ruptured during one of these sessions, illustrating how sensitive Ernest was to my rhythm of verbal and nonverbal dialogue during this early phase of our relationship. Ernest initiated the aaah-choo game as usual, and I thought I was participating as usual. But, after four or five repetitions, he stopped pulling on the rope and sat relatively still. Some minutes later I sang "aaah,"

FIGURE 2–1   Ernest: the "aaah-choo" song.

hoping he would pull down on the rope, but he remained silent for the rest of the hour. Subsequently, while reflecting on how I had participated in the aaah-choo game, it occurred to me that during the previous evening, I had been dealing with a stressful family problem, and I realized that my emotional tone had been affected. I thought, however, that when I started the session I had managed temporarily to set the problem to one side. But apparently I was not myself, and Ernest noticed it. Fortunately in the sessions that followed I was able to participate as usual and was successful in repairing the rupture that had occurred in our relationship.

At one point, Ernest introduced the first enactment representing his wish to enter the outside world. On his way through the playroom to the Therapeutic Garden, he paused, handled several toys, and picked up a tennis ball, which he carried with him in one hand while holding our rope in the other. Sitting in the cave, we played the aaah-choo game for about 10 minutes. After remaining silent for a while, he rolled the tennis ball out of the cave and whispered, "Out." Although I was not sure what he had in mind, I immediately crawled out of the cave, retrieved the ball, crawled back, and handed it to him. A moment later, he again rolled the ball out and whispered, "Far." Again I crawled out of the cave to retrieve the ball. Then he rolled the ball out of the cave and now whispered, "Near." I retrieved it. He repeated this enactment 15 or 20 times during the remainder of the session; each time he whispered either "Near" or "Far."

To encourage Ernest to help me understand the meaning of this activity, when I handed him the ball during one enactment, I pretended that the ball was exclaiming fear, "Gee, I was far away from you guys!" Then I expressed relief, "Thanks for getting me back!" In retrospect, I was expressing the emotions of both fear and relief because I was influenced by Ernest's having devoted so much energy to hiding himself behind the couch and now in a cave. I assumed that it was frightening for the ball to leave the safety of our container. Whenever I expressed fear and then relief, Ernest sometimes grinned. His reaction encouraged me to elaborate my facial and emotional expressions and gestures.

During each of the next several sessions, Ernest, repeating "aaah-choo" and "near–far" enactments, shifted from one to the other during the hour. And with the "near–far" game, I continued to express my confusion, fear, and anxiety about what was out there. Then, in one session, he introduced a new enactment that clearly represented the traumatic meaning we were negotiating. Without giving me any warning, he suddenly crawled out of the cave and scampered up the bank behind the cave. I ran after him. For a moment he scurried among the cluster of pine trees located above the cave (area F, Figure 1, Introduction). Then he suddenly stopped at the face of one tree, thrust the palms of his hands onto the pine needles, and screamed, "Ouch!" I did the same and raced back into the cave, with Ernest following me. He initiated this enactment about five times interspersed with playing "near–far," and each time I joined him, racing back to the cave. Eventually the "ouch" enactment occupied most of four sessions. Significantly, on several occasions, once he had run to the evergreen trees and enacted "ouch," Ernest fell to his knees and asked me to "kiss boo-boo" on his hands, which I did, expressing concern and nurturance.

Weeks later, Ernest introduced another enactment, expanding the metaphor that the outside world inflicted pain and danger. He noticed a lawn sprinkler located in a section of the Therapeutic Garden, which is flat and open (area L, Figure 1, Introduction). The water had already been turned on, and the sprinkler was sending an arc of water that sprayed back and forth high into the air. Standing near the sprinkler, Ernest was obviously waiting for the spray of water to arch over him. When the water reached overhead, he screamed, "Poison!" and frantically ran about. I raced to a clump of large evergreen trees located at the edge of this area (area K), shouting, "Over here! It's safe!" Ernest ran after me (Figure 2–2). I do not recall consciously thinking about how I should respond when he screamed, "Poison!" In retrospect, it seems to me that, since he had ventured into the outside world and was now enacting that danger was imminent, I spontaneously responded by enacting that we could find a safe place in that world. Apparently my intervention turned out to be productive because Ernest repeated this enactment more than a dozen times in this session. Moreover, he initiated this enactment during the next several sessions, and we had to set up and turn on the sprinkler each time. Whenever we ran from the water, we shouted in fear and expressed relief when we reached the clump of trees. On several occasions, after we had reached the safety of the trees, he asked me to carry him to "our house" (the cave), which I did. Whenever we entered the cave, he sat in silence for a few minutes before running off again to enact the "poison" game.

FIGURE 2–2 Ernest: "run to safety . . . water is poison."

Two enactments that occurred while we were playing the poison game expatiated the symbolic meaning of this first phase of treatment. On one occasion, after we had run to the clump of trees to escape the poisoned water, I reached down and picked up a couple of acorns and showed them to Ernest. I was not conscious at the time of any theoretical concept that had guided me in doing that. He took the acorns and held on to them. In the next session, after running from the poisoned water to the cluster of trees, I noticed that Ernest had gathered three or four acorns. When I carried him to the cave, at his request, he carefully placed them in a concave area of the boulder on which we sat. When the session ended, he kissed and gently patted the acorns to reassure them and commented, "I like my house." Imitating him, I also kissed the acorns and commented in a reassuring tone that they were safe in our house, and we could figure out how to be safe when we are outside. With the second enactment, after running from poisoned water to the safety of the cluster of trees, Ernest spontaneously sat at the base of the trunk of a large elm tree (area L, Figure 1, Introduction), and, nestling himself into a concave area, said, "Nice."

The enactments Ernest introduced during this phase captured several themes: that the outside world was dangerous and painful; that our shared world now included our container as a home base plus a safe area located in the outside world; that Ernest was defining me as someone who could help him find safety; and that our relationship could help him find a solution to the quandary presented by his wanting to enter and explore the outside world.

The symbolic significance of the rope. Throughout this phase, Ernest continued hiding behind the couch in the waiting room at the start of each session, and I lowered the rope behind the couch, following which we walked into the Therapeutic Garden, each of us holding one end of the rope. A few developments occurred with the rope that symbolized the embodied attachment Ernest was developing with me, an attachment he began to transfer to his mother. Several weeks after treatment had started, when Ernest and I walked into the waiting room, each of us holding one end of the rope, he spontaneously said to Nancy, "String keeps me and Seb together." At the end of one session, while we walked toward the waiting room, Ernest said to a staff member, "Seb and me tied together."

After the 20th session, I received a telephone call from mother, who reported that Ernest was experiencing difficulty falling asleep; prior to treatment, he had not been having a problem. Now Ernest insisted that all the lights in his bedroom remain on throughout the night. I described to mother the "ouch" game Ernest had recently introduced as one possible reason for his current nighttime fears and proposed that he was beginning to consider entering the outside world but was very frightened because of the pain and danger he believed existed there. I told mother that I would ask Ernest to take our rope home and place it under his pillow so we could "stay together" and that he could bring it back whenever he and I had a meeting. After the next session, he took the rope with him, and the intervention proved successful. Mother subsequently reported that his nighttime fears gradually diminished and that Ernest was verbalizing more than ever what he liked and did not like. In addition, he asked mother to obtain a piece of rope and initiated a ritual that took place at home at least once a day. He directed mother to hold one end of the rope while he held the other as they walked about the house touring different rooms. During several of these excursions, Ernest spontaneously commented, "our rope" (referring to the rope he and mother were holding) and "Seb's rope and my rope," referring to the rope in his other hand, which he held while walking with mother. Mother reported that during one of these walks, he spontaneously commented, "Seb likes me."

Phase II

Metaphor	I prepare myself to enter the outside world and ensure that my relationship with my therapist can save me.
Period	Early September to mid-October.
Age	4 years, 8 months to 4 years, 9 months.
School	Reenters preschool program.

Overview

Ernest continued to crouch behind the couch in the waiting room before each session. When I entered to greet him, mother or Nancy routinely handed me our rope, which Ernest had been taking home

with him after each session to cope with his fears at bedtime. I continued to lower one end of the rope behind the couch, and Ernest continued to stand with the other end in hand. In this phase, Ernest shifted
our location from the Therapeutic Garden to the playroom, where he
engaged in several play themes and elaborated the metaphor of the
previous phase. We saw that, for Ernest, entering the outside world
resulted in pain (the sting of pine needles) and imminent danger (poisoned water), but that it was also possible to find "places" that provided safety from these hazards. By shifting our location to the
playroom, Ernest took a step forward, enacting two interrelated
themes. With one, he practiced interacting with the outside world;
with the other, he practiced being rescued by our therapeutic relationship. Also during these sessions, I noticed that his echolia gradually
decreased, and his use of interactive speech increased.

Summary of Sessions

On entering the playroom, standing by the doors leading to the garden, I expected Ernest to go outside and continue with the poison
game. Much to my surprise, he did not. Instead he stretched our rope
along the floor, removed 9 or 10 toy vehicles from the bins (trucks,
bulldozers, helicopter, cars), and carefully placed each one along the
rope, forming a row. He sat on the floor, and I joined him. He took a
truck, rolled it out of the line to face a car, and commented, "Hi. I'm
a truck." For the rest of the hour he moved toy vehicles about, each
greeting the others, and at times interacting (e.g., "What do you do?"
"I move dirt"). During the sessions that followed, he shifted back and
forth between playing with vehicles and two other activities.

In one activity, he constructed two towers with wooden blocks
and placed a bulldozer next to each. Taking one bulldozer, he slowly
pushed one tower toward the other. I spontaneously pushed the
other tower with my bulldozer toward his. We spent many minutes
inching the towers forward. When the towers met, he moved them
back to their original locations, exchanged bulldozers, and directed
that we continue pushing the towers toward each other. At first I
concentrated on inching my tower toward his and paid little or no
attention to what he was doing with his tower. But then I noticed
that Ernest was vocalizing sounds of frustration and irritation, and
on occasion his tower of blocks toppled. These behaviors caught

my attention, and I wondered to myself if he had noticed that I was not paying attention to him. Accordingly, I decided to use gestures to convey that I was paying close attention to his efforts and occasionally commented, "Wow!" after Ernest had successfully moved his tower forward an inch. Ernest soon imitated me so that this activity developed into a symbol of ritualized reciprocity; each of us took turns being a passive observer and cheering the other's efforts. In the other activity, Ernest walked about the playroom labeling items. For example, standing before a toy cash register, he called out the numbers on the keys ("zero, five, nine"); touching the buttons on a stuffed toy bear he commented, "coplinks"; turning a door knob, "door knob"; and he called out the letters of alphabetical blocks he arranged on the floor.

In the last sessions of this phase, Ernest interrupted these activities to introduce a different but related, representation. He walked over to the large rug on the playroom floor and began stepping along its edge. I imitated him, chanting, "Walking on the sidewalk." I recalled that I had been impressed during the previous sessions with Ernest's engaging the outer world by having vehicles interacting and by labeling items including letters of the alphabet. I thought that the meaning I was now enacting (walking on the sidewalk) might relate to walking into the outside world. Soon Ernest began to sing along with me. Then I reminded him of the game we had played during the evaluation when we pretended that the blue background of the rug was "water" and the medallions "stones." Continuing to walk along the edge of the rug, I now enacted that I was being careful not to fall into the water. Suddenly he fell on the rug, exclaiming, "Help, sharks!" I quickly seized our rope, tossed one end of it to him, and enacted pulling him to safety. Repeating this theme many times, he expressed intense fear while on the rug and relief and joy when pulled to safety. I joined him in expressing the same emotions.

After spending several sessions primarily enacting the shark theme, Ernest returned to the toy vehicles and introduced a new metaphor related to my rescuing him from sharks. At one point he held a toy truck and said, "Help! I'm sick." I immediately pretended I was a "Car Doctor," took a stethoscope that was available among the toys, carefully examined the vehicle, and played that I was fixing it. After each of these "medical procedures," Ernest rolled the vehicle at a vigorous pace, representing that it was all better now. Each time a vehicle sped about the room after having been healed, I commented with feeling, "Wow! We made it better." Ernest enjoyed my expressions of pride and expressed his own surges of excitement.

Phase III

Metaphor	I negotiate self-assertion and testing aggression and then attack the forces in the outside world that have terrorized me.
Period	Mid-October through February of the next year.
Age	4 years, 9 months to 5 years, 1 month.
School	Continues in preschool program.

Overview

Ernest spent all except four of the sessions of this phase in the Therapeutic Garden notwithstanding that on some days there was snow on the ground. In the previous phase he had enacted that he was ready to enter and interact with the outside world and that our relationship could provide him with the means to repair and overcome the damage that he had experienced. In this phase, his enactments focused on negotiating self-assertion and testing his aggression in the service of destroying the dangerous forces located in the outside world that had terrorized him. Ernest also elaborated his attachment to me, his expression of emotions, and the subjective world we had been constructing.

Summary of Sessions

When I entered the waiting room to greet Ernest, I expected that he would be crouching behind the couch, as he had been from the start of our relationship. Instead, much to my surprise, he was lying on the couch and had covered himself with pillows. As soon as I greeted him, he sat up, pushed the pillows to one side, and showed me three thin, stemlike branches clutched in his hand. I asked him what he had brought for us, and he replied, "Arrows, shoot arrows." I explained that we needed to make a bow, which we attempted to construct with one of the sticks he had brought with him, but it proved to be too fragile. So we went into the garden, searched for an appropriate branch, and made a bow. He asked me to teach him to shoot arrows, which I did.

In the sessions that followed, he continued shooting arrows with the bow we had made but was not satisfied with the distance traveled by the sticks. He rummaged through the bins in the playroom and obtained a crossbow that shoots large (18-inch) Styrofoam arrows and a toy pump gun that shoots plastic balls. He took these items to the top of the mount (area M, Figure 1, Introduction), where I demonstrated how to use the crossbow. I expressed wonder as each arrow spiraled upward. Ernest soon mastered the technique and became very involved in sending arrows soaring through the air. He screamed with delight as I had (Figure 2–3). At the same time, he asked me to shoot plastic balls as far as I could. In the following sessions whenever we engaged in this activity, we took turns shooting arrows and plastic balls from the top of the mount and continued to marvel at how high and far the arrow or plastic ball had flown.

During one session Ernest interrupted the shooting game to introduce a new but related enactment. He announced that he was a "little train engine." I announced that I was a "big train engine" and wanted to go with the little train engine everywhere it went. We

FIGURE 2–3   Ernest: "shooting arrows as high as possible."

jogged side by side along pathways throughout the Garden (areas F, G, K) with Ernest leading us. Significantly, he traversed areas in the garden he had not penetrated before.

For a little more than three months, Ernest oscillated between the shooting and the train engine activities; he gradually modified and elaborated the embodied meanings being expressed. With the shooting game, Ernest directed that, using a stick decorated by a piece of colored yarn, we mark the location of the plastic ball or arrow that had traveled the greatest distance. He transformed the train engines into "jumbo jets," which we enacted by running over pathways with our arms outstretched. In another elaboration, he introduced wooden geometric cutouts (obtained from the playroom) as "signals" that the train engines or the jumbo jets were to follow, each cutout representing either stop, go, or a particular tempo. Sometimes Ernest set the wooden cutouts on a pathway in advance of a run, and sometimes, jogging in front of me, he held up one or another signal, which we followed.

During one session, while playing jumbo jets, Ernest focused his attention on the shadow his outstretched arms and body formed under the pale winter sun. I imitated him. At one point, I spontaneously initiated an elaboration that at the time I experienced as representing the deepening attachment I felt with Ernest. While each of us, with outstretched arms, focused on our shadows, I maneuvered myself so that my shadow shook hands with his. Ernest screamed with delight. In subsequent sessions, whenever sunlight was available, he made a point of initiating having our shadows shake hands.

During the last six weeks of this phase, Ernest transformed the shooting game, with its emphasis on distance and ascendance, into a game of hunting for and destroying danger, a transformation representing a significant turning point in his progress. When I look back at this development, it seems to me that the time we spent shooting arrows and plastic balls as high and far as possible, running through the garden as train engines and jumbo jets, and joining our bodyselves with our shadows must have enabled Ernest to cultivate enough self-assertion and confidence to enter the outside world and confront the fear and danger it contained for him.

At the start of one session, as we stood on the mount armed with the crossbow, pump gun, and sword, which Ernest had begun to carry with him, he designated areas of the Therapeutic Garden as "desert," "forest," and "jungle," in which, he announced, lived "Monstro," who wanted to hurt us. He directed that we search throughout the garden to find and destroy this danger. As we cautiously explored all corners of the garden, from time to time, Ernest abruptly stopped, pointed to a tree or bush and shouted, "There's Monstro!" Then with cross-bow, pump gun, or sword, we attacked the bush or tree (Figure 2–4).

Throughout this phase Ernest displayed several behaviors from time to time that elaborated the metaphors we were negotiating. During the winter months, experiencing confidence, he sometimes spent 5 or 10 minutes carefully walking on the ice covering the pond. He pretended he was ice-skating and experimented with sliding down the mount on a sled. Also, while we were hunting Monstro, he declared that we needed to take a rest and led us to the cave, where we sat for several minutes. The cave also became a safe haven when-ever he proclaimed that a storm was coming.

He also spontaneously joined me in inventing shared language symbols, reflecting that we were successfully constructing a shared, subjective world. At one point he asked for a lollipop. I handed it to him and commented, with a grin, "Here's your popolino." He laughed heartily. In subsequent sessions when, for example, we were

FIGURE 2–4   Ernest: "fighting with Monstro."

hunting Monstro, he exclaimed, "Holy Spackoletti. There's one!" (i.e., a monster), and we continued sharing this verbal symbol during our hunting game. He frequently called me Seborino and on one occasion spontaneously kissed me on the cheek and commented, "Feels good."

Two other developments that occurred during this phase suggested that Ernest had been developing strong attachments with others as well as with me. Ernest mentioned that he felt "sad" because Nancy was returning to Ireland. Shortly after her departure, during a session he dictated a letter for me to write down, and with much feeling we walked to the corner mailbox.

In another development, which occurred several weeks later, I informed Ernest that I would be taking a two-week vacation the following month. We marked a calendar to track when I would leave and return. When I first informed Ernest of my vacation plans, he did not express any thoughts or feelings verbally. In the next several sessions, however, when it was time to return to the waiting room, he lay on the ground in the garden and refused to end our session. I sat next to him, held his hand, and acknowledged that it was hard for us to be away from each other because we liked each other a lot and that we get sad and mad when a friend leaves. At the next session, Ernest threw snowballs against a tree trunk in the garden and yelled to me, "I hit your house!" In response, I threw snowballs at the tree and yelled, "I'm mad at you, Seb, for going away." He soon joined me in yelling the same thing and throwing snowballs with vigor. I added that it would help if we could find a way to feel together even though I was away. I offered Ernest a stone from a rock collection he had admired in my office. I pointed out that the stone was like our rope, helping us to feel together even when we were not in the same room. He took the stone, spontaneously kissed it, and then kissed me on the cheek. When I returned from my vacation, Ernest greeted me while holding the stone I had given him. He asked me where I had been, and I readily shared details with him.

Phase IV

Metaphor   Having destroyed my fear of the outside world, I define and nurture a new body-self.

Period   March to mid-May.

Age   5 years, 2 months to 5 years, 4 months.
School   Approaching the close of preschool.

Overview

Ernest spent most of the sessions of this phase in the playroom; he used the Therapeutic Garden only during the last five sessions. In the previous phase, he had developed self-assertiveness and tested aggression in the service of destroying dangerous forces (Monstro) that existed in the outside world and that had prevented him from entering that world. In this next phase, Ernest engaged in activities symbolizing that he had been born again, so to speak, experiencing a new subjective "me," defining and nurturing his body-self. At the close of this phase he projected this new, nurtured self onto bushes in the Therapeutic Garden; he nurtured them as he had been nurtured. He also elaborated his growing attachment to and affection for others.

Summary of Sessions

It was a beautiful spring day. Since we had been hunting Monstro for the past weeks and anticipating that we would continue our enactment, I had taken out the crossbow, pump gun, and swords and placed them on the table in the playroom. When I greeted Ernest, I noticed that he had a book in his hands. Entering the playroom, he ignored the items on the table, sat down, and asked me to read to him from the picture book he had brought from home. With large, colorful drawings, the book depicted the stages of a butterfly's birth and development. As we examined each several times, Ernest spontaneously described the particular stage of development we were considering—for example, "Butterfly lays eggs," "Eggs hatch," "Now a caterpillar," "Now a cocoon," "Then baby comes out with wings," "Wings grow big." Significantly, each time we examined the picture showing a butterfly emerging from a cocoon, Ernest spontaneously got up and ran around the playroom, flapping his arms and pretending he was a newly born butterfly in flight. After examining the butterfly book several times, he announced, "I'm hungry." I took him to the clinic's kitchen, where we gathered grapes, granola bars, crackers, and fruit juice. Ernest nibbled some of each before the session ended.

In the next session he asked if we could gather our food first and snack while reading the butterfly book, a ritual that lasted several weeks. At least once during each session, but more often on several occasions, he asked me to feed him. I fed him with pleasure, enacting motherly affection. Ernest sometimes lifted his head and opened his mouth, imitating, it seemed to me, the expression and response of an 18-month-old. After we examined the butterfly book and ate our snack, Ernest initiated several other activities during each session. Two of these related to food. He held a large plastic spaceship and, with arms outstretched, walked about the playroom "flying" what he called the "restaurant" and announcing that it contained food—"bread," "cereal," "milk." The other enactment had to do with the plastic pump gun that he had previously used to hunt Monstro. With each thrust of the handle, he sent a ball sailing across the playroom and exclaimed that each was a food item.

On other occasions, after we examined the butterfly book, Ernest would initiate an enactment transforming a previous one that represented the outer world as dangerous. He again imagined that the large blue rug on the floor of the playroom was a body of water. Now, however, he jumped down on the rug and rolled about, pretending he was swimming. He invited me to dive in and swim with him, which I did. He also placed toy rubber seals (each about 12 inches long) on the rug and pretended they were swimming with us. (The sharks that were swimming in the water during the earlier phase had now become seals.) Ernest expressed considerable pleasure as he frolicked about, swimming, and, on a number of occasions, he held a toy seal to my face, kissed me with it, and asked me to do the same with him. When I entered the waiting room during the later part of this phase, I noticed that, instead of holding the butterfly book in his hands, Ernest had a watering can next to him. I expressed interest and wondered why he had brought it with him. He replied, "Plants are hungry." During this and the remaining sessions of this phase, he entered the garden and watered the bushes.

Two developments deserve highlighting. When we reviewed the pages of the butterfly book, Ernest displayed many signs of his keen intelligence and the sophisticated vocabulary he was developing. For example, after examining a page depicting a butterfly drawing nectar from a flower, he commented that the butterfly had a "big proboscis." Also during this phase, Ernest occasionally had difficulty terminating sessions, suggesting that the new self he was developing had become very attached to me and had not yet adequately negotiated separation. At the end of one session, for example, he sat on the floor and declared, "I'm staying. I leave on Friday." This particular session was on a Thursday and the next was to be on Monday. In an effort to help him, sometimes I drew a picture of a butterfly or gave him a granola bar or a stone from my stone collection to take with him along with our rope. Usually these interventions worked, but on three or four occasions they were not successful. He was steadfast in refusing to leave. Because I had another appointment waiting, I carried Ernest to the family car.

Phase V

Metaphor	I negotiate separation-individuation and begin to differentiate good and bad forces in the outer world.
Period	Mid-May through January of the next year.
Age	5 years, 4 months to 6 years.
School	Completes preschool in June. Enters kindergarten in September.

Overview

Before sketching a summary of this phase, it should be useful if we summarize Ernest's developmental achievements thus far. From confining himself within a container (the cave) because the outer world presented danger, he stepped out, developed self-assertiveness, destroyed the fear the outside world contained, began constructing and nourishing a new self, and deepened his attachment to me. At the same time, he experienced intense anxiety when these achievements required him to separate. In this next phase a noticeable shift occurred in how Ernest interacted with me as he negotiated separation-individuation. In addition, differentiating the outside world as a place containing both dangers and good forces, he allied himself with the latter. He also oscillated between spending several sessions in the Therapeutic Garden followed by one or two sessions in the playroom. Two thirds of the sessions took place outdoors.

Summary of Sessions

Ernest continued watering the bushes in the garden. Soon, however, he oscillated between preferring to be left alone and inviting me to join him in some activity. He asked me to wait for him on the terrace (area B, Figure 1, Introduction), and I complied. During these moments he seemed to be in a contemplative mood, engaging in solo activities. He slowly walked back and forth along the rill, sometimes dipping his fingers in the running water, and he stretched out alongside the rill where it emptied into the pond. I thought to myself he probably was listening to the water ripple over the rocks. On occasion he would sit by the pond, holding one end of our rope and putting the other end in the water; he was (it seemed to me) playing that he was fishing. He also stretched out on the tall grass at the top of the mount and looked up at the sky.

When he invited me to participate with him, he directed several activities. He took a Frisbee from the playroom and climbed to the top of the mount. He said that the Frisbee was a "bird" and it was going to fly "where it wants to go" (Figure 2–5). He pointed in the direction where I should throw the Frisbee, and, when I hurled it through the air, he expressed much excitement. He repeated this "fly-the-bird" game many times.

In another enactment, Ernest armed himself either with the plastic pump gun or the crossbow and handed me the other. (Recall that these are the same objects he had used previously to hunt Monstro.) Armed and determined, Ernest prowled through the garden, hunting "bad mosquitoes" and "bad rabbits." As we stalked through the garden, carefully slipping between bushes and ever on the ready, Ernest suddenly stopped and exclaimed, "There's a bad rabbit get him!" or "There's a rabbit! Wait! It's a good one! Don't shoot!." In still another enactment, he stood at the top of the mount and shouted either "Go away bad wind" or "Hello good wind." Before or after shouting at the bad wind and greeting the good wind, when there was snow on the ground, he sometimes sat on an inflated rubber tube and slid down the mount, clearly enjoying himself.

When Ernest spontaneously elected to remain in the playroom instead of going outdoors, he engaged in two activities that appeared to expand his negotiating separation-individuation and defining good and bad. Using a large set of wooden cubes and cutouts of different shapes,

FIGURE 2–5   Ernest: "bird flies where it wants to go."

he constructed a train he called "Ernest the UPS Train"; a bus, "Ernest Bus"; an army truck, "Ernest Army Truck"; a fire engine, "Ernest Fire Engine Puts Out Forest Fires"; and a bulldozer, "Ernest Bulldozer Plants Corn and Wheat." He also constructed towers using lettered blocks that contained the spelling of his name and authored a game in which a toy rubber eagle (wingspan of about 12 inches) searched for "bad mice" to catch. He asked me to hide bad mice (wooden cutouts) in different places in the playroom, which I did while he kept his eyes closed. Holding the eagle overhead, Ernest ran about the playroom. Whenever he spotted a wooden cutout, he had the eagle swoop down, pick up the wooden cube, and drop it into the "bad box."

　　In concluding my discussion of this phase, I would like to point out that sometimes our sessions were scheduled for 5:00 p.m. Therefore, during the winter months it was dark at this hour although lights illuminated the terrace. Nonetheless, Ernest still went into the Therapeutic Garden to play the fly-the-bird game and to hunt "bad rabbits and mosquitoes."

Phase VI

Metaphor	Now that I have individuated, I consolidate and conceptualize my body image.
Period	February to mid-April.
Age	6 years, 1 month to 6 years, 3 months.
School	Continues in kindergarten program.

Overview

During this phase, Ernest shifted the location of our meetings from the Therapeutic Garden to the playroom. Having negotiated separation-individuation, he now became very curious and invested in learning the details of human anatomy and physiology, activities that appeared to consolidate and allow him to conceptualize his body image. In addition, he continued to enter the outside world and to experience others in more differentiated ways. For the first time since the start of treatment, he discussed experiences with classmates at school.

Summary of the Sessions

One day Ernest arrived announcing that he had been learning about the human body with a computer program his parents had obtained for him. I had learned in a meeting with the parents a few weeks earlier that Ernest had been asking questions about the human body and body parts, including the penis. In response, the parents obtained a computer program about human anatomy designed for children. After making his announcement, which I soon learned ushered in a new metaphor, Ernest sat in the playroom and discussed what he had learned about human anatomy. He continued with this topic for the next several weeks and asked for textbooks on human anatomy, which we obtained from my office. While examining and discussing the pictures, he sometimes stood up and assumed the tone and manner of someone giving a lecture. "The stomach is protected by the lining inside of it. If acid goes up, the ulcer gets very bleeding and painful. It's very bad." "This is the cochlea; this is the tympanic membrane; sounds vibrate the membrane and it sends signals to the brain. The brain says, 'Oh, what am I hearing?'" "The tube that goes to the mouth from the stomach is the esophagus" (he spelled esophagus correctly!).

When he was not examining pictures and lecturing on human anatomy, Ernest engaged in another activity that seemed related to the metaphor of consolidating and conceptualizing his body image. He asked if we could build a model of a ship. We went to a hobby shop, and he selected models of a battleship and a rocket. During almost every session, Ernest spent about 20 minutes carefully examining the directions and gluing pieces together. As had been the case when we examined pictures in the anatomy textbooks, Ernest focused on the interrelationships among various parts we were gluing together. When we completed the models, he took them home with pride.

While we were working on the models, Ernest initiated discussions about incidents occurring at school that concerned him. This was the first time he introduced events from his outside world for discussion, except for comments he made about family vacations or the departure of his au pair a year earlier. One incident he mentioned concerned a boy in his class who had been teasing him for the past several weeks. Ernest gave me very detailed directions to the boy's home in the event that I wanted to visit the boy and talk to him. (The parents subsequently confirmed the accuracy of these directions.) Over several sessions, I noted that it was not possible for me to visit the boy at his home, but I was sure that Ernest and I could figure out what he might do to handle this kind of situation.

We discussed that, as he continued interacting with kids at school, he would experience being teased and observe other children being teased. Inasmuch as teasing always goes on, it helps to learn how to tell the difference between someone who is teasing in "fun" and someone who is teasing to be mean. I related our discussion to our enactments in the previous phase that involved distinguishing between "good wind and bad wind" and "good rabbits and bad rabbits." If we could tell the difference between good and bad people, we could learn how to handle these two forms of teasing.

Ernest decided that the boy was being mean and elected to send him a letter, which he dictated and I printed on a large sheet of paper. He gave the letter to his mother to mail. I learned later that Ernest's parents and the parents of other children in the class had decided to tell the teacher of their concerns about this boy's behavior. The teacher intervened, and, in the weeks that followed, the boy's behavior changed to some degree. Ernest was pleased; he felt that his letter had made a difference.

In a meeting with me, the parents reported that Ernest was noticeably more verbally interactive at home; the teacher reported to them that he was interacting with classmates and not showing the detached behavior he had shown the previous year. Ernest also became more verbally interactive during this phase before and after sessions. He stepped into the office of the clinic on a regular basis and engaged the administrator and office staff in chitchat. They clearly enjoyed his visits, and he enjoyed conversing with them.

Phase VII

Metaphor   I extend my new embodied self into nature and relationships and express to others the caring I received.
Period   Mid-April through June.
Age   6 years, 4 months to 6 years, 6 months.
School   Completes kindergarten.

Overview

Ernest shifted our location from the playroom to the Therapeutic Garden once again. Having negotiated separation-individuation and consolidated his body image, he extended these gains into interactions with plants in the Therapeutic Garden and with another boy. His interactions with this boy are striking because Ernest repeated and shared with him the beginnings of his own treatment as if to say, "This is where I started, and now I can share with others the power of healing and growing that I have internalized."

Summary of Sessions

After completing the models, Ernest entered the garden and wandered about for a while. Deciding that he wanted to play "Guard of the Garden," he examined each bush and touched leaves. He pointed out, "I'm making sure they're growing okay." In addition, he talked reassuringly to each bush. He commented, for example, "I'll be here every week" or "Gee! You are growing good!" He also busied himself removing leaves and lilies from the edge of the pond so that the fish could "breath better."

Midway through this phase, while walking about, he approached a young boy who happened to be working in the garden with another therapist. I should note that from the beginning of treatment, another child and therapist happened to be in the garden on several occasions. At these times, Ernest ignored these children and therapists and remained totally preoccupied with his own activity. This time, on seeing this child, Ernest invited him to tour the garden, and the boy accepted. As they walked about, Ernest paused before one bush, then another, as he brought to the boy's attention how well the bushes were growing. Then, much to my surprise, Ernest asked me to sit in the cave with the boy and show him our aaah-choo game, which Ernest and I had not enacted for two years. The boy obliged, and, laughing, we played the aaah-choo game for several minutes. Deciding that he wanted to take a video of us playing the game, Ernest took a stick, held it in front of his face as if it were a video camera, and pretended to film us. Then Ernest asked me to video him and the boy, which I did as, laughing heartily, they played the aaah-choo game.

After our session in late June, Ernest and I would not be meeting until early September because his parents had planned several extended trips. Accordingly, I introduced our upcoming interruption during May to give us an opportunity to prepare for a constructive separation. When I first mentioned it, Ernest shared the places that he would be visiting with his parents. Later in that same session he commented, "I'm hungry." Except for a couple of occasions, he had not asked for food since our sessions a year ago when he ate while we examined the butterfly book. We ate fruit and cookies, and I noticed that Ernest gobbled his with obvious vigor. At this moment I chose not to interpret the possible connection between his gobbling food and our upcoming separation.

During the next sessions, he again said that he was hungry. While we munched on fruit and cookies, I said I also was hungry for something to eat but I was also hungry because in a couple of weeks I wouldn't have our friendship to fill me up and make me feel good like the fruit and cookies we were eating. Ernest asked how I stay filled up "when a friend is gone." I suggested that memories of what my friend and I have done help me to stay filled up. I reminded him of how we had handled our separations in the past: he took with him our rope and a stone from my collection; he wrote a letter to Nancy, whom he liked very much, when she returned to Ireland. Over the next couple of sessions I noticed that, when Ernest walked about playing "Guard of the Garden," he spontaneously commented about activities and games he and I had played in the past. He was collecting memories, so it seemed. For example, "Remember when we rolled down the hill in the snow?" And, laughing, "Remember when we went swimming with the seals?" Joining him recalling other moments we shared, I decided not to make any further interpretations.

During the next session, I introduced another intervention related to our upcoming interruption. I initiated drawing a picture of Ernest and me that he could take home with him. I hoped it would provide him with a transitional object representing our relationship. In the session after that, Ernest arrived with a picture in hand (Figure 2–6). He commented that he had drawn the picture at school to show the two of us in a rainbow and wanted me to keep it in my office.

The last session of this phase coincided with Ernest's attending the last day of school before the summer break. He arrived wearing a blue ribbon around his neck on which was printed, "Principal's Award." Pointing to the ribbon with pride, he informed me that he

FIGURE 2–6   Ernest: "while I am away, keep this picture of us in a rainbow."

had won the prize for "listening and paying attention." I compli-
mented him and told him how proud I was that he had done so well in
school. Ernest busied himself during this hour by walking about the
garden and picking flowers. He gave several to the administrator with
whom he had been chatting before and after sessions for many weeks.
He also gave flowers to each of two staff members who were sitting in
a nearby conference room, several to me, and several to his mother
when we entered the waiting room. I wished him a good time on his
trip, and he waved as he walked away, holding our rope in his hand.

Phase VIII

Metaphor   Having individuated, I renegotiate with nonhumans and
            humans rather than a mythical figure the danger the
            outer world contains.
Period   September through March of the next year.
Age   6 years, 9 months to 7 years, 2 months.
School   Begins first grade and continues successfully.

Overview

Having constructed and consolidated his body image and entered
the relational world and relating to others the nurturing he had received, Ernest renegotiates the fear and danger he construed the
world contained now by interacting with humans rather than mythi-
cal figures.

Summary of Sessions

When I entered the waiting room, Ernest was behind the couch—
behavior he had not displayed for almost two years. This time, however, his sneakers were placed side by side on the back of the couch
with the toes pointing forward. Given the gains he had made since
the start of treatment, I thought, this behavior represented, "find
me" and related to his having been away. I greeted the new au pair,
Maria, and dramatized, "Where is Ernest? I really missed him!"
Maria replied, "He's around, but I don't know where." Expressing
hope, I purposefully looked behind chairs and expressed frustration.

I continued fussing and searching for a few moments and then, picking up one of the sneakers, declared, "He's got to be here! His sneakers are here!" At this moment an inflated balloon emerged from behind the couch, and then Ernest's hand holding the balloon. He stood up, grinning from ear to ear.

After initiating our hide-and-seek game for several sessions, which allowed us to work through our separation of more than two months, Ernest shifted to the following enactment. He announced that he was "Officer Dandelion," who would search for "dangerous weeds," and I was his assistant. Ernest, ambling through the garden, carried the toy crossbow and Styrofoam arrow. When he discovered a bad or dangerous weed, he would shoot the Styrofoam arrow into the air as a signal. In response I would race to the spot where Ernest stood, pointing to the dangerous weed. My job was to flip my knife into the ground, as close to the weed as I could get, and dig it out (Figure 2–7). While engaged in this activity, he commented on occasion that we were getting rid of things that could be dangerous to the garden. During my participation, I tried to be as accurate as possible when I threw my knife and expressed relief whenever we got rid of another dangerous weed.

FIGURE 2–7   Ernest: "Officer Dandelion."

After enacting Officer Dandelion, Ernest shifted the location of our sessions indoors for the remainder of this phase. He brought in picture books about sharks and whales and informed me that he was learning about them from books he and his father were reading. Ernest asked me to read to him, engaging me in discussions with nearly every page. As the weeks passed, he spontaneously stood up at times and, focusing on the dangers presented by certain fish, "lectured" about what he was learning at home and from the books we were reading. About those dangers he said, for example, "There are two types of whales; one has teeth; the other strains microscopic organisms. Of course, you need to stay away from the ones with teeth" or "There is the banded butterfly fish, the snapper. The good news is the snapper hides by day and feeds by night, so it's hard for him to kill you." During these weeks, the parents reported that Ernest had begun wetting his bed, a symptom very likely related to his mounting anxiety about bodily danger.

After the turn of the year, Ernest shifted his focus away from the danger posed by fish and introduced what he called the "scare-them" game, which took place in the clinic's open hallways connected by a flight of stairs. A person standing on the second floor hallway could look down onto the corridor below, which led from the entrance of the building to the waiting room. In the scare-them game, Ernest would balance several pillows on the banister of the second floor. He assigned me the role of informing a staff member that she or he was wanted in the waiting room. I informed the staff member and said I would appreciate it if he or she would participate in an enactment. Each available staff member readily agreed. As the person walked along the hallway to the waiting room, Ernest pushed pillows from the banister onto the staff member below. In response, the staff member, following my suggestion, exclaimed surprise and fear. Ernest burst with anxious excitement and laughter. This activity became a ritual for several months. Ernest asked me to record in a notepad the name of each staff member, the date when the staff member participated, and how well the person coped with and endured the fear, the intensity of which Ernest decided by assigning a number to each episode. At the start of each session, he examined his record book, noted who needed to be frightened, inquired whether or not the person was available, and reviewed the adequacy of the person's last performance. Since staff members were accustomed to, and had experience with, our using the building and the Therapeutic

Garden in our work with children, all of them did an excellent job participating in this enactment by expressing anxiety and fear with vocal tones and gestures as the pillows tumbled around them and by conveying their ability to cope.

Phase IX

Metaphor   Once I was afraid of the outside world. Now I enter that world with a new self and sail on my own on the River of Life.
Period   April through October.
Age   7 years, 3 months to 7 years, 9 months.
School   Completes first grade. Enters second grade.

Overview

Having resolved to a satisfactory degree his struggle with body anxiety, which had occupied much of the previous phase, Ernest introduced during this last phase of treatment enactments that symbolized his having constructed a new self and his now being equipped to sail on the River of Life, so to speak. The world he once construed as painful and dangerous he now experienced as providing warmth and support. Moreover, the enactments he introduced appeared to demonstrate that he had successfully resolved the quandaries he had introduced at the start of treatment. The result was that he had constructed a new, embodied self that enabled him to step out of the autistic-like world in which he had been hiding and participate in new, growth-fostering experiences. Evidence of the growth he had displayed within the treatment sessions, plus feedback that he had performed well during the first grade, contributed to my decision to introduce termination early in June. Ernest and I would have five months to negotiate a growth-fostering conclusion to our work together.

Summary of Sessions

At the start of a session in early April, Ernest introduced a new beginning in two ways: when I greeted him, he commented that he did not want to play the scare-them game and also that he wanted to go outside. As we walked into the Therapeutic Garden, he brought attention to the new belt he was wearing. "It gives me security," he said. I recalled to myself that he had used the same phrase months earlier when referring to our rope. (I learned later that Ernest had asked his parents a week before this session to buy him a new belt.) I noticed, however, that he still held on to our rope, which he had been including in our sessions from the start. Given that almost three months had passed since Ernest had entered the garden, I wondered to myself what he was planning to do. Soon he busied himself by watering plants; removing leaves and blades of grass from the pond with a net "to help the fish breathe"; removing twigs and leaves from the rill, which he now called "singing river"; and pointing out that if he did not keep the rill clear it would become "clog river."

During the next weeks, Ernest originated two activities that seemed to represent developing competence, confidence, and participating in relationships. With one, he raced from the mount to the cluster of trees that I had designated as a safe place during the first phase of treatment, when we escaped from poisoned water (area K, Figure 1, Introduction). He asked me to time him during each race and record his time in our "race book." He was obviously proud whenever he shaved a second or two from his best time. With the other activity, he removed a propeller (about 12 inches in diameter) from a toy helicopter. While we stood on the mount, each of us took turns hurling the propeller into the air and judged whether the throw had resulted in the propeller's remaining in flight longer than any of our previous throws. Ernest also sat along the edge of the pond, "making friends" with frogs. He gave each frog a name. Because one was blue-green, Ernest called it Blue Boy. He became especially excited whenever he spotted this frog; he greeted it and inquired how things were going. At one point he asked me to take a picture of him while his friend, Blue Boy, was sitting on a lily pad, so I ran to get a camera and photographed him (Figure 2–8).

I met with Ernest's parents in June to discuss the report they had received from school indicating that during first grade Ernest had made steady gains socially and had performed extremely well academically. Given these gains and what Ernest had accomplished in treatment, we discussed terminating treatment in the fall if Ernest continued to do well at the start of second grade. During one session in June, I brought up with Ernest that we would be ending our meetings in a few months. I made this announcement in a context that I

FIGURE 2–8   Ernest: "making friends with frogs."

hoped conveyed the gains he had achieved. I mentioned that we had
played many games showing he was getting stronger. I noted, for example, his best time when racing from the mount to the trees and
how long the helicopter propeller continued flying when he threw it.
Reviewing the school year that he had just completed, I emphasized
that he had done really well with class work and developed friendships with kids in his class, as well as with the frogs in the pond. Ernest did not respond directly to my comments and continued to talk
to his frog friends.

When he returned for the next session, however, he began an
activity that could be interpreted as his response to my introducing
termination. Walking along the rill, he removed twigs and leaves
from the water much as he had done in previous weeks. This time,

however, after spending a few minutes cleaning the rill, he took a leaf, which he called Champion Sailor, walked to the start of the rill, which he called the River of Life, and placed the leaf in the water. As the leaf floated along, he cheered loudly. At times the leaf stalled because it became lodged against a pebble or another leaf. During these moments he shouted, "Danger! Danger!" When this first happened, I bent over to remove the obstacle. Ernest stopped me: "Let him do it on his own!" He repeated this enactment many times during the next sessions and commented, "Let's see how the Champion Sailor does today." During each sailing, Ernest and I cheered as we watched the leaf struggling along the rill toward the pond. On a few occasions, whenever the leaf became lodged, I intentionally bent over and commented, "I'll clear the way for Champion Sailor." I was interested in learning if Ernest would change or elaborate his response. Each time he held to the same theme, "Champion's got to do it!"

In addition to racing from the mount to the cluster of trees, hurling the helicopter propeller from the mount, engaging his frog friends, and sailing the Champion Sailor down the River of Life, Ernest began to create a map of the garden. He assigned a name to each section: the mount was labeled "Mountain—because you see the whole world from here"; areas covered with peat moss were labeled "Swamps—there's mud pythons in there"; pathways of grass between the areas of peat moss were labeled "Safety Roads," because you could walk on them and avoid the pythons. On a number of occasions, guiding me along these pathways, he reassured me that the pythons would not get us.

Three weeks before we were to terminate, Ernest introduced an enactment that dramatically represented the crown, so to speak, of the psychological growth he had accomplished by interacting with the landscape provided by the Therapeutic Garden. After visiting the frogs and cheering Champion Sailor along the rill, he wandered up the slope above the cave (area F, Figure 1, Introduction). He paused in front of the cluster of pine trees that, at the start of treatment three years earlier, were a source of pain. I trailed behind him. He paused in front of one of the pine trees and, slowly pressing his body, hands, and face against the pine needles, said, "This feels warm and good." I embraced the pine tree next to his and exclaimed that the tree made me feel warm and good too. Then he said we should explore the garden and search for other trees and bushes that made us feel good. Asking me to wait by the patio, he explained that, when he found a tree or bush that gave warmth, he would call me.

With his first discovery of a bush, he made what he labeled "my finding call." The sound he made reminded me of the friendly howl of an animal. I ran to him, and we both embraced the bush he had located. At this point he instructed me to respond with an "answer call" whenever I heard him sounding the "finding call." He took great pains to teach me how to make the correct "answer call," a sound that reminded me of a baby's high-pitched wail. We enacted this "finding" game during the next four sessions; we embraced the bush or tree he had located and commented on the warmth and good feelings it gave us.

During the last meeting, I mentioned to Ernest that it seemed to me that we had learned that it was possible to find warm and good feelings out there not only from trees and bushes but also from people. Ernest agreed. I asked him if he wanted to take our rope with him to keep, that it would be like having a picture of our friendship, of our connection, and of all the different games we had played. He grinned and said he would like that very much.

Concluding Comment

I would like to share a communication I received from Ernest's parents when Ernest was in sixth grade, several years after treatment had been concluded. They reported that he continued to invite friends to his home and was invited to the home of friends, and he continued to do very well academically, scoring at the 98th percentile in standardized achievement tests. The parents also reported that ever since treatment ended, Ernest had never been without some kind of string or rope or belt. Moreover, in his room he kept a "tattered piece of clothesline that is fraying significantly at both ends." The parents believed that this rope was the one Ernest and I had used throughout treatment. I believe the rope symbolized that Ernest had internalized his interactions with me and the natural landscape and had constructed a new self that allowed him to continue successfully on the pathway of development.

3   Vera

Abandoned at the Doorstep of an Orphanage, I Battled the Abuse I Embodied to Gain My Freedom

Vera was referred for an evaluation and possible treatment at the age of five years, eight months. For almost three years, she had been experiencing difficulties at home that her adoptive parents understood stemmed from physical and emotional stresses she had experienced in a government-operated orphanage located in an Eastern European country. The parents decided that they should arrange for a psychological consultation because teachers of the kindergarten program Vera was attending became very concerned when they observed her inability to handle routine classroom activities and peer relationships.

My Interview with Vera's Parents

After making the necessary administrative arrangements through an international adoption agency, an endeavor that took the parents almost a year, they traveled to the orphanage to meet Vera and bring her to the United States. She was 36 months old. During this visit they noticed that she had bruises on her head and body, which the staff explained were due to Vera's falling down or running into furniture. Physical examinations conducted in the United States produced negative results except that Vera had a slight hearing loss in one ear. The parents focused on Vera's eating habits, which concerned them. When food was placed before her, she would touch neither it nor the silverware set next to her plate. Usually she sat still, sometimes tilting her head back with her mouth wide open. The parents patiently fed her. They related Vera's eating difficulty to recent media reports describing the conditions in orphanages in Vera's country of origin and how the infants and toddlers were fed. At mealtime the children were lined up in a row and required to tilt their heads back. A staff member would walk back and forth along the row of children, placing a spoonful of food into the mouth of each child. If the child reached forward to touch the bowl, the child was restrained or the staff member tapped the child's hand with the spoon.

After living for about a year with her adoptive family, Vera began to touch food and feed herself. She continued to show difficulties with eating, however. She took long pauses between mouthfuls and sometimes required up to two hours to complete a meal. She frequently became restless and spilled her soup or toppled her glass of milk. When Vera seemed to be extremely restless, the parents occasionally arranged for her to eat her meal in her room; they hoped the arrangement would help Vera feel less anxious. Once Vera was in her room, the parents typically heard the toilet flushing many times, following which Vera appeared in the kitchen with a clean plate. When asked if she had flushed her food down the toilet, Vera always denied doing so, although it seemed clear she had.

In addition to her difficulty eating meals, Vera had been enuretic for several years, sometimes stole items, and broke toys. One particular behavior puzzled the parents. On occasion, after returning to her bedroom and closing the door, Vera barricaded the door with furniture, wastebasket, and shoes. The parents discovered this barricade one evening when they opened the door to check whether she was all right and asleep. When they asked her why she had piled items against the door, she would not respond. The parents realized that the stress Vera had experienced in the orphanage very likely affected her psychological development. Yet they remained hopeful that their love, attention, and caring would help her overcome the effects of those early experiences. They also noted that, in spite of her difficulties, Vera had developed an attachment with each parent and could at times be related, affectionate, and playful. Then, too, the parents wondered if Vera was of low intelligence and handicapped by a delay in cognitive development. These questions had gradually taken shape because they noticed that Vera did not respond well to instructions and had difficulty paying attention.

To learn about Vera's academic and social functioning in kindergarten, I met with the school psychologist who had urged the parents to obtain an evaluation. He reported that, because of her limited academic performance, Vera had been transferred to the slow-learning group. When called on by the teacher, Vera was very slow to respond, and, if she raised her hand and was then called on, she typically commented, "I forgot what I wanted to say." In addition, Vera was very shy and guarded in the classroom and typically stood alone by a fence during recess. She had formed no friendships with the exception of a special-needs girl who sometimes pulled her own hair and rhythmically tapped her head on a desktop, behavior that Vera imitated. Considering Vera's overall performance in kindergarten to that point, the teacher had recommended that she enter a transitional program in the fall instead of first grade.

Vera's Psychological Evaluation

Vera worked individually with a female examiner and with me. The manner in which she interacted with each of us was pretty much the same: inhibited, shy, and anxious. She repeated one behavior at the start of each session that seemed particularly significant, replicating what she had been doing at home after going to bed. Whether working with the female examiner or with me, on entering the playroom, she immediately placed chairs, pillows, and wooden blocks against the door, clearly in an attempt to construct a barricade. Once the barricade was completed, she allowed the examiner to address her and introduce test procedures. As we learned later, this behavior forecast a metaphor she enacted during treatment over many sessions.

Because of Vera's intense anxiety, the female examiner and I spent our first two sessions with Vera in a nondirected play format in order to build an alliance. During these sessions, Vera examined various toys and games but did not initiate play. She accepted, however, the examiner's invitation to play a board game. Once the psychological tests were introduced, she worked with all the procedures we administered and completed most of them. It seemed clear, however, that with each examiner she continued to experience considerable anxiety from one session to another, anxiety reflected, for example, by her constantly kicking one leg back and forth when seated.

Vera showed above-average intelligence (112 Verbal IQ, 110 Performance IQ, 113 Full Scale IQ), which surprised us, given her shy and anxious presentation, and also surprised her parents and school personnel. She became noticeably more anxious and withdrawn when dealing with personality tests, whether I or the female examiner administered these procedures. With the Rorschach Inkblot Test, she struggled with each card and typically responded, "I don't see anything," suggesting the degree to which she avoided or repressed representing unconscious meanings. After the examiner provided support, however, Vera did construct a few images representing unconscious meanings she had assigned to past traumatic experiences—for example, "Part of the inside of a person. It's a very bad part. It hurts" and "A bug; someone stepped on it. The head and front legs are there; the body is squashed."

When asked to look at pictures and make up stories about what was going on, she rejected about half the cards. In the stories she did construct, the main character was either sad or frightened about something that Vera did not or could not specify. With another procedure the examiner spoke aloud sentence stems and Vera was asked to complete each one in anyway she chose. She had considerable difficulty with this task and responded "I don't know" to most of the sentence stems, examples of which are, "I know it's silly, but I'm afraid of . . ."; "What I want to happen the most is . . ."; and "The thing I can do best is . . ." Sometimes she gave a hint of underlying difficulties she seemed to be aware of and was willing to share with the examiner. For example, to the stem "When I think about my body, . . ." she responded, "That one is really a hard one," and shared that if she paid attention to her body, she would become "mixed up" and "nervous."

The battery of cognitive tests administered was designed to assess how a child surveys information, focuses attention in the face of distraction, and holds information in memory while experiencing different emotions and fantasies evoked by test stimuli (Santostefano, 1988,

1998b). The results did not support the hypothesis that Vera's overall cognitive development was delayed but indicated that particular cognitive dysfunctions were the result of significant emotional conflict. Vera's performance with one set of tests designed to evaluate how a child holds information in memory and relates this information to present perceptions is illustrative. Vera was asked to examine 63 pictures displayed consecutively, five seconds for each display, and to report any changes she noticed. Four tests, each presenting a different scene, were administered: a house; two females smiling and greeting each other; two females in a shootout; and a female child sprawled on a sidewalk, blood dripping from her mouth and with a startled adult standing by. Vera's performance with the scene of a house and the scene of two women greeting each other indicated age-adequate ability to scan, focus attention, and hold information in memory when dealing with stimuli that arouse emotions and fantasies concerning interpersonal affiliation. But her performance fell well below age expectation (fifth percentile) when test stimuli aroused emotions and fantasies concerning aggression and trauma.

On the basis of the results, we concluded that Vera was of above-average intelligence and was struggling with intense anxiety and severe emotional conflicts very likely related to physical and emotional abuse she had experienced early in life. She was managing these conflicts, for example, by holding memories outside awareness and avoiding interacting with others and with food. The parents accepted our recommendation of intensive therapy. We also recommended that she be allowed to begin first grade in the fall pending the outcome of the first months of treatment, a recommendation that school personnel accepted. I began working with Vera two sessions a week and increased the frequency to three sessions a week and then four when indicated.

I met with Vera for two sessions with the intention of giving her some feedback about the results of the evaluation and introducing her to our meeting weekly. At the start of each session, she again barricaded the playroom door with chairs and pillows, and I joined her by expressing with gestures and emotional tones that I was more than willing to join her subjective world and help her deal with the fear she was experiencing. I raised the lids of the storage bins by way of inviting her to explore their contents. I commented that she had played a lot of games I had asked her to play, and now it was her turn to decide what we would do. For the most part, she handled toy animals sometimes walking one along the floor. While she was walking a toy baby elephant, I walked a toy horse toward the elephant and said, "Hi!" Vera joined the play and, speaking for the elephant, asked, "What do you want?" I replied, speaking through the toy horse, that the baby elephant had worked hard and had done a great job, that I know the world she lives in is very scary, so I would like her to visit every week because I want to help. Speaking for the baby elephant, Vera responded, "We'll see."

The Pathway and Course of Vera's Treatment

When participating in treatment sessions with Vera, as was the case with Ernest, I was influenced by my commitment to the models of development and relational psychoanalysis discussed in the first chapter. My goal was to join Vera in constructing a subjective world we could share, and within which we could eventually relive and resolve the traumatic embodied life-metaphors interfering with her development, so that she could develop a new self. Accordingly, I continually reminded myself that it was important to regulate my emotional tone and physical movements in an effort to help Vera join me in mutual regulations and to repeat enactments that summarized and represented some constellation of actions, sensations, and emotions related to traumas she had experienced when interacting with others in the orphanage. As I had done with the treatment case discussed in chapter 2, I organized Vera's treatment into phases, each defined by the embodied life-metaphor she enacted and negotiated. Vera continued to barricade the door and elected to remain indoors for eight months, although she understood that the Therapeutic Garden was available.

Phase I

Metaphor	I relive the regimentation of my early, embodied experiences. Who am I? Who are others? I wish to escape.
Period	March through September.
Age	5 years, 10 months to 6 years, 4 months.
School	Completed kindergarten. Entered first grade.

Overview

Consistent with the model of Sander (1962, 1964), when in the orphanage, Vera apparently did not have opportunities to negotiate
initial adaptation, focusing others on her needs, and reciprocating.
In this phase, she constructed and relived an embodied metaphor
representing interactions as severely regimented and devoid of empathy. From this experience, she and I introduced solutions that
gradually transformed the embodied metaphor of a confined, regimented core self into a core self that could direct activity, recipro-
cate, and participate in mutual regulation. That Vera successfully
resolved this first level of traumatic experiences she had endured is
supported by a development that occurred during the latter part of
this phase. Vera ate food with pleasure during sessions and initiated
fantasy play in which, with much excitement, we pretended to prepare
and share meals representing the ethnic background of each of us.

Summary of Sessions

When Vera arrived for the first treatment session, she again barricaded the door to the playroom, and I again joined her. As I had done
previously, I also raised the lids to the storage bins by way of inviting
her to explore their contents. She slowly walked about the playroom
in silence, ignoring me and peering into each bin. After about 10 minutes, she walked over to the bin from which she had removed the toy
elephant during our previous session, examined a dozen other toy animals, and carefully placed each in a line on the floor. She seemed to
be preoccupied with ensuring that the space between animals was
exactly the same. Then she took the baby elephant and walked it
along the floor, placed it in front of a toy bear in the line, and asked,
"What's your name?" Speaking for the toy bear, she replied, "My
name is Mufasa." In a similar fashion, walking the baby elephant
along the line of animals, she asked each its name and responded for
the animal. A seal replied, "Nalla"; a giraffe, "Simba"; a lion, "Leone";
a horse, "Sebastiano"; a colt, "Serabi."

I sat on the floor nearby paying attention with much interest, but
I did not comment or gesture. I did note that, when the toy horse
responded, she had used my first name. I had used the toy horse

in the previous session to talk to her about coming every week. I thought her use of my first name suggested that she was beginning to include me in her world. At the close of this session, Vera asked if we could save the toy animals for our next meeting. I obtained a large plastic container into which Vera carefully arranged the toy animals, and I commented that the animals would be pleased to know we were going to see them again.

When I greeted her in the waiting room for the next session, Vera was holding a book in her arms. We took out the container of toy animals and entered the playroom. Again Vera barricaded the door with my help. She sat down, I sat next to her, which she accepted, and she began examining the pictures in the book. Each page depicted an animal or insect with its offspring. Vera examined the pictures in silence for the most part. On a few occasions she commented, for example, "That's nice," while looking at a picture of a kangaroo with a baby in its pouch, or "Wow!" when she turned to a page that depicted a scorpion on whose back were 12 offspring.

Setting the book to one side, she removed two toy seals, designated one as the "mama" and the other as "baby," slowly walked them side by side across the floor, and called out their names, which she had assigned in the previous session. She repeated this activity with other pairs of animals. She located each immediately behind the previous pair, gradually constructing a column of two. Again, she seemed to focus on ensuring that the distance be exactly the same between pairs, and I noticed that she correctly recalled the names of all the animals.

Dramatically, Vera would occasionally place a seal next to a cow, for example, and a calf next to an elephant. She would exclaim for the "baby" animal, "Hey! Who are you? You're not my mother." I assumed at the time that Vera was representing the confusion she very likely had experienced in the orphanage because of the rotating staff. Accordingly, the next time she located one animal next to another of a different type, I tied a piece of pink yarn around the neck of the toy animal designated as the "baby" and a piece of green yarn around the toy animal designated as the "mother." "So we can tell them apart," I said. She readily joined me in tying the appropriate piece of yarn around each animal. In the following session, while constructing a column consisting of pairs of animals (mother and baby), Vera repeated and elaborated this metaphor. She tied a strand of pink yarn around her wrist and a strand of green yarn around my wrist.

During the next weeks, Vera increasingly invited me to participate. She asked me to retrieve particular animals, locate them side by
side in the column, and tie a piece of yarn around the necks of the animals she designated as mother or baby. Occasionally I tried to learn
more about the metaphor we were enacting. For example, I took a
baby animal from the column and, galloping it across the floor, said
with a tone of frustration, "Let's get out." As another example, when
she held a mother doll that slapped and yelled at a baby doll, I vigorously wiggled the baby doll and exclaimed confusion and fear. But
Vera did not respond. A couple of times she did not tie yarn around
the neck of a few animals, who milled about in confusion, exclaiming,
"Hey! Who are you?"

In one session, Vera, modifying the metaphor, changed the organization of the toy animals. Instead of placing pairs of toy animals in
two columns, she located each in a single file on the floor. After constructing a column of about 10 animals, she moved each animal a few
inches, beginning with the animal at the head of the column and continuing, in turn, with each of the other animals (Figure 3–1). In this
way, the column "crept" across the floor, up the steps of a climber,

FIGURE 3–1   Vera: "animals must stay in line and move slowly, inch by inch,
toward the barn."

across the top platform, and into a large box she located there and that she called the "barn." Joining Vera, I did my best to imitate the stilted tempo of her arm when I moved a toy animal an inch or two.

Continuing this theme, she added a few animals to the column during each of the following sessions. While we were quietly moving the column of toy animals across the floor, on one occasion, I held an animal and addressed the animal immediately behind, "Hey, are you Nalla, or are you Simba?" By using names Vera had used weeks earlier, I intended to encourage her to elaborate the meaning of our activity. But Vera exclaimed, "Shhh!" Clearly irritated with me, she continued to move each animal in the column one painstaking inch at a time. At other times, I would hold an animal and express its wish for the opportunity to play, but Vera either told me to be quiet or ignored me. Eventually I realized that it was important for her repeatedly to enact this embodied meaning representing interactions as severely regimented and expressions of affiliation as forbidden.

Vera introduced still another elaboration of our play activity that poignantly symbolized the constriction her body-self had endured. She took a large (24-inch-tall) female cloth-doll from the bin, leaned its back against the wall, and placed a pair of toy handcuffs on its wrists. Vera turned away from the doll and continued moving the column of animals. When the session ended, she removed the handcuffs without comment and returned the doll to its bin. I chose not to do or say anything, with the hope that she would spontaneously relate to this activity in some way, but she did not. In the following sessions, when she again handcuffed the doll, I exclaimed, "Hey!" and, expressing despair, wiggled the doll. Vera did not respond and continued moving the column of toy animals.

Vera was working with a column of 34 toy animals when she introduced a major revision in this fantasy play. As she lined up three animals, I thought she was going to continue her theme. Instead, placing a toy dish before each of the animals, she commented that it was time for them to eat. On each plate she put the same number and type of wooden beads. Gradually she added other animals to the line and carefully examined the beads to ensure that each dish had exactly the same items (Figure 3–2). During the following sessions, sometimes she jiggled an animal and then slapped and toppled it while exclaiming, "Don't move!" I participated in this enactment during these sessions; I angrily scolded the animals or slapped them when they moved.

FIGURE 3–2   Vera: "animals in a row; fed exactly the same food; slapped if touch food."

With another major play theme, Vera introduced feeding us, reenacting the same metaphor she had expressed when feeding the toy animals. This development appeared to have been stimulated, at least in part, by an enactment I introduced. In one session I purposely put a couple of sticks of gum in my mouth and chewed conspicuously. My intention was to learn if Vera would assimilate my gesture into her fantasy in ways that involved her body-self. As I chewed away, Vera and I busied ourselves lining up animals and ensuring that each had the same beads. At one point, she asked, "What's in your mouth?" I replied, "Gum," and she asked for some. I gave her a stick, which she chewed vigorously, imitating, it seemed to me, her view of how I was chewing. Over the next sessions, she gradually increased the number to five sticks, which she chewed vigorously in one large mass. At one point, after stuffing her mouth with sticks of gum, she interrupted her play with toy animals and sat on the floor. I sat alongside her. She placed a plate before each of us in which she carefully placed the same wooden beads she had been using to feed the animals. She asked me to feed her. I held a bead near her lips, and she pretended to munch on it. Then she held a bead to my lips, and I did the same. She repeated this play theme for a number of sessions, adding a salient elaboration.

On one occasion, as she raised a bead to my lips, I spontaneously moved my hand ever so slightly and touched the bead with my fingers. Although I had learned from Vera's parents months before that children in the orphanage were sometimes struck with a spoon if they touched food, I was not consciously aware at that moment of intending to replicate this part of her history, but that could have been my unconscious intention. In any event, Vera slapped my hand and yelled, "Don't touch!" When I raised a bead to her lips, she clearly intentionally placed her fingers on the bead. Influenced by what Vera had just enacted with me, at first I thought I would slap her hand. Instead I scolded her in a very melodramatic way. Vera, however, insisted that I slap her hand, and I did. She immediately transformed these interactions into a play theme that was repeated many times for several weeks along with our feeding and scolding animals. She directed me to touch my beads, or to push them off the plate, following which she yelled at me and slapped my hand. And she directed me to do the same with her. On two occasions she abruptly slapped my face. I responded by playacting that I had frozen to attention.

Apparently by repeating this enactment with our bodies as well as with toy animals, Vera was able gradually to resolve the trauma she had experienced when being fed at the orphanage, an inference supported by a significant transformation she introduced. In one session, when I placed a stick of gum in my mouth and offered her a stick, I anticipated that we would continue enacting the same metaphor. Much to my surprise, Vera said that she would like some fruit. I went to the clinic's kitchen and returned with a handful of grapes and strawberries. In the meantime, Vera had already lined up the toy animals with a dish before each one. While nibbling on the fruit, she continued to place beads in the plates and feed the animals. At the start of each of the next several sessions, Vera asked for something to eat. She gradually included, in addition to fruit, such items as crackers and granola bars, which she ate with obvious pleasure. She also invited me to join her as she ate.

Given the obvious change that had taken place in the meaning she was giving to eating, on several occasions, in an attempt to learn how she now experienced being fed, I held a grape to her mouth. She accepted the grape and chewed it with pleasure. She also fed me. In addition, and significantly, she began one session by announcing that we were going to prepare food from her country of origin and from mine. During the previous weeks, as we sat eating, Vera had asked questions about my country of origin and the meals I enjoyed eating. Using the same wooden beads, she played that we were cooking several courses from each of our ethnic backgrounds. We "ate" with pleasure while discussing the taste of various items. Vera repeated this theme for several sessions when she introduced a very different metaphor that ushered in a new phase.

Phase II

Metaphor	I long to escape into freedom, but there is much danger and evil in the outer world.
Period	October.
Age	6 years, 5 months.
School	Continued in first grade.

Overview

This phase is defined by two significant developments: (1) for the first time Vera did not barricade the door of the playroom, and (2) we entered the Therapeutic Garden. Having successfully worked through the regimentation she had experienced during the first years of her life, and the anxiety associated with eating, Vera now revealed the meaning of barricading the door. During this brief, four-week phase we are considering now, she introduced an enactment that represented the obstacle to her achieving psychological freedom—namely, that the outside world was filled with danger and evil persons.

Summary of Sessions

Instead of preparing menus from her country of origin and mine, Vera announced at the start of one session that she wanted to make a book. Carefully threading a piece of yarn through the holes of several sheets of notebook paper, she bound them together. On the first page, using phonetic spelling, she printed, "I want to run away." She asked me to finish the story. I invented a story of a girl who was trapped in a building with other children and who wanted to escape. Participating in coauthoring this story, Vera spontaneously exclaimed, "They live in a orphanage!" I agreed and, pronouncing each word very slowly, carefully printed that sentence. As I continued the story, Vera sat close to me clearly focused on my every word. I continued that the girl crawled out of a window and ran into a nearby forest. Vera again spontaneously added, "People in the orphanage are yelling, 'Come back, come back!'" Again, slowly printing and enunciating each word, I recorded her contribution.

Then I continued my story. A bird came along and asked the girl why she was upset and scared. The girl explained that she had been trapped with a lot of other kids for a long time, and now she wanted to find a place where she could live without being afraid. The bird sympathized with the girl's predicament, expressed confidence that they could find that place, and invited the girl to follow. The story ended with the girl walking along a pathway and following the bird, which fluttered overhead, while the two of them chatted and developed a friendship. When I finished printing my story on the pages of the book Vera had prepared, she printed at the bottom of the last page, "I luv yoo."

In the next session, Vera again did not barricade the door. She said that she would like to go outside to look for and save bugs "like the bird saved the girl." Her decision really surprised me because we had not entered the Therapeutic Garden since the start of treatment. Vera gathered a handful of wooden beads, which she had previously used to represent food, and asked for a jar to save the bugs in. Tiptoeing to convey that we needed to be very careful, she led us into the Therapeutic Garden, jar and beads in hand. She sat under a large bush located just beyond the terrace, and I sat alongside her. She immediately placed the wooden beads on the ground in a row before us and said, "Now no one can see us." She scanned the garden for a number of minutes and exclaimed, "Look, in the bush over there! Danger eyes! They're looking at us!" She asked me to draw a picture of the bush and eyes. I replied that I had to crawl back to the playroom for a pad of paper and pencil. Vera handed me a wooden bead to make me invisible as I crawled to the playroom and then returned to our bush. There I sketched the bush and the "danger eyes." Then Vera pointed out two other bushes with their danger eyes, which I also sketched (Figure 3–3).

Vera later clarified our mission. From session to session, we sat under a different bush in the periphery of the garden and made drawings of bushes that she said contained danger eyes staring at us. While engaged in this activity, Vera always placed wooden beads

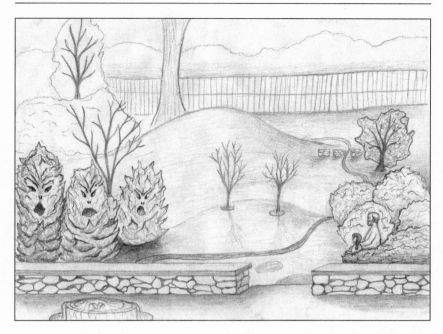

FIGURE 3–3   Vera: "the world is filled with danger and evil."

around us to ensure that we were invisible. Eventually we had sketched nearly every area of the garden. Of note, it was during this five-week period that Vera's parents reported that she was wetting her bed at night. In addition, she had had two accidents at school; she had urinated while seated at her desk. The appearance of this symptom seemed clearly related to the increase in anxiety and fear Vera was experiencing that stemmed from our enacting that we were entering a world fraught with danger.

Phase III

Metaphor	I experience the routine of first grade as regimented as the orphanage. I also strengthen my attachment to my therapist in order to prepare myself to deal with the evil in the outside world.
Period	November through mid-April.
Age	6 years, 6 months to 6 years, 11 months.
School	Continued in the first grade.

Overview

Anticipating that we would go into the Therapeutic Garden and continue searching for "danger eyes," I greeted Vera with pencil and paper in hand. Vera, however, asked that we go to my office—a request that I thought at the time served to interrupt our "running away from the orphanage," expressed in the story we had written previously. But, as it turned out, what Vera produced in this phase indicated that it was necessary for her to resolve first the embodied metaphor of interpersonal regimentation as it applied to her human landscape, namely, school. Vera had been coping with first-grade demands for two months and was enrolled in a class reserved for children designated as "slow learners." School personnel had decided that, given her difficulties in kindergarten, a class with fewer demanding activities than mainstream classes would be most appropriate. After asking to go to my office, Vera devoted many sessions enacting that, from her point of view, the routine of first grade was the same as the regimented, restrictive, and abusive environment of the orphanage. In addition, she focused on strengthening her attachment to me in order to prepare herself, once she resumed her escape, to deal with danger in the outside world.

Summary of Sessions

Throughout this phase Vera engaged in activities either in my office or in the playroom; she spent several consecutive sessions in one setting and then in the other. When in the playroom, Vera, arranging the furniture to replicate a classroom, placed chairs in a row. She asked me to pretend I was a student and placed a doll, to which she had assigned a name, in each of the other chairs. She played at being a teacher, and when she called out the name of a doll, my job was to respond for that doll and do what Vera asked that doll to do.

In this "classroom" setting, Vera enacted metaphors that contained ingredients of the previous theme, in which animals were lined up and controlled. For instance, speaking in a sharp voice, she announced to the students, "I'm teaching you to write letters," and cautioned them to hold their hands still on their desks and not pick up their pencils until she gave the order. She printed several letters on the easel and directed the child (doll) in the first seat to copy the first letter on its sheet of paper, the child in the second seat to record the second letter, and so on. Sometimes she asked me to be the teacher, and she played being the student, purposefully picking up her pencil without permission and then directing me to scold her and hit her hand with a ruler.

Of special note, she had the children eat "snacks" at recess time. During these enactments, Vera as the teacher repeated the stern behavior she had used when feeding the toy animals during the first phase. She directed, for example, that one of the students (played by me or a doll that I manipulated) spill food. In response, Vera screamed angrily and sometimes slapped our wrists with a wooden pointer. At the same time, while we set up the classroom, or as we put items away at the end of each session, Vera continued to eat and enjoy snacks.

After the winter school recess, Vera introduced a new activity that transformed the representation of a classroom from stern and abusive to flexible and caring, suggesting that she had begun to resolve experiencing school as regimented and harsh. She invited me to join her in constructing "kids" out of popsicle sticks and told me that the children we were constructing had recently moved into the neighborhood and were visiting our school. For the first time, Vera referred to our school in this play theme by the name of the school she was actually attending. As I manipulated the stick figures, Vera spoke for the dolls in the classroom, who warmly welcomed the newcomers. She also reminded everyone that, since the stick figures were new to the community and the school, they felt out of place and lonely. In response the dolls gave these newcomers tours of the neighborhood and helped them with their homework.

As I noted earlier, Vera sometimes located our activities in my office, where she examined rocks and shells from a collection housed in baskets. She also examined pictures on the wall, books on shelves, and items on my desk and asked questions about each. She expressed special interest in several items. On one shelf were framed photographs of a village in Sicily from which my family of origin had emigrated. She examined these pictures many times and asked numerous questions about the village and my relatives. At the same time, she described family gatherings that included relatives of her adopted family. A globe also received considerable attention. Pointing to different areas, she asked me for the name of each country and information about its culture. Gradually she focused on the countries of her origin and of mine and frequently commented, "They are really near to each other."

Vera also asked questions about my daily activities and professional work. At one point during these conversations, she mentioned that her mother had told her that I was a "feeling doctor." Vera said that, in response, she had told her mother that was not the case, that I was a "doctor of body parts." (The parents confirmed this conversation in one of my meetings with them.) In the hope of learning what she meant by this linguistic metaphor, I asked Vera if she could tell me more about how she thought a doctor of body parts helped children, but she ignored my question. I wondered to myself if she was construing me as someone who would help her construct a new body-self.

When I entered the waiting room, a month before this phase came to a close, Vera's nanny handed me a copy of the *New York Times*. She said that Vera's parents wanted me to see an article discussing the orphanages from which Vera had been adopted. I took the newspaper with me. Vera went to my office and again involved herself in examining various items. Since Vera had seen the nanny give me the newspaper, and heard her comment about what was in it, I asked Vera if she knew why her nanny had given me the newspaper. Vera responded, "I don't want to hear about it." During this and the following sessions, as Vera examined items in my office, I occasionally referred to the newspaper article. I mentioned, for example, that her parents and nanny must have been talking about the orphanage she lived in; that I knew it is very upsetting to hear people talk about it; that I was sure she and I could find a way to do something about what had upset her a long time ago. Vera did not refer to the newspaper article or to my comments. I did notice, however, that, during the sessions following the nanny's handing me the newspaper, Vera spent more time in my office examining items and asking questions about my background and less time playing school.

Apparently, Vera worked through, with some degree of success, the demands of first grade through the lens of the regimentation she had experienced in the orphanage. This inference was supported by my learning through the parents that Vera had made steady gains socially and was performing academically at a level that surprised school personnel, given that they originally wondered if she could handle first grade. In addition to achieving some resolution to her construing school demands as regimented, Vera apparently strengthened to a considerable degree her attachment to me. Having revised her core self, which entailed identifying me as having resources to battle the trauma she had endured, Vera introduced a radical change in the metaphor that guided our interactions.

Phase IV

Metaphor   I travel from the present to my embodied past and enact and resolve my interpretation of the physical and emotional abuse I endured.
Period   Mid-April through October.
Age   6 years, 11 months to 7 years, 5 months.
School   Completed first grade. Began second grade.

Overview

With the benefit of a strengthened alliance, Vera was able to return to, elaborate, and enact the unconscious meanings associated with her barricading the door and seeing "danger eyes" outdoors. In this phase, the enactments Vera originated lent strong support to the inference that her experiences in the orphanage, as she construed them, must have included physical and emotional abuse. The sequence of locations in which Vera enacted this metaphor is particularly significant. Initially, she enacted in my office that we were repeatedly being attacked by dangerous men. Then she repeated this enactment in three successive locations: the hallway outside my office on the second floor; the playroom on the first floor, and again in the terrace of the Therapeutic Garden. This sequence of locations suggests that, step by step, Vera was moving closer to and eventually entered the outer world where imminent danger was finally defeated.

Summary of Sessions

At the start of one session, on entering the playroom, Vera asked if we could carry the easel to my office. As I carried the easel upstairs, I wondered to myself what the meaning could be of Vera's now playing school in my office instead of the playroom. Once in the office, I soon learned that she was launching a new enactment that represented an embodied metaphor at the root of her difficulties. I should pause to describe the easel because of the meaning Vera assigned to it. The easel consisted of two large wooden panels joined at the top by hinges, each panel set on two wooden legs. When the panels were spread apart, they formed an A-frame structure standing almost five feet tall. Once I set up the easel, Vera asked me to drape a large table cloth over it while she placed pillows under it. She asked me to sit next to her under the easel, where we remained silent for several minutes until Vera commented, "This is our village. It's safe here."

Vera curled up on the floor and rested her head on a pillow. I lay down next to her and also rested my head on a pillow. She asked me what I had done today and listened as I shared the details of the day. Suddenly she thumped her feet on the floor five or six times and gasped, "Bad guys! Trying to get in our village!" I jumped to my knees and, peering out from the tablecloth, exclaimed, "I'll stop them!" I quickly crawled out and thrust a vigorous punch at the imaginary enemy. Vera screamed, "Get them!" I continued throwing punches, attempting as best I could, with body movements and grunting, to enact that I was engaged in a fierce battle. After fighting the bad men for a minute or two, I commented, "Okay, they're gone. We're safe." Vera directed us to lie down and go to sleep again. After sleeping for a few minutes, she thumped her feet again and announced that bad men were attacking our village. And again I crawled out to battle them. Vera repeated this enactment at least 10 times during this session.

During each session that followed, Vera constructed the village in my office and at least a dozen times repeated this enactment, which she elaborated in several ways. For the physical makeup of our village, she placed large plastic crates around the outside of the easel and added blankets, more pillows, and utensils. For our enactment, on occasion she asked me to pretend I was a "bad guy." As I tried to sneak into the village, Vera would "kill me" with "magic rays" emitted by a shell or stone that she held in her hand and that she had obtained from the collections in the office. Recall that, during the previous phase, she had carefully examined these items. Most of the time, however, Vera directed that I battle the bad men.

At this point, I should note that sometimes after a battle Vera made clear that she disapproved of how I had fought the bad men. She criticized me for not being sufficiently vigorous. She conveyed this opinion by complaining directly, "You're not punching hard enough!" or declaring that the bad men had run off and were preparing to attack again. She then ordered me to leave our village and resume the battle. When I look back at these moments, I realize that sometimes, after having engaged in seven or eight battles in the course of 20 minutes, I became tired and found it difficult to maintain the degree of authenticity and sincerity required by Vera, who apparently was paying close attention to my emotional style and physical vigor. When Vera criticized how I fought, I agreed with her and continued to try.

In one session Vera introduced an elaboration of the metaphor of bad men attacking us that represented our attackers with a more reality-based symbol. She searched through magazines and newspapers, cut out particular photos, glued them to pieces of cardboard, and called them ID cards, which she directed were carried by the evil men. Vera limited her selection to males who could be considered to represent a stereotyped Eastern European appearance.

She directed that, whenever someone approached our village, we were to check the person's ID card first to determine if he was a "bad guy." While most of the persons approaching our village proved to have identifications qualifying them as bad, some were declared to be good and were permitted to enter. This elaboration of our play theme, to my mind, was a turning point because it symbolized, on one hand, that Vera was now representing evil in forms that more closely referenced real persons; on the other hand, this elaboration symbolized that Vera was beginning to differentiate evil versus good, rather than projecting that only evil surrounded our village. Now, when someone approached our village (always signaled by Vera's thumping her feet as we lay under the easel), I crawled out of our village, obtained from the imaginary person the ID card (which Vera had already placed on the floor), and handed it to Vera. She passed the card under a "stone machine" (she had obtained stones from my collection). If the machine beeped, the man was "bad," and I was to beat him up. During any given session, our village was approached 15 or 20 times while we were trying to sleep.

During the remaining weeks of this phase, using the same easel and material, Vera relocated our village in the hallway area just outside my office (Figure 3–4), then in the playroom, and, finally, on the terrace of the Therapeutic Garden. In each location she directed the same enactments: we lay under the easel trying to sleep; Vera

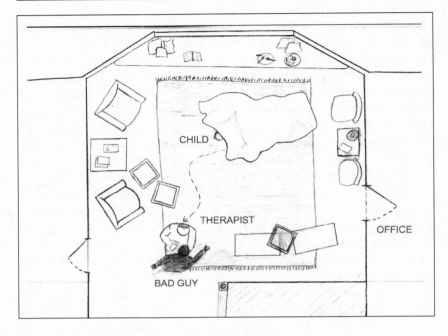

FIGURE 3–4   Vera: the "village" in the hallway.

thumped her feet announcing that someone was coming; I crawled out to check the person's ID card and beat him up if the stone machine identified the man as bad.

During the last sessions of this phase, while our village was located in the Therapeutic Garden, Vera introduced a new activity that forecast the next phase in her treatment. As we will see, this new activity symbolized that she had conquered the danger she construed the world contained. Between attacks, she announced it was mealtime and instructed me to set plates in a row along the terrace for the children in the village and to prepare "oatmeal." I placed about 10 sheets of paper in a row outside our tent. She then directed me to give each child (who we imagined was sitting opposite a sheet of paper) "one spoon of oatmeal." At the time, I recalled to myself that this enactment replicated what Vera's adopted parents and the *New York Times* article had described as occurring in the orphanage. The enactment also related to Vera's early fantasy play when she lined up animals and fed them the exact same beads. Vera pretended that some of the children were making noise, crying, or grabbing their plates. She instructed me to scream at them whenever these behaviors occurred or to "strap them with a belt." During these episodes, Vera surprised me. When I stood before a sheet of paper and screamed at a child, who Vera had decided was being naughty, Vera spoke to me as herself in a calm voice, "They're only kids. Calm down." She also spoke to the imaginary child, "Don't worry. We're getting out of here. I know where there's a better village."

Phase V

Metaphor	Having defeated the impact of early trauma, I enter and interact with a predictable, safe, and friendly world and acknowledge my adoption.
Period	November through the following May.
Age	7 years, 6 months to 8 years.
School	Continues in and completes second grade.

Overview

Vera ushered in this phase when she shifted our location from the Therapeutic Garden back to my office and the adjoining hallway. She used the same materials that formed our village to construct what she now construed as "our home" and retraced the same sequence of locations she had used while battling evil men. From my office and hallway, she relocated our home to the playroom and then to the Therapeutic Garden. In each location, we were mother and father with children, engaging a world that was friendly, safe, and predictable. In addition to using the same materials to construct our home, Vera transformed the meaning of actions and objects she had used in the previous phase, supporting my opinion that she had overcome the effects of the trauma she had endured in the orphanage. She announced the approach of visitors to our front door by thumping her feet on the floor in the same way she had announced the approach of evil men. The wooden beads she used in phase I to feed animals in a regimented way became meals for visitors. And Vera called our imaginary daughter by the name she had been given at the orphanage. Last, when our home was eventually located in the Therapeutic Garden, Vera enacted adopting a frog she had fished out of the pond.

Summary of Sessions

At the start of one session, Vera asked if we could set up our "things" in my office. I thought to myself that the weather could not be a factor since it was a sunny, autumn day. I soon learned that she was initiating a new metaphor. She arranged the easel and other material much as she had when she labeled the location "our village," but she now commented that "no bad guys are coming" and referred to the location as "our home." She designated areas in the office and hallway as our "bedroom," "kid's bedroom," "living room," "kitchen," and "TV room." These designated areas became the location for various play themes during the next several weeks. She directed that she was mother and I father. We set the table, prepared dinner, fed ourselves and the children, read the newspaper, went to sleep, and woke up when the alarm clock sounded in the morning. After breakfast, Vera handed me a pillow to serve as a briefcase, and I left for work. Sometimes, when she needed to leave our house to go shopping, she instructed me to "take care of the kids." We also drove our children to school. Now and then someone would come to our front door. It is noteworthy that Vera announced the arrival of a visitor by thumping her feet, much as she had done in the previous phase to announce the approach of a bad man. People came to our home for various reasons; for example, a woman arrived to help us clean the house, a serviceman arrived to check the furnace, and a neighbor visited for the evening.

Vera initiated other enactments that deserve highlighting because of their symbolic significance. In one session, Vera told me to visit a toyshop to buy a doll for one of our children. When I returned with a doll, which I had obtained from the playroom, Vera gave the doll to our imaginary daughter, whom she called Cristina. Vera spent a great deal of time interacting with our imaginary daughter, feeding her with differently colored wooden rods ("baby bottles"), each color representing a different food (e.g., milk, orange juice). Usually Vera fed the doll while humming softly and rocking. Sometimes she directed me to hold the doll and feed it a particular drink, which I did, enacting as best I could being a caring, giving father. In a routine meeting with the parents, I asked if there was anyone Vera knew by the name of Cristina. The parents informed me that Vera had been given that name by personnel of the orphanage. In another enactment, on four separate occasions, Vera noticed a child accompanied by her therapist farther down the corridor and spontaneously invited them to "look at our home." Sometimes, when we sat in our living room to play a board game, she set sheets of paper on the floor, much as she had done in the previous phase when we fed children in our village, and placed fruit and granola bars on each sheet. While we played our game, she ate with obvious pleasure, and I joined her.

Vera then used the same material to build "our house" in the playroom, which became the location of our activities for the next several months. Significantly, she now designated the door leading to the Therapeutic Garden as our "front door" and located a "mailbox" just outside. With our house now in the playroom, she directed several play themes in addition to my going to work or her leaving to shop. We received and read mail from friends each day. With another theme, she directed me to play a person who had just moved into the neighborhood, invited me into her home, served me dinner, and discussed, for example, the school her children attended and the best places to go shopping. When serving these meals, Vera used the same wooden beads as food that she had used at the start of treatment to feed the toy animals she had lined up. Now, however, a salad, for example, consisted of a mixture of beads. And Vera surprised me at the start of one session when she directed that we take our children for a ride in the park. She led us into the Therapeutic Garden and walked to an area she designated, "where our kids could have fun." This enactment forecast another change in the location of our home.

In mid-March, Vera used the entire Therapeutic Garden to define "our home." She designated different areas as our kitchen, living room, bedroom, our kid's bedroom, the school attended by our children and the park (Figure 3–5). With our home now encompassing the entire Therapeutic Garden, she directed a number of the same play themes: I went to work and telephoned her from the office or she telephoned me; sometimes Vera went shopping while I took care of our children; neighbors visited; and we drove our children to school and to the park. On a couple of occasions, when we were sitting at the foot of the mount talking to our children in their bedroom, passing my hand through the grass, I commented how good that felt. Vera passed her hand through the grass and agreed. In the following sessions, she frequently touched the leaves of bushes or passed her hand through the grass and asked me to do the same while she commented how "nice" it felt.

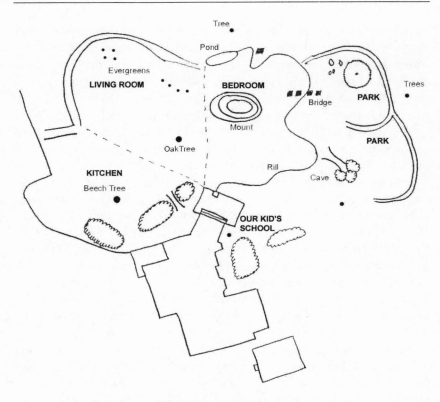

FIGURE 3–5   Vera: "our home."

Vera introduced a new enactment into this routine that literally related to her having been adopted. She became fascinated by the frogs and fish in the pond. Using a net attached to a pole, she attempted many times to scoop up a frog. Eventually she caught one and placed it into a large plastic container along with grass and water. She named the frog Lucky. After talking with the frog in a friendly and playful way, she returned it to the pond. During each of the following sessions, she again scooped at the water until she caught a frog and, repeating the same enactment, talked to the frog in soothing tones much as a mother would talk to a very young child. Interacting with each frog, she gradually elaborated that "Lucky is an orphan" and "needs a home." Vera assigned herself the role of "mother" who "adopts Lucky." Toward the end of this phase, using toy animals, human toy figures, and toy furniture, Vera constructed a farm alongside the rill and played out several themes. Mother and daughter worked

FIGURE 3–6   Vera: the "village" in the garden.

around the house and prepared meals, while father taught the son how to milk cows, tend sheep, and plant vegetables (Figure 3–6).

Phase VI

Metaphor   I reenact with microactions the meaning of being attacked and continue practicing using my new self to benefit from relationships.

Period   June to the following June.

Age   8 years, 1 month to 9 years, 1 month.

School   Begins and completes third grade.

Overview

Near the close of the previous phase, during the month of May, I scheduled a meeting with Vera's parents to discuss her progress since the start of treatment and my recommendation that we develop a plan for termination. The parents told me that in their opinion Vera had shown steady improvement. They informed me that a "Flexibility Award" is given by the school principal each year to the second-grade student who has shown the most progress socially and academically. With excitement, they announced that Vera had won this award. She seemed to be thriving and appeared to be in a happy mood most of the time.

The parents were also excited to report that Vera had told a friend of hers that she had been adopted. To the parent's knowledge, this was the first time Vera had openly acknowledged her adoption. In this connection, I shared with them Vera's enacting that she was a mother who adopted a frog named Lucky, and they noted that she had already shared this with them. They also said that she had been eating food with pleasure and was more related when interacting with neighbors and relatives.

After reviewing Vera's progress, I recommended that I discuss with her that we meet until she completes third grade and that we gradually reduce the frequency of our meetings to one session weekly, then to one session biweekly, and finally to one session a month during the last two months. I explained that, given the traumatic interpersonal experiences to which she had been exposed during her first years of life, and given the attachment we had developed, I thought a gradual terminating process would likely make a more constructive contribution to her continued development. The parents accepted my recommendations.

Summary of Sessions

During the sessions immediately following my meeting with the parents, while Vera continued playing with the village she had located alongside the rill in the Therapeutic Garden, I introduced termination. I pointed out to her that she had done really well during second grade and how proud I was that she had won the Flexibility Award. I noted that in much the same way she had worked hard in our meetings so that now she experienced the world as a place where she was not afraid of being hurt and where she could enjoy friends and eating delicious food, even American food. At the latter comment, Vera laughed, joking that she would limit herself to eating only food from her country of origin and mine.

I took out of her folder the story we had written earlier about the girl who escaped from the orphanage. Reading it slowly and with feeling, I said that the girl in the story could be Vera and the bird could be me, and that we had now found that happy place. I reminded her of the time when we huddled, afraid, in our village but now we had a home in the garden visiting our children's school, going to the park, and meeting friends. In this context, I pointed out that, because our work would soon be finished, we would meet less often and then stop our meetings at the same time that she finished third grade.

Vera seemed to listen carefully. Although she did not respond to my comments verbally, I thought she responded through activities. For example, one day she arrived with a box in which were six or seven stones. Showing them to me, she commented that she had started a rock collection, "just like you have," and that the rocks came from her neighborhood. She looked over my rock collection and compared it with hers, and I offered several rocks, which she happily added to hers. At the start of the next several sessions, she arrived with her box of rocks under her arm and entered the Therapeutic Garden to look for rocks she could add to her collection. We searched under bushes, scratched the soil with sticks, carefully examined each rock we found, and selected a number for her collection. On occasion I shared that I was really glad that she would have rocks in her room at home that come from the place where we built our village.

When Vera was not in the garden looking for stones, she directed three activities that took place in the playroom. One seemed to represent with microactions the same meaning she had represented earlier with macroactions—namely, struggling to escape from a restrictive, painful environment. She placed on the floor about seven blue wooden beads selected from the set she had used in earlier phases of the treatment. Around these beads she carefully placed three and sometimes four concentric circles of "guard" beads. Vera explained that the blue beads were children who wanted to escape, "Get out of where they were, like that girl we wrote a story about." The other beads were guarding them so they could not escape. My job was to try to penetrate the circles of beads with other beads Vera gave me and rescue the blue pieces. From one session to the next I tried different strategies as Vera and I imagined different situations. For example, when she noted that the "guard beads" were taking a break and having a snack, I moved three of my pieces toward the guards from one direction and engaged them in conversation while moving several other pieces, inch by inch, from the opposite direction to infiltrate each circle. When I reached the innermost circle, however, Vera said that one of the guards had sounded an alarm. As we repeated this fantasy play, Vera typically said that my pieces had been thwarted in some way. Each time I set out to invent another strategy to rescue her pieces, and Vera seemed to focus on and derive pleasure from my perseverance.

In another enactment, Vera directed me to play being a "good" student or a "bad" student, while she played being the teacher, staging a number of events occurring in the classroom or playground that involved good behavior versus bad behavior. This play activity seemed to provide Vera with an opportunity to enact and work through situations with which she was coping in third grade. With the third play theme, Vera initiated our playing board games that emphasized constructing strategies and competing (e.g., Mastermind, Stratego). Sometimes Vera interacted in ways that seemed to me to be obstinate, defiant, and rude. Initially I was annoyed, but, after reflecting on my reaction, I recognized that I had become accustomed to and enjoyed my role in our relationship as the fighter, with Vera enacting the role of someone who was helpless and in need of protection. I soon realized that she was negotiating self-assertion and testing aggression. Accordingly, when playing these board games, I responded to her defiance and rude behavior with playfully aggressive comments and gestures, sometimes allowing her a victory and sometimes challenging her. Gradually, the rudeness disappeared, but her assertiveness remained.

While playing the board games and the fantasy of my wooden beads trying to rescue hers, Vera also initiated discussions about friends at school and home and continued to eat fruit, granola bars, and candy with pleasure. One issue Vera introduced for discussion was particularly significant. Her parents had asked her if she wanted to attend a sleep-away camp during the coming summer. Vera had never been away from home for more than an evening at a friend's home. Because Vera indicated that she would be interested, the parents enrolled her in a camp. But, as summer approached, she became more anxious about the prospect of leaving home. As Vera shared her anxieties, associations, and fantasies about sleep-away camp, she and I came to the formulation that, in her mind, going to sleep-away camp was like being in an orphanage. She gradually resolved this conflict while we repeatedly examined and discussed the camp brochure and the different activities and programs she could enjoy. I also suggested that it would help if she took with her to camp the rock collection she had been constructing. Vera decided she would take some of the rocks to "keep me company" and asked me to help her select rocks that originated from her yard and from the Therapeutic Garden.

When Vera arrived for one of our last sessions, she proudly handed me a story she had written for an assignment in school:

Vera and the Carpet

It was a good day and I was done with all my work. I decided to go on a trip to the past. I wanted to fly way back when I was born. I was just a baby. I grew up to when it was the day I got spanked with a belt. So, I quickly went to my carpet and flew back to when I was a little older. Now my new parents come. I was taken care of.

I read her story aloud slowly and with feeling. When I finished, Vera and I talked about the metaphor of her story. We noted that she had gotten hurt a "long time ago." Vera responded, "Maybe with a belt but I don't remember anything about it." We emphasized that she did escape into a family and a world that cares a lot about her. I thanked her for the story and told her I was really happy that together we had gotten so much done. I joked that she was graduating from our meetings, and, for her diploma, I wanted to give her one of my rocks that I had brought back from Sicily. She held it tightly and with a big smile said goodbye.

Concluding Comment

During the years that followed, Vera's parents occasionally contacted me to discuss her progress. She continued doing well academically and socially and became very invested in gymnastics and piano lessons. The parents also reported that, in her interactions with peers, she tended to give advice and reassurance, "behaving like a therapist."

4 Ernest and Vera from the Vantage Point of Environmental Psychology and Ecopsychology

The treatment cases presented in the previous chapters illustrated how each child's interaction with indoor and outdoor environments, as well as with the therapist, contributed significantly to the success of the treatments. Given my focus on the importance of the location in which treatment takes place, two schools of thought are relevant: environmental psychology, which addresses the relation between environments and behavior, and ecopsychology, which addresses why interacting with nature promotes well-being. In what follows, I summarize the main concepts of each school and ask you to imagine an environmental psychologist and an ecopsychotherapist discussing, from each of their respective viewpoints, the main themes Ernest and Vera generated during treatment. Following each presentation, a relational psychoanalyst responds to these formulations. My goal is to illustrate that, although environmental psychology and ecopsychology address the significance of the location in which therapy takes place, each school of thought leaves unanswered questions that are important in conducting child psychotherapy in indoor and outdoor environments, questions for which relational psychoanalysis provides answers.

New Directions in Environmental Psychology

Emerging in the 1950s, environmental psychology was committed to constructing a scientific understanding of the relationship between human behavior and environments and addressed questions faced by all disciplines seeking to understand such relationships. Should we see behavior as creating environments or environments as causing behavior? To answer this question, as Werner and Altman (2000) pointed out, environmental psychology was required to select one of Aristotle's two conceptualizations of determinism: "efficient cause," a process by which something impinges on a person, causing some outcome, and "formal cause," a process by which elements are seen as forming a holistic organization so that an influence exerted on any part influences the total unit. Environmental psychology elected to follow the view that environments determine behavior (Bonauito and Bonnes, 2000; Werner and Altman, 2000). For example, Sako (1997) compared the behavior of children attending small schools with that of children attending large schools and reported that small schools stimulate students to participate more responsively. Other examples are found in studies comparing behaviors observed in urban environments with those observed in rural environments (Wapner et al., 1997). Although the view that environments cause behaviors has dominated environmental psychology, a few voices have argued that studies should follow Aristotle's other concept of determinism. For example, more than 40 years ago, Heidegger (1962) proposed that a person and the environment should be understood only in terms of the holistic relationship they form, or what he called *dasein* ("being-the-world").[1]

Recently, investigators following Heidegger have proposed a holistic model referred to as "transactionalism," a model that in my

---

[1]Notice that, when enacting embodied life-metaphors, as defined in chapter 1 and illustrated by Ernest and Vera, when each of them and I participated in an enactment we "became" and "lived" in the meaning and its environment; we were "being-the-world."

opinion carries the most potential for our interest in addressing the issue of the physical location where psychotherapy is conducted (Wapner, 1995; Wapner and Demick, 2000). At the foundation of this model is the assumption that the unit of analysis consists of the person-in-the-environment, and a change in one part of the system affects the whole system. On this foundation three core concepts are constructed that integrate personal experiences, environments, and self-concept.

Within the person-in-the-environment system, a person gathers experiences and operates at three interrelated levels (Table 4–1): (1) physical (e.g., a person's unique physical makeup; actions a person takes); (2) intrapersonal (e.g., sensorimotor, perceptual, conceptual, and emotional experiences); and (3) sociocultural (e.g., the roles of others to which a person responds, and the role the person assumes when interacting). Environments are also defined at three levels: (1) physical (e.g., natural and man-made); (2) living organisms (e.g., peers, siblings, pets, wildlife); and (3) sociocultural (e.g., rules of a family, community, or society). With the third concept, body experiences are conceptualized as resulting in self-experiences at three levels. The first involves body actions and movements in relation to the environment (e.g., tactile experiences, moving the body and body parts at different tempos, gestures). The second level involves perceptions of the body as an object (e.g., the location of the body in space; the shape and size of the body and body parts; perceptions of touching or being touched). The third level involves conceptualizing body

TABLE 4–1
Proposals from the Transactional Model of
Environmental Psychology

- Person and environment form an indivisible system.
- Within this system, a person functions and gathers experiences at three levels: *physical* (actions), *intrapersonal* (meanings given to environments), and *sociocultural* (roles enacted by others).
- Within this system, the environment is defined at three levels: *physical* (man-made, natural), *interpersonal* (persons operating within that space), and *sociocultural* (rules governing relationships within the environment).
- Within this system, body experiences result in self-experiences at three levels: *body actions,* tempos, sensations; *perceptions* of the body as an object; and *conceptualizations* of body experiences (body image, self-concept).
- When development occurs, the system shifts from a global organization to a more differentiated and integrated one.

experiences that form a person's body image (e.g., fantasies, and linguistic metaphors representing body experiences).[2]

Transactionalism also proposes that each level of body-self experiences does not replace but integrates earlier levels, a view converging with embodiment theory, which we considered in chapter 1. In addition, transactionalism proposes that people interpret environments in terms of personal intentions and act on environments according to those interpretations. Moreover, to define change, the transactional model relies on the orthogenetic principle (Werner, 1957), which holds that, whenever development occurs, the entire system shifts from a global, undifferentiated state to a more differentiated and integrated state. As the person-in-the-environment unit becomes more differentiated and integrated, the person shows more flexible modes of coping, multiple ways of taking action to achieve the same goal, and multiple goals that satisfy the same need or intention. In studies following the transactional model (e.g., Wapner and Demick, 2000), differences in the behavior of two diagnostic groups of adult, hospitalized patients were examined prior to and following the physical relocation of the entire psychiatric community. The transactional model has encouraged psychotherapists "to address the role of personal space and other environmental factors in the context of psychotherapy" (Demick and Andreoletti, 1995, p. 65).

What a Transactional Psychologist Has to Say About Ernest and Vera

Relying on the concepts of transactional psychology, I raised the following questions. Is there evidence that Ernest and Vera entered treatment having already established a person-in-the-environment

---

[2]In thinking of body experiences as leading to self-experiences at three levels, notice that transactionalism relies on James's formulation (see chapter 1). The first (which involves movements of one's body in relation to the environments) and the second (which involves perceptions of one's body as an object) are related to James's (1890) concept of the Me-Self. The third (which involves conceptualizing body experiences) relates to James's concept of the I-Self.

unit? What experiences did each of them gather at the physical level, the intrapersonal level, and the sociocultural level? Did the body experiences they accumulated result in changes in their respective body images? Did the unit each of them constructed with environments change from a global to a differentiated-integrated form?

Ernest-in-the-environment. Ernest's initial detached, autistic-like state indicated that he had not constructed a person-in-the-environment unit. In the first phase of treatment, however, when he and the therapist sat in the cave while holding a rope, he showed a global, person–environment system. Later this system became slightly differentiated when Ernest pulled down on a branch with the rope, resulting in the "aaah-choo" game that gave Ernest and therapist the first opportunity to construct a meaning representing an emotion and body movements they could share.

Ernest differentiated his person–environment system further on two occasions: with the "near–far" activity, he redefined the environment to include space outside as well as inside the cave; with the activity involving pine needles and poisonous water, he elaborated his definition of the environment to include pain and danger as well as safety. His physical actions accepted running from painful needles to the safety of the cave and from poisoned water to the safety of a cluster of trees. Of special importance, Ernest included interpersonal body experiences during these activities when he occasionally asked the therapist to "kiss the booboo" on his hand, which had been hurt by pine needles, and when he asked the therapist to carry him to the safety of the cave after they had escaped from poisoned water.

When the therapist introduced acorns into their world, Ernest immediately accepted and interacted with them, indicating that his previous body experiences with the therapist were resulting in self-experiences related to Ernest's emerging body image. Guided by this image, he kissed the acorns and welcomed them into "our house," symbolizing that he experienced the therapist and cave as a safe holding environment. Similarly, by nestling in the concave area of a tree trunk, Ernest also expressed the embodied percept that, although surrounded by danger, he was being embraced by the arms of safety and warmth. At the start of this phase, sociocultural rules defined the world as only dangerous and painful, but roles played by

Ernest and the therapist eventually symbolized that safe places could be found and relationships could be caring.

In the next phase, Ernest relocated his person-in-the-environment system from the Therapeutic Garden to the playroom, where he expanded his interpersonal world to include toy vehicles that were ill. In response to the therapist's assuming the role of a "car doctor," healing vehicles, Ernest immediately accepted this meaning and pushed each vehicle along the floor in a demonstration that it was now competent. He also differentiated his environment further, now including a blue rug as shark-infested ocean water into which he fell, setting the stage for the therapist to rescue him.

While the sociocultural rules still defined the world as dangerous, these rules also defined a more differentiated role for the therapist as someone who not only found safe places in the environment, but also who could enable Ernest to become competent once he entered the outside world. It is especially important to recall that, since the start of treatment, Ernest held on to one end of a rope while the therapist held on to the other. This body experience created an embodied sense of attachment to Ernest's self-concept. We saw a hint of this when, while at home, Ernest was able to manage his anxiety at bedtime by placing the rope under his pillow.

Having confirmed that he would have assistance if he expanded his environment from the safety of the cave to include the outside world and the danger it presented, Ernest relocated his person-in-the-environment system from the playroom back to the Therapeutic Garden. The sociocultural rules now defined this environment as providing opportunities to cultivate assertiveness and competence by standing on the mount and shooting Styrofoam arrows with a bow and plastic balls with a pump gun, as well as by running through pathways like a train engine. With these physical actions, Ernest's body experiences and body perceptions contributed to the further development of his body image at a conceptual level. For example, he imagined that his shadow and the therapist's were joined, symbolizing their attachment, and he invented symbolic language that he shared with the therapist. Especially significant is that, after cultivating confidence and assertiveness, Ernest performed the physical action of marching over the pathways of his interpersonal world to hunt for and battle "Monstro," a more differentiated, humanlike form of danger that must be defeated before the outside world could be fully explored and relationships developed.

In the next brief phase, Ernest relocated his person-in-the-environment system back to the playroom, where he examined a book about the birth and development of butterflies, flapped his arms pretending to be a newly born butterfly, and ate snacks and pretended to be swimming with and kissing toy seals. During the last sessions of this phase, he reorganized and relocated his environment to include a related activity in the Therapeutic Garden. He busied himself by watering bushes he construed as hungry. The sociocultural rules that defined Ernest's environment and roles during this phase indicated that he was now ready to give birth to a new embodied self and enter a world that provided supplies and included living organisms that took care of each other.

During most of the next year of treatment, Ernest located his person-in-the-environment system in the Therapeutic Garden. Thus he further differentiated his world, his relationship with the therapist, and his body image. The sociocultural rules now defined that Ernest could stand as an individuated self, that the outside world consisted of both good and dangerous forces that could be distinguished, and that affiliation and empathy govern interactions so that people give as well as receive. Sometimes Ernest preferred to be alone, slowly walking along the rill. At other times he asked the therapist to join him in several activities—for example, hurling a Frisbee that Ernest imagined was a bird flying "where it wants to go" and shouting at the "bad wind" to go away while welcoming the "good wind."

Emerging from an accumulation of diverse body experiences that entailed interacting with the therapist and with features of indoor and outdoor environments, Ernest's body image eventually achieved more differentiated expressions, integrating previous body actions and body perceptions. Recall that he constructed, for example, "Ernest the UPS Train," "Ernest Fire Engine Puts Out Forest Fires," and "Ernest Bulldozer Plants Corn and Wheat." He constructed models of a battleship and a rocket and examined pictures of, and gave lectures on, human anatomy. Calling himself "Guard of the Garden," he reassuringly interacted with bushes and plants. Elaborating his self-concept further, he enacted being "Officer Dandelion" and assigned the therapist the role of throwing a knife into and removing "bad weeds." In another significant elaboration of his person–environment system, he invited another boy into his subjective world by playing the aaah-choo game in the cave. And, expanding his interpersonal world further, he chatted more often with office personnel before and after each session and gave them flowers he had gathered outdoors. These behaviors reflected that he was now using multiple ways to achieve the goal of interpersonal affiliation and had multiple goals to satisfy this need.

During the second part of this phase, Ernest located his physical environment in the hallways of the clinic and increased the number of persons interacting in his world by including clinic staff. The actions Ernest now performed involved frightening others by dropping pillows on them from the second floor. This activity represented at all three levels a much more differentiated and integrated person-in-the-environment system than Ernest had displayed at the start of treatment. From sitting in the cave and fearing a global, undifferentiated world that he avoided, he now saw the world as consisting of many persons performing diverse roles and coping with challenges. Ernest prescribed different doses of anxiety and fear to others and identified with and internalized the coping ability each person demonstrated. At the sociocultural level, the world now included many rules that defined an elaborate system of interpersonal interactions and varying degrees of anxiety.

In the last phase, Ernest selected the outdoors as the physical environment and performed many actions representing a wide range of meanings and emotions, such as ambition, competence, and affiliation. For example, he raced to a cluster of trees while being timed by the therapist. He sailed a leaf he called Champion Sailor down the rill, which he called the River of Life, and insisted that the leaf complete the journey without assistance. He established friendships with frogs in the pond and with clinical staff. He assigned a label to different sections of the Therapeutic Garden and constructed a world of "roads," "tunnels," "peaks," and "villages." He engaged pine needles, which give warmth and a sense of well-being when one touches them.

In summary, from the start of treatment to its conclusion, the indivisible unit that consisted of Ernest-in-the-environment underwent a complete transformation. Within this unit, Ernest became transformed from a withdrawn, detached self to a differentiated, individuated self with diverse emotions, needs and motivations. Over the course of treatment, he developed multiple modes to achieve the same goal, multiple goals to satisfy the same need, and an interest in establishing and maintaining attachments with others. Also within this person-in-the-environment unit, the environment became transformed from a global source of pain and danger to a differentiated organization of persons, rules for interacting, and various meanings and emotions, such as good, bad, pleasure, unpleasure, assertion, ambition, warmth, and nurture.

Vera-in-the-environment. During most of the first seven months of her treatment, the physical environment Vera constructed included the playroom and a barricade of furniture set against the door leading to the outside. The sociocultural rule defining this world, shared by toy animals and dolls, declared that individuality was not recognized. Initially the actions Vera performed represented regimentation, restriction, and body confinement (e.g., moving a line of toy animals an inch at a time across the floor and physically punishing them if they stepped out of line). The same sociocultural rule was extended to toy animals that were each fed exactly the same food and slapped if they touched it, and then extended again to Vera and the therapist, who were fed in the same regimented way and slapped if they touched the food.

By shifting from dolls to her body and that of the therapist, Vera's embodied experiences moved from a distal level to a proximal level so that in the treatment situation she physically experienced eating food in a very regimented way. From these actions, Vera accumulated self-experiences and bodily perceptions that resolved the embodied meaning that interpersonal interactions are severely regimented, and she developed the ability to experience eating as enjoyable. In addition, while preparing imaginary meals, Vera integrated her ethnic background with that of her therapist in a symbolization that the sociocultural rules changed dramatically during this phase, now permitting individuality, mutuality, and reciprocating.

In the next, very brief, phase, when Vera asked her therapist to write a story, which she titled "I Want to Run Away," she expressed her wish to achieve individual and emotional freedom. She located her environment outdoors with the intention of "rescuing" bugs, living organisms she added to her interpersonal world and that represented her intention to rescue herself. This intention was blocked, however, because sociocultural rules now defined that danger in the form of "danger eyes" existed everywhere as Vera directed that she and the therapist sit under bushes while the therapist drew the location of danger eyes peering at them from other bushes. The outer world, therefore, could not be engaged at this time.

During the months that followed, Vera located the physical environment in the playroom and the therapist's office, each defined by different sociocultural rules. The playroom was defined as a classroom that was as regimented as the previous environment in which toy animals had been fed. Here Vera's actions repeatedly expressed regimentation and restriction now imposed by a schoolteacher onto pupils who were played by dolls and the therapist.

In contrast, sociocultural rules defined the therapist's office as a shared world. Here Vera examined and discussed collections of stones and seashells, photographs of the village from which the therapist's family of origin had emigrated, and a globe that displayed the proximity of Vera's country of origin and that of the therapist. In addition, Vera declared to the therapist and to her parents that the therapist was a "doctor of body parts," signifying that her body experiences, which derived from interactions with the therapist since the start of treatment, resulted in self-experiences suggesting that her damaged, body image could be repaired. Eventually the sociocultural rules that defined the classroom shifted from regimentation to reciprocating and affiliation, as Vera directed that children who were newcomers to the neighborhood be warmly welcomed into the classroom.

During the next six months, Vera constructed a physical environment consisting of an easel draped with a large table cloth, which she labeled "our village." She constructed this village in a sequence of locations and spent a number of weeks in each: from the therapist's office, to the hallway just outside the therapist's office, to the playroom, and finally to the terrace in the Therapeutic Garden. In each location the sociocultural rules required that the village be surrounded by a more differentiated form of danger than the global "danger eyes" of the previous phase. Beginning with the village located in the office, and in each location thereafter, Vera directed the same actions. While she and the therapist attempted to sleep inside the village, she thumped her feet on the floor to signal that a "bad man" was coming. In response the therapist battled the imaginary attacker. Vera differentiated this person-in-the-environment system when she cut out photographs of men she found in magazines and used them as ID cards to determine if the person approaching was good or bad. By repeating this set of actions dozens of times during each session and in each location, Vera accumulated body experiences resulting in self-experiences that eventually viewed the world as safe.

During the next seven months, Vera used the same material to construct the same village in the same sequence of locations, but instead of sociocultural rules defining each location as under attack, each was now defined as "home." She labeled areas surrounding the easel as "kid's bedroom," "kitchen," and "living room." Guided by new sociocultural rules, Vera and the therapist now assumed the roles of "Mom" and "Dad" and enacted daily routines, including taking care of their children. As the physical location shifted from the office and hallway to the playroom, and therefore closer to the outside world, Vera's interpersonal world differentiated. She announced the arrival of neighbors by thumping her feet as she had done to announce the approach of bad men, now indicating growth by using the same action to achieve a different goal. Vera also directed the therapist to buy toys for their daughter to whom she gave the same name she had been given when in the orphanage. The body experiences Vera accumulated during this phase, when integrated within previous experiences, resulted in self-experiences and a self-image that enabled her to acknowledge she had been adopted—an acknowledgment that gained expression when she enacted being a "mother" who adopted a frog named Lucky. At the close of this phase, she differentiated and integrated the outside world further when, defining the entire garden as her home and neighborhood, she designated particular locations as "kitchen," "bedroom," "school," and "park."

During the last phase of treatment, Vera introduced a game defining a sociocultural world that presented the same issue that had dominated the early phases of treatment: namely, living organisms are confined and long to escape into emotional freedom. This meaning, however, was now expressed with actions at a much more abstract level, with Vera using wooden beads to represent persons. She assigned the therapist the task of manipulating other beads, representing rescuers, who persisted undauntedly to help Vera's beads escape. This game, cast in microactions and fantasies, indicated that Vera had resolved at the embodied level the impact of the trauma she experienced when in the orphanage and, therefore, could now represent these meanings in an abstract form instead of with physical actions involving her entire body. This achievement is illustrated by the story she wrote for a third-grade assignment. She expressed with words her understanding that during therapy she returned to the orphanage of her past to relive frightening experiences and that she had been rescued from that world of danger and abuse.

A Relational Psychoanalyst Responds to a
Transactional Psychologist's View of Ernest and Vera

Transactional psychology contributes to an understanding of one aspect of the treatment process constructed by both Ernest and Vera that psychoanalytic-relational psychology does not emphasize—namely, that Ernest and Vera, and each of the environments in which they interacted, formed indivisible systems and these systems were gradually transformed from global to more differentiated and integrated forms, signifying growth of the two youngsters.

Two other concepts that are part of the scaffold of transactional psychology, and are used to understand what Ernest and Vera did during treatment, are virtually the same in the framework of relational psychoanalysis. One is the assumption of constructivism that a person continually interprets environments and acts on those environments according to those interpretations. We saw, for example, that Ernest interpreted the outer world as painful when he touched pine needles and dangerous when he ran from water he construed as poison.

The second concept of transactional psychology that is the same in relational psychoanalysis proposes that body experiences are the foundation on which self-experiences are constructed, which, in turn, result in a child's body image. Unlike transactionalism, however, relational psychoanalysis emphasizes that body experiences that occur during interactions in the first years of life establish the meanings assigned to interpersonal experiences later in life. Moreover, relational psychoanalysis also emphasizes that meanings, specifically embodied life-metaphors, constructed early in life are extended by a child into environments and interactions so that the child can continue negotiating particular unconscious developmental needs the metaphors represent, whether these needs concern promoting growth or resolving the impact of traumatic experiences that impede the child's growth.

The concept that a child introduces and represents early experiences into enactments and interactions relates, in turn, to other concepts within the model of transactionalism that do not adequately deal with the treatment process. With one, transactionalism typically examines a single change from one person–environment unit to another, a change typically introduced by people other than the person forming a unit with the environment in question—for example, behaviors associated with children making the transition from first grade to second grade. During treatment guided by relational concepts, illustrated by Ernest and Vera, the child, not someone else, decides with which particular environments he or she forms a series of person–environment units. Transactional psychology, then, does not contain concepts that help us to understand changes in environments that a child introduces during treatment.

Nor does transactionalism provide therapists a way to understand the significance of the sequence of person–environment units a child constructs. This issue is particularly important because, when several locations are available, most children would very likely construct a sequence of different person–environment units during the course of treatment. For example, the sequence of environments with which Ernest formed indivisible units included behind a couch, to a cave, to pine trees that inflicted pain, to spraying water that could poison you, to a playroom with toy trucks that were ill, to the top of the mount where he shot arrows and hurled Frisbees, to pathways in the garden where he hunted Monstro, to the playroom and a book about the birth of butterflies, to the mount where Frisbees thrown by the therapist were birds flying where they wanted to go, to the playroom and books about human anatomy, and so on.

The view that a child initiates a particular series of changes in person-in-the-environment units relates to the need to address several interrelated questions about the treatment process (Table 4–2). While we agree with tranactionalism's view that a person interprets

TABLE 4–2
Questions That Call for Answers in Response to Transactionalism's
Evaluation of Ernest's and Vera's Treatment

- How can we understand that, unlike as propounded by transactional psychology, the child decides which changes in environments take place and with which environments he or she forms an indivisible unit?
- While relational psychoanalysis agrees that the environment a child enters is interpreted in terms of personal intentions, could the meanings guiding these interpretations be operating at an unconscious level?
- How can we understand why during treatment a child shifts through a particular sequence of person–environment units and how a particular sequence helps the child develop?
- How should the therapist participate during a particular sequence of child-in-the-environment units?
- Should the therapist initiate changes in environments, thereby directing the child to form a different person-in-the-environment system?

environments in terms of personal intentions and acts on the environment according to those interpretations, is the person always consciously aware of the intentions guiding the interpretations, or could the intentions be operating at the unconscious level? How can we understand the way in which a particular sequence of person-in-the-environment units a child constructs, and the interpretations that guided how a child acted within each unit, help that child address his or her difficulties during interactions with the therapist? Should the therapist discourage a child's shifting from one person–environment unit to another? Should the therapist guide the child to a particular, new environment? In psychoanalytic-relational psychotherapy, the child decides who interacts within the environment and the sociocultural rules defining those interactions. How can we understand the living organisms the child introduces within the person–environment unit and the sociocultural rules the child formulates to govern the interactions that take place?

Ecopsychology and the Healing Power of Nature

Ecopsychology recently emerged to focus on the healing power of nature and the view that there is an intimate connection between a person and the places with which that person interacts.[3] The rallying cry for this emerging school was sounded by Roszack (1992), who stated,

> The goal of ecopsychology is to awaken the inherent sense of environmental reciprocity that lies within the ecological unconscious. Other therapies seek to heal the alienation between person and person, person and family, and person and society. Ecopsychology seeks to heal the more fundamental alienation of person and environment [p. 320].

---

[3]The roots of ecopsychology can be found in propositions such as the one by the architect Frederick Law Olmsted, who in 1865 stated, "[Nature] employs the mind without fatigue and yet exercises it, tranquilizes it and yet enlivens it; and thus through the influence of the mind over the body, gives the effect of refreshing rest and reinvigoration to the whole system" (quoted by Ulrich and Parsons, 1992, p. 95).

Roszack (1995) also urged psychotherapists to integrate the natural world into their work. A number of responses to Rozak's urging can be found in the literature: for example, clinical psychology was reminded that its focus on individualism ignores the contributions of nature to well-being (Carr and Schumaker, 1996); a synthesis of traditional psychology and ecopsychology calls for a paradigm that includes the concept of an "ecological self," or one's unique relationship with nature (Fenwick, 1999); Gestalt therapy, which employs methods for reconnecting with one's body perceptions, has been proposed as fertile ground for the emerging field of ecopsychology (Swanson, 1995); and the viewpoints of ecopsychology have been related to the concepts of Carl Jung (Yunt, 2001) and the fields of psychiatry (White, 1998) and clinical psychology (Merkl, 1995). Of particular relevance here is Conn's (1998) discussion of how ecopsychology urges psychotherapists to expand their focus beyond a person's internal landscape by exploring the person's interactions with the natural landscape. And Spitzform (2000) compared the propositions of ecopsychology with those of relational psychoanalysis—a proposal we considered in chapter 1. In addition, ecopsychology has stimulated a growing number of clinicians and researchers to study how passive and active contact with nature serves therapy with children and adults and has given rise to a set of concepts as well as a model of therapy (Table 4–3). The momentum of ecopsychology has reached a pitch that has resulted in newspaper articles informing the general public how flowers have power and how gardening can improve a person's mental health (Walzholz, 2003).

The Benefits of Passive Contact with Nature

Studies have documented that passive contact with trees, bushes, wildflowers and water, for example, promotes a sense of well-being, reduces stress, and enhances physical health.[4] Here are a few examples. After completing a demanding cognitive task, adults who walked through an area filled with trees and vegetation were more relaxed than were subjects who read magazines, listened to music, or walked in an urban area. Adults sitting in the waiting room of a dental

---

[4]For example, see Kaplan and Kaplan (1989), Hartig, Mang, and Evans (1991), Relf (1992), Ulrich and Parsons (1992), and Flagler and Poincelot (1994).

TABLE 4–3
Proposals from Ecopsychology and Ecopsychotherapy

- Preferences for natural landscapes emerged during human evolution; survival was promoted by our learning that danger can exist in enclosed places whereas open landscape provides safety, invites exploration, and is more readily understood.
- Passive context with features of nature has a positive effect on everyone and restores well-being because (a) a passive context is less intense and complex than are man-made environments and provide diverse stimulation to the senses, and (b) when one is experiencing these features, attention shifts away from internal turmoil and toward sensations that bring pleasure.
- To facilitate this shift in attention, nature-based tasks are designed to increase sensual awareness and provide pleasurable experiences through the senses.
- Nature-based assignments are designed by the therapist on the basis of activities the patient identifies as bringing pleasure to the senses.
- The primary therapeutic relationship is between patient and nature. The therapist serves as tour guide.
- Instead of trying to remove conflict, therapy focuses on experiences that bring enjoyment.
- The therapist offers metaphors to the patient that symbolize how nature-based assignments represent a journey through life.

clinic were less stressed when a large mural depicting mountains and trees was hung on the wall than were subjects who sat in the same waiting room when the wall was blank. University students who were experiencing mild stress because of a final exam recovered to a greater degree after viewing slides of rural settings than did students who viewed slides of urban scenes. And hospitalized surgical patients who had available a view of nature from their windows required fewer hospital days postoperatively, and less medication, when compared with patients who did not have a window view available.

Consistent with these observations of adults, studies also document that children and adolescents prefer outdoor sites. For example, Schiavo (1988) asked children and adolescents what they liked best about their neighborhood: 46 percent of the total sample described such places as ponds and woods where they could play, and 86 percent reported having places in their neighborhood where they could explore. Schiavo also gave a camera to all the youngsters and asked them to photograph "any place in your neighborhood that is important to you." The sites photographed most often by each age group involved natural landscapes. Along the same lines, when children living in Great Britain were asked to draw their favorite place, only 4 of the 96 children drew a picture depicting the interior of a building (Moore, 1990). A number of studies[5] involving children in the United States have reported similar results, and a preference for natural landscapes has also been observed in Italian, Australian, and Pakistani children.[6]

Why Children and Adults Prefer Contact with Natural Landscapes

Although emphasizing different viewpoints, theories explaining why children and adults prefer contact with nature converge with the idea that contact with vegetation relieves stress (Ulrich and Parson, 1992). One view proposes that environments with high levels of noise, movement, and visual complexity fatigue human sensory systems and that restoration is fostered by plants and trees, which are low in intensity, complexity, and movement. Another view holds that contact with nature diverts a person's attention away from stress-producing thoughts. And still another emphasizes that people form a positive association with the landscape during vacations, whereas they form stressful associations with manufactured environments because of noise, traffic, and fast pace.

In contrast to theories emphasizing environmental features that inherently have a negative or a positive influence, other viewpoints conceptualize that natural landscapes satisfy "needs" intrinsic to human psychology, such as a desire to find out more about one's surroundings and constructing a sense of certainty and predictability (Kaplan and Kaplan, 1989). Such theories relate to the "biophelia hypothesis," proposing that preferences for natural landscapes emerged during human evolution: survival was promoted when *Homo sapiens* learned that enclosed places might contain predators whereas open landscapes provided secure places in which to live (Orians and Heerwagen, 1992; Lewis, 1994).

---

[5]For example, see Maurer and Baxter (1972), Berg and Medrich (1980), Bernaldez, Gallardo, and Abello (1987), Owens (1988), and Chawla (1992).

[6]For example, see Moore (1990), Purcell et al. (1994), Woolley and ul Amin (1995), and Herzog et al. (2000).

Psychological Therapies Conducted Outdoors

Given the accumulating evidence that adults and children alike prefer and benefit emotionally from contact with natural landscapes, it is not surprising that using the outdoors as the location for psychological treatment has been growing steadily.

Horticultural therapy. Horticultural therapy typically involves growing, harvesting, and processing plant life and has been part of the treatment of a wide range of patient populations, including child and adolescent psychiatric inpatients.[7] According to Stamm and Barber (cited in Mattson, 1992), horticultural therapy activates and exercises several psychological functions—for example, *regularity* (plants require nurturance and continuous care to survive), *impulse management* (gratification is delayed as a person learns that it takes time for plants to grow), and *anxiety reduction* (physical labor helps reduce anxiety and stress). As Mattson noted, the "value of a bushel of tomatoes is more than just dollars and cents" (p. 167). In contrast to the relatively widespread use of gardening in the treatment of adults, the approach has been used on only a few occasions to treat children with emotional disabilities (e.g., Muleski, 1974; Jesse et al., 1986), to help stuttering preschoolers (Rozhdestvenskaya and Pavlov, 1967) and to promote the cognitive and social development of toddlers (Wortham and Wortham, 1989).

Adventure and wilderness therapy. Adventure and wilderness therapy programs are typically preferred for children and adolescents and involve activities much more vigorous than gardening, such as hiking, rock climbing, and canoeing.[8] These programs have been viewed by some as providing adolescent sexual offenders opportunities, such as during rock climbing, to empathize with victims and to experience intimacy (Lambie et al., 2000). These programs enable adolescent survivors of sexual assaults to experience a physically challenging situation that evokes the same feelings of helplessness they experienced during

---

[7]For example, see Beckwith and Gilsten (1997), Stein (1997), Riordan and Williams (1998), and Simson and Strauss (1998).

[8]For example, see Kiewa (1994), Fine, Coffman, and Aubrey (1996), Williams (2000), and Ewert, McCormick, and Voight (2001).

the assault, but with the program they now have an opportunity to conquer those feelings (Levine, 1994). In addition, adventure programs have been used to help inner-city adolescents to develop a sense of self-definition (Harris, Fried, and Arana, 1995), to promote self-esteem and social cooperation in learning-disabled children (Chisholm, 1985), and to strengthen trust and teamwork in high-risk youths (Davis, Ray, and Sayles, 1995). Such programs have also been incorporated into family therapy programs (Teeple, 1989; Burg, 2000; Burns, 2000). A review of the literature revealed that both anecdotal and empirical data support the view that treating adolescents in a wilderness setting is more effective than treatment in an indoor facility (Williams, 2000).

Ecopsychotherapy. Ecopsychotherapy was formulated by Burns (1998) on the grounds that "nature [is] an initiator of health, healing, and well-being" (p. 201). Although his model is for treating adults, I give it particular attention because his conceptual framework incorporated various applications of outdoor treatment and provides a context that raises questions addressed by the model I outline for conducting child psychotherapy outdoors as well as indoors. In broad terms, ecopsychotherapy proposes that it is beneficial to shift attention away from internal personal problems toward sensory experiences that bring pleasure. He writes, "While psychotherapy has traditionally looked within the individual for answers, ecopsychotherapy explores how the answers may be found in our relationship with the natural environment" (p. 76). To facilitate this shift from personal turmoil to pleasurable external experiences, ecopsychotherapy cultivates a person's senses to enhance the experience of pleasurable environmental stimulation. Burns states that ecopsychotherapy is effective, brief, solution oriented, and based on promoting experiences that are pleasurable and empowering ("The primary relationship, unlike the case in psychoanalytic therapies, is not between client and therapist. The therapist serves a role perhaps akin to a traveler's guidebook," p. 29).

From this conceptual base, the main therapeutic strategy involves encouraging the patient to engage in nature-based assignments such as sitting and looking at a spider's web or walking along a beach to search for seashells. To help a therapist determine which attributes of nature could be useful for a given patient, the patient is asked to list activities for each sensory modality from which he or she obtains pleasure. Relying on this data, the therapist designs tasks to help the patient focus attention on experiences that promote a sense of well-being. From Burns's point of view, nature-based assignments provide opportunities for learning that are not available in the consulting room and "ought to be pleasurable experiences or at least have a pleasurable outcome" (p. 103).

Burns presents case illustrations for each sensory modality. For the sense of sight, he instructed a depressed 40-year-old woman to rise before dawn, walk to a riverbank, and watch a sunrise. When she returned to the next session, the patient described herself as "certainly much better," and Burns noticed an improvement in her emotional state. For the sense of hearing, Burns describes a man with a history of experiencing stress related to sounds because as a child he was frightened by the sounds of bombing raids in England. When a family with teenagers moved next door, the sound of rock music booming from the house was so stressful he wanted to move. Burns assigned this man the therapeutic task of walking along a river and focusing on sounds he found pleasurable.

Using the concept of the "experiential metaphor," Burns also addresses the meaning that a patient gives to nature-based experiences. In his model, unlike in psychoanalytic therapy, the therapist guides the patient in constructing a metaphor of his or her experiences with nature. As an example, Burns described his work with Wayne, who had crashed into a lamppost, endured physical injuries, and became depressed. Since Wayne had already decided to trek through the Himalayan Mountains, his plan satisfied the first step in constructing a metaphor, namely, planning a "journey." Burns writes, "In many ways the journey through nature parallels our trek through life and can thus serve as a metaphor about life" (p. 127). In Wayne's case, then, Burns joined his patient in planning details for his journey to the Himalayas.[9]

What an Ecopsychotherapist Has to Say About Ernest and Vera

Relying on the concepts of ecopsychology, three questions guide an examination of the activities of Ernest and Vera during treatment

---

[9]As discussed in chapter 1, the concept of metaphor that I use in my model for child psychotherapy is quite different from Burns's.

sessions. Is there any evidence that Ernest's and Vera's relationship with nature had been ruptured and that during treatment each of them healed this alienation? Did Ernest and Vera show evidence that their sensual awareness had increased and, accordingly, that they had become more able to engage nature and derive enjoyable sensations through the senses? How well did the therapist play the role of tour guide, making suggestions that could enhance their sensual awareness of various features of nature?

Ernest from the viewpoint of ecopsychotherapy. People prefer natural landscapes because we are influenced by inherent needs that promote our functioning and ensure survival. One of those needs concerns finding out more about one's surroundings. Ernest was driven by this need when, peering through branches at open landscapes, he demonstrated that he wanted to engage experiences provided by nature. Ernest's behavior exemplified that of a person whose relationship with the environment had been ruptured and who needed to heal this fundamental alienation.

Ernest clearly accomplished this repair by the last phase of his treatment. Laying by the rill, he listened to water bubbling over rocks; he felt warmth and affection while pressing his hands and cheeks against pine needles; and he experienced affiliation and companionship when interacting with frogs. Perhaps one of the most vivid illustrations of Ernest's having resolved his alienation from the environment was his assigning a name to each part of the Therapeutic Garden—creating a map, as it were, of a world he now embraced. That Ernest resolved his alienation from the environment supports Burns's (1998) position that nature-based experiences provide options for learning about life, survival and enjoyment that are not available in the office or the playroom.

Next we should notice that throughout treatment Ernest made use of features of nature in ways indicating that the ability of his senses to perceive stimulation steadily increased, as did his capacity for pleasure. He climbed the mount many times and ran over hilly pathways playing at being a train, both activities that provided pleasurable kinesthetic sensations. He munched on snacks, sometimes had the therapist feed him, and experienced the pleasure of taste. Obviously enjoying the sound of rippling water, he lay down by the rill. Standing on the mount, he shouted greetings to the wind, as he felt it caressing his face and body. And he gently touched leaves and watered bushes when he played "Guard of the Garden." Incidentally, some ecopsychotherapists would add that Ernest was practicing aspects of horticultural therapy in that he was experiencing nurturing and caring for the life of plants as important emotions.

In terms of the therapist's role as a tour guide, he appeared to have performed his duties relatively well. When Ernest rolled the ball out of the cave in the near–far game, for example, the therapist repeatedly crawled out to retrieve the ball. Thus he illustrated to Ernest a sense of confidence that the environment, with its natural features, could be engaged as a source of pleasurable sensations. The therapist also handled acorns and placed them in Ernest's hands, and Ernest continued interacting with these acorns, nestling them in a concave area of a rock. In general, by introducing various ways of engaging landscape and by joining Ernest when he engaged landscape, the therapist increased Ernest's sensual awareness and opened up possibilities for Ernest to experience the environment with pleasure rather than fear, pain, and anxiety.

Vera from the viewpoint of ecopsychotherapy. Vera's behavior during the first months of treatment provides another excellent, and even more dramatic, example of a person whose relationship with the natural environment had been ruptured and who eventually healed this fundamental alienation. Initially, before each session, she barricaded the door leading to the outside; she avoided going outdoors for six months. When she finally entered the garden, she made use of this location for only four weeks. Then she remained indoors for a year before she returned to the outdoors, again for only a brief period. It was not until another year later that she finally constructed what she called "her home" and designated various areas in the garden as kitchen, living room, bedroom, and so on. And while engaging these features of the garden, she played "house" much as a child her age would with a doll house. With this activity she clearly demonstrated that she had healed the alienation between her senses and the natural environment.

One of her behaviors at this time is especially important from the standpoint of ecopsychotherapy. Vera caught and fed frogs and talked to each one in a friendly and affectionate way before returning it to the pond. During these activities, she imagined the frog was an orphan, and she was a mother adopting the frog. This behavior reflects one concept of ecopsychotherapy—that a playroom or office would not have made available such opportunities for Vera to learn about life and the caring an orphan requires to survive. Vera seemed to be stimulated in particular by the sense of touch. She handled stones from the therapist's collection several times and at the conclusion of treatment constructed a collection of stones from her yard and the Therapeutic Garden.

Whenever Vera did make use of the outdoors, the therapist seemed to serve as an adequate tour guide, suggesting possibilities to Vera that helped her increase her sensual awareness. As one example, she and the therapist gave tours of the "neighborhood" to imaginary visitors. When Vera and the therapist sat on the mount, the therapist passed his hand through tall grass and pointed out how "good it feels," an experience Vera imitated. One interaction occurred indoors that also illustrates how the therapist served as a tour guide. The therapist began chewing gum, which opened up the possibility to Vera that she, too, could enjoy the sense of taste. Vera's enjoying the taste of gum resulted in her and the therapist feeding each other and in Vera's overcoming her difficulty eating food.

A Relational Psychoanalyst Responds to the Ecopsychotherapist's View of Ernest and Vera

Psychoanalytic-relational psychology agrees that Ernest and Vera initially showed that each of their relationships with natural environments had been severely ruptured. We also agree that during treatment each child healed this alienation, experienced pleasurable sensations made available by features of nature, and developed a sense of well-being. But several concepts of ecopsychotherapy seem to be contradicted by behaviors Ernest and Vera displayed during treatment.

To begin, ecopsychotherapy maintains the view of positivism that enclosed places inherently evoke a sense of danger whereas open landscapes provide a sense of safety and security. Yet Ernest made clear at the start of treatment that he experienced the cave as safe and open terrain as dangerous. Then there is the assumption that particular features of nature evoke a sense of pleasure and well-being—for example, seeing trees swaying in the wind, touching the leaves of bushes, and smelling vegatation. Yet, instead of seeking stimulation in nature that brought pleasure, Ernest and Vera initially searched for stimulation that caused pain and aroused fear and anxiety. Ernest devoted many sessions to touching the needles of pine trees while screaming in pain, and he ran in fear from water, which he experienced as poisonous. For several months, Vera barricaded the door of the playroom against the outside and avoided the natural landscape altogether. And when she finally entered the outdoors, she felt anxious and fearful because, for her, danger lurked everywhere.

An ecopsychotherapist could respond that these behaviors, and others by Ernest and Vera, were simply expressions of the alienation that existed between each of them and their natural environments. Psychoanalytic-relational psychology would rebut this response and raise several questions (Table 4–4). First, do these behaviors by Ernest and Vera express something other than their alienation from natural environments? As used in ecopsychology, alienation means insensitivity to, or a detachment from, stimulation offered by nature. If we examine these behaviors closely, we could argue that, rather than being detached from nature, Ernest and Vera were very much in touch with environmental stimulation and actually searched for, preferred, and engaged stimulation that evoked pain, anxiety, and fear.

TABLE 4–4
Questions That Call for Answers in Response to Ecopsychology's
Evaluation of Ernest's and Vera's Treatment

- Why do some children, when interacting with nature, seek forms of stimulation that provide minimal variation, low intensity, and static and predictable sensations, which are opposite from the forms that are assumed to be inherently beneficial?
- Why do some children experience features of natural landscape as painful and frightening instead of as providing pleasure and enjoyment?
- Why do some children search for and prefer to reexperience negative stimulation when engaging nature?
- If a child's destination in therapy is to resolve the alienation between himself or herself and nature, and if the child searches for stimulation that causes anxiety, what can a therapist do (in addition to suggesting that the child engage in stimulation that should bring pleasure) to enable the child to reach that destination?
- Why do some children require many months of treatment, while others are reported to overcome their emotional difficulties after only a few experiences with natural landscapes?
- Once a child resolves his or her alienation from natural environments, what does it mean for the child to have a relationship with nature that is free of conflict, anxiety, and fear?

With this in mind, the question could be phrased in another way. Why did features of the natural landscape that most persons experience as pleasurable activate fear and anxiety in Ernest and Vera? Is it possible that the alienation between a person and nature cannot be healed unless the conflicts and disagreements that exist among meanings within a person's self are healed first?

A related issue is reflected by the patient Burns (1998) described who experienced anxiety and fear whenever he heard rock music booming from next door. To help this person "switch off" the cause of stress, Burns assigned him the nature-based task of walking along a river and listening to birds chirping and the rustle of the wind in the trees. In contrast, rather than switching off the source of stress, Vera preferred to hear, over and over again, the thumping of feet, which announced that danger was arriving and evoked in her intense fear. About this issue, relational psychoanalysis would ask, is it possible that a person needs repeatedly to reexperience unpleasant stimulation, rather than switching it off, in order to resolve the particular meaning of that stimulation?

Still another question arises if we consider Ernest's and Vera's behaviors in the context of the characteristics of the nature-based stimulation by which ecopsychology explains why contact with nature is associated with a sense of well-being: variation, intensity, and anticipation of the unexpected. Yet Ernest sat in a cave at the start of treatment. He clearly preferred less variation, intensity, and unexpected happenings. As for Vera, not only did she avoid entering nature, but initially she became totally preoccupied with lining up and moving toy animals an inch at a time. With this behavior she actively avoided variation, intensity, motion, and the unexpected; she preferred, instead, regimentation and constancy. Although Ernest and Vera finally experienced enjoyment when engaging the landscape, what pathway did they follow, beginning with each of their painful starting points, to reach their respective, successful destinations?

The pathway a person should follow eventually to enjoy nature has to do with the point proposed by ecopsychotherapy that a therapist should serve as a travel guide. To carry this analogy further, does the therapist simply suggest to a child enjoyable experiences based on what the child has already found pleasurable—attend a summer camp, visit the seashore, or go to a zoo or a museum? Are there guidelines to help a therapist decide which experiences should be emphasized for a given child to increase the likelihood he or she will reach the final destination—that is, resolving the alienation between himself and herself and natural environments? And, once this alienation is resolved, what does it mean for a child to have a relationship with nature that is free of conflict, anxiety, and fear?

Is it possible to restore the relationship between a traumatized child and nature in a brief period of time? Although addressing the treatment of adults, the treatment examples that Burns (1998) gave could apply to children. Recall the depressed woman who described herself as "certainly much better" after she had walked to a river-bank before dawn and watched the sunrise. And Burns describes a woman who experienced panic attacks when riding buses but was able to ride buses after only three sessions during which she was guided to focus on the pleasurable smells in her backyard. As we saw, Ernest and Vera required at least three years to resolve the alienation that existed between each of them and nature. Why did they need so much time?

Concluding Comment

The questions raised by psychoanalytic-relational psychology are addressed by a model for conducting psychotherapy with children outlined in the next chapter. The model I propose includes aspects of environmental psychology's transactionalism that follows the assumptions of constructivism but does not include the positivistic concepts and techniques of ecopsychotherapy.

5 A Psychoanalytic-Relational-Developmental Model for Conducting Child Psychotherapy

The model I propose to guide child psychotherapy has at the center of its foundation the concept that the process that takes place between child and therapist is fundamentally the same as the process of "growing together" that takes place between infant or toddler and caregiver.[1] In his concluding remarks to the participants at the first World Congress of Infant Psychiatry held in Carcais, Portugal in 1980, Erik Erikson (1983) shared a view that converges with psychoanalytic-relational psychology and relates to the model I propose: "As we learned to treat children . . . we found that [therapeutic] intervention in the widest sense really means involvement in the overall dynamic of 'growing together' . . . which alone can heal" (p. 425). If child and therapist are to grow together so that the child can heal, we must ask, how should we map the child's self, the therapist's self, and what child and therapist do as they grow together to achieve their goal (Wilson, 1995; Santostefano, 1998a)?

---

[1]Related views have also been proposed by Stern (1985), Spiegel (1989), and Nahum (1994).

Since I advocate that child psychotherapy should take place outdoors as well as indoors, this mapping requires that we find a way to
integrate a child's "outside" environments, viewed by ecopsychology
as containing stimuli that promote well-being, with a child's "inside"
environments, viewed by psychoanalytic-relational psychology as
consisting of a landscape of intrapsychic and interpersonal meanings
given to experiences. To map the self and mind of both child and
therapist, and to integrate environments in which they grow together, I do not ask what knowledge a therapist should provide a
child to help the child overcome his or her difficulties. Rather, I ask
how child and therapist should interact with each other and nonhuman landscapes while growing together so that the child resolves
conflicts and assumes a growth-fostering developmental pathway.

Another question emerges from this viewpoint. In what language should child and therapist communicate as they grow together? Although Aragno and Schlachet (1996) were addressing
psychodynamic psychotherapy with adults, they made an important point related to this question: "Defining our therapies as the
'talking cure,' our theories do not address the question of the language in which the talking should be done" (p. 23). Observing how
adult patients for whom English was a second language participated
in psychotherapy, they reported, "We found these patients were
able to access intense, emotional meanings when encouraged to re-
count early, traumatic experiences in their language of origin" (p.
31). Similarly, I propose that child and therapist should interact in
ways that encourage the child to access and relive his or her traumatic experiences in the child's *interactive language of origin,* including physical enactments, postures, gestures, rhythms of nonverbal
and verbal behaviors, and emotional tones. But much as is the case
when treating bilingual adults, I am reminded that the interactive
language of origin that a child brings to treatment is a second language for the therapist and vice versa.

A Therapeutic Model for Learning a Child's
Interactive Language

The foundation of my model follows assumptions of psychoanalytic-relational psychology (see chapter 1) and relational-developmental theory (Overton, 1998). Subscribing to constructivism,

relational-developmental theory defines development as change that takes place within the meanings a person assigns to his or her interactive experiences, the modalities that express these meanings, and the functions these expressions serve. This position also holds that relational means dialectical: "From a relational point of view, a one-person psychology and a two-person psychology are alternative perspectives of the same psychological whole" (Overton, 1998, p. 72), a position articulated by others (e.g., Aron, 1996; Frank, 1999).

The Goal of Psychoanalytic-Relational-Developmental Child Psychotherapy

The goal of treatment is to help a child construct a new matrix of embodied life-metaphors within his or her self (as defined in chapter 1). This goal includes developing more interactive flexibility within the child's embodied self and also between that self and available human and nonhuman environments. To achieve this aim, the therapeutic process must first help the child relive meanings and emotions representing stressful relationships and traumatic experiences that the child internalized. The process must then guide the child in enacting solutions to the quandaries presented by these experiences. Once constructed, this new self equips the child to interact and participate within a diverse range of human and nonhuman environments, providing new ways for the child to negotiate embodied life-metaphors that promote continued development and resulting in new meanings representing new experiences. A relationship negotiated during treatment that does not give rise to new ways of being and relating "is a rearrangement of old furniture" (Summers, 2001, p. 639).

The goal I propose, then, is to help a child construct new furniture or new embodied life-metaphors that become integrated within his or her matrix of embodied life-metaphors. My aim, and the emphasis I give to a child's expressing in action conflicts and solutions, is supported by research illustrating that, as child and parents grow together, the child's self is not promoted if the parents relieve stress by providing immediate comfort, but, rather, if the parents first allow the child to experience distress and then help the child develop ways to resolve it (Demos, 1992; Summers, 2001). My intention and methods also are supported by research demonstrating that much of learning and change occurs through action and nonverbal interactions rather than through "insight" (Reiser, 1990; Holinger, 1999; Summers, 2001).

The roots of my model are located in a viewpoint introduced by Sándor Ferenczi (1920, 1931) and elaborated by others.[2] He proposed that therapists use what he called the "active technique," which had the therapist asking a patient either to engage in an enactment or to avoid taking some action, whichever facilitated reliving an experience. Ferenczi believed that, as patients relived the experiences in question, they could free-associate more easily, thereby analyzing more thoroughly the issue with which they were struggling. For example, Ferenczi might encourage a patient to stroke his or her face or hands, or, if a melody came to the patient's mind, encourage him or her to sing the melody aloud.

Ferenczi's proposal was elaborated by Michael Balint (1932, 1934), who in the 1930s pointed out that a therapist's task was to create an interpersonal climate in which the patient could experience the therapist as analogous to an infant's caregiver. Within this interpersonal climate, Balint argued, the patient could heal his or her "basic fault" and construct more flexible patterns of interacting with others, an achievement he termed a "new beginning." Then the therapist could provide the patient opportunities to engage in new experiences during treatment sessions that could have therapeutic value. To take one example, Balint asked an inhibited young woman to perform a somersault during a treatment session, following which she showed a sharp increase in her progress.

In the 1950s, Franz Alexander (1950, 1956) described the technique of constructing a "corrective emotional experience" to help a patient develop new ways of interacting and relating. First the therapist modified his or her ways of relating in order to create an interpersonal atmosphere in which the patient could reexperience attitudes and behaviors of others he or she had encountered in the past that were the cause of the patient's maladaptive ways of responding. Benefiting from a phase of reexperiencing, the patient corrected his or her ways of interacting. With this technique Alexander hoped to demonstrate to patients that they misunderstood

---

[2]Bacal (1990) provides a review from which I have drawn the summary of positions presented by psychoanalysts who followed Ferenczi.

current relationships and could develop new ways of responding based on new perceptions.

For W. R. D. Fairbairn (1958), the main goal of any form of psychoanalytic treatment that maintained a relational orientation was to help the patient reintegrate the parts into which his or her original self had been split by traumatic events (see also Aron, 1998b; Stern, 2002). Along with Alexander and Balint, Fairbairn argued that interpretations and discussions were not sufficient to help a patient reintegrate those parts of the self that were disconnected. Rather,

> [it is] the actual relationship between the patient and the analyst [that] constitutes the decisive factor. . . . By this "actual relationship" Fairbairn means . . . the total relationship between the patient and analyst as persons; in particular [a] relationship with a reliable and beneficent parental figure [Bacal, 1990, p. 367].

Techniques to Help a Child Resolve Psychological Turmoil and Develop a New Matrix of Embodied Life-Metaphors

To set the stage for a discussion of techniques in conducting child psychotherapy that derive from the proposed relational-developmental model, let us begin with a statement by Aron (1998b):

> Gradually patient and analyst mutually regulate each other's behaviors . . . such that each gets under the other's skin, each reaches into the other's guts . . . the analyst must be attuned to the nonverbal, the affective . . . [and] to his or her bodily responses, so that these may be . . . gradually utilized to construct metaphors and symbols that may be . . . exchanged by [patient and therapist] [pp. 25–26].

My model defines three broad phases in which child and therapist participate and during which each gets under the skin and into the guts of the other. They thus are enabled to construct and enact traumatic embodied life-metaphors and solutions to the conflicts represented, and eventually grow together. In the first, the child and the therapist develop a shared interactive language and repair the link that was disrupted between the child's I-Self and Me-Self. In the second phase, the child and the therapist relive embodied life-metaphors the child enacts that represent stress and trauma that the child internalized, and the therapist enacts solutions to each conflict. As the child identifies with and internalizes each solution, the total constellation of solutions serves the child in constructing a new matrix of embodied life-metaphors and a new self. In the third phase, the child, equipped with a new self, gathers new experiences within and outside treatment while interacting with human and nonhuman environments, experiences that promote the child's continued development.

To define the cycles of interaction in which child and therapist participate throughout the three phases, I have integrated Louis Sander's (1962, 1964, 1989) model of issues that a toddler and caregiver negotiate and Stern's (1985) model of the senses of self that emerge from negotiations, both of which we discussed in chapter 1. I also subscribe to Stern's position that cycles of relatedness between infant and caregiver remain active throughout development: "none are lost to adult experience. Each simply gets more elaborated" (p. 31). Accordingly, although dominant at particular times during treatment, each interactive cycle remains active and becomes elaborated throughout treatment.

Finally, the dialectical interactions I describe do not result in a child's acquiring new knowledge. Rather, by developing a new self, a child changes how he or she understands and gives meaning to experiences. At the same time, changes in how the child understands contributes to the child's developing a new self (Goldberg, 1987). Moreover, as demonstrated by infant research, change also results from the interacting and negotiating that give rise to "implicit relational knowing" that stems from perceiving and understanding what takes place between one's body and the bodies of others during mutual regulations and recognizing each other's motives and desires that direct action (Stern et al., 1998).

Cycles I Through III: Developing a Shared Interactive Language and Repairing the Relationship Between the Child's I-Self and Me-Self

At the start of treatment, in cycles I through III, a therapist sets out to enter and discover himself or herself in the child's matrix of embodied life-metaphors by seeking opportunities to negotiate initial adaptation and reciprocal exchange—for example, being charmed, antagonized, or frustrated when interacting with the child. At the same time, the therapist facilitates the child's discovering himself or herself in the therapist's matrix of embodied life-metaphors. Aron (1998b), addressing how therapists help adult patients repair their self-reflexive functioning, sets the stage for my view concerning children. He points out that the therapist should convey that he or she understands what the patient is feeling and experiencing, which, in turn, stimulates the patient's Me-Self to engage that feeling and the patient's I-Self to perceive it. Aron emphasizes that ideally the therapist should convey a "visceral" understanding to the patient "through a good interpretation, but it may also be done by expressing a feeling of one's own . . . or even through a more direct bodily response, such as a sudden gasp, a change in posture, breathing, or facial expression" (p. 29).

I propose that, when working with children, as opposed to adults, during these first cycles, therapists should avoid interpreting and discussing and instead focus on registering and conveying with bodily expressions a "visceral" understanding of the children's unformulated emotional experiences. With a sudden gasp or a change in posture, breathing, or facial expression, a therapist should enact rhythms of gestures, movements, and dialogue that are coordinated with the child's so as to communicate nonverbally, "I feel what you feel; show me more." This recommendation is founded on studies demonstrating that, as early as 12 months of age, infants interpret the actions of others in the context surrounding the interaction (Woodward and Sommerville, 2000) and that rhythmicity between child and caregiver as they negotiate developmental issues is a crucial factor in the child's development (Acredolo and Goodwyn, 1998; Jaffe et al., 2001). Nahum (1994) writes, "How [the infant's] action patterns are recognized and responded to determine in an important fashion the nature of the infant's self and self awareness" (p. 10).

Requiring a therapist to communicate with body language that he or she understands what the child feels and means, however, typically runs into an obstacle that is also faced by any caregiver attempting to grow together with an infant. Initially infant and caregiver, as well as child and therapist, communicate in an interactive language that is not totally familiar to either. The interactive language of the child and that of the therapist is a second language to the other. M. E. Johnson (1993) notes, "It is virtually inevitable

that the child therapist will work with a client who has a social, ethnic, or cultural background different from her or his own" (p. 68). I,
however, propose that in the beginning of treatment child and therapist are always of "different interactive cultures" whether or not they
are of the same social or ethnic background.

In the first months of treatment, then, child and therapist are
faced with the same task that infant and caregiver face—namely, negotiating a shared interactive language, and especially the shared
rhythmicity that requires, in particular, that child and therapist negotiate reciprocal exchange and direct each other's actions, gestures, facial expressions, and emotions (see chapter 1). This requirement is in
the service of translating each other's nonverbal vocabulary, as is the
case with the development of communication during the first 18
months of life (e.g., Acredolo and Goodwyn, 1996). Notwithstanding
this similarity between the child–caregiver dyad and the child–therapist dyad, there is an important difference. Although the caregiver has
already constructed a matrix of embodied life-metaphors, with its interactive vocabulary, the infant has not. In contrast, at the start of
therapy, child and therapist each have already constructed a unique interactive language that evolved during past interactions and that is being shared with others outside treatment. It is necessary, therefore,
that they first participate in negotiations conceptualized in the first
three cycles of my model.

As shown in Table 5–1, let us imagine a circle as representing a
shared, interactive matrix with its unique vocabulary. In the beginning, child and therapist, although interacting, are standing outside
this circle (cycle I): the child discusses a school trip while playing a
board game, and the therapist asks questions about the trip and participates in the game. But during these interactions the child and the
therapist are not learning each other's interactive language. During
the second cycle, the child steps into the circle, usually without conscious awareness, to negotiate some aspect of his or her interactive
vocabulary, but the therapist fails to step in and communicate an understanding: while relating a comment the teacher made that day,
the child slowly passes her right hand back and forth over her left
arm, which has a bruise; the therapist remains focused on the child's
description and does not respond to the gesture (Table 5–1, cycle II).
Conversely, sometimes, with or without awareness, a therapist steps
into the circle to negotiate some aspect of his or her interactive vocabulary. For example, because the therapist's laugh is more subdued

than the child's, at one point she spontaneously bursts out laughing loudly. The child's behavior suggests that he did not experience and perceive the difference in sound volumes.

Throughout these initial interactions, then, a therapist should focus as much as possible on being authentic while taking special care to notice whether and how his or her matrix of embodied life-metaphors influences how he or she experiences the child's and also influences how the child experiences the therapist's.[3] Along the same lines, much like the case in the first phase of negotiations between caregiver and infant (chapter 1), while negotiating initial adaptation and reciprocal exchange, the therapist should make an effort to distinguish between what is unique about the child's interactive language, on one hand, and, on the other, what the therapist prefers the child to be.

At one point, as child and therapist continue interacting, they both step into the circle and "contour" themselves to some aspect of each other's nonverbal, interactive vocabulary, much as infant and caregiver do (Stern, 1985). Each responds in ways indicating that his or her Me-Self has registered and experienced unique qualities of the other's interactive language and emotional experience which his or her I-Self interprets (see Table 5–1, cycle III). Each gets to know and understand, for example, how the other walks and moves when excited or when tired and how the other sighs, laughs, and glances when disappointed or when pleased. This is an interactive process analogous to Stern's (1985) "core relatedness" between infant and caregiver. During this process, techniques a therapist might use include imitating a gesture or facial expression the child typically performs during a moment of excitement or physically enacting in a genuine way an emotion or fantasy the child is experiencing.

Each time the therapist expresses a gesture, facial expression, or emotional tone during dialectical interactions, it is crucial that he or she be as consistent and authentic as possible. To recall the discussion in chapter 1, a child conserves and constructs a mental representation of an interaction, concerning some particular part of the vocabulary of the interactive language being negotiated, only when the constellation of actions, sensations, and emotions is repeated

---

[3]Similar views have been expressed by others treating children (Maroda, 1998) and adults (Aron, 1996; Knoblauch, 1997; Frank, 2002).

TABLE 5–1
Cycles of Interacting, Negotiating, and Enacting Embodied Life-Metaphors: How a Child Develops a New Self That Overcomes the Impact of Psychological Difficulties

Cycle	Dialectical Circle/ Shared Interactive Matrix (•Child, ■Therapist)	Types of Interactions and Goal	Issues Negotiated	Sense of Self and Relatedness
I	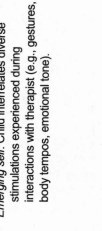	*Repairing dialectical relationship between child's I-Self and Me-Self.* Child and therapist interact, but each remains in his or her respective world with its unique interactive vocabulary; therapist focuses on experiencing and understanding the child's nonverbal vocabulary.	*Initial adaptation* →	*Emerging self.* Child interrelates diverse stimulations experienced during interactions with therapist (e.g., gestures, body tempos, emotional tone).
II	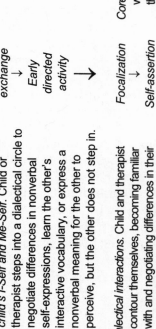	*Repairing dialectical relationship between child's I-Self and Me-Self.* Child or therapist steps into a dialectical circle to negotiate differences in nonverbal self-expressions, learn the other's interactive vocabulary, or express a nonverbal meaning for the other to perceive, but the other does not step in.	*Reciprocal exchange* → *Early directed activity* →	→
III		*Dialectical interactions.* Child and therapist contour themselves, becoming familiar with and negotiating differences in their respective nonverbal interactive languages, coordinating rhythms of nonverbal and verbal behaviors, and constructing a shared interactive language.	*Focalization* → *Self-assertion* →	*Core self/core others.* Repeating experiences with the therapist in the subjective world they are sharing, child summarizes and conserves these experiences in representations of interactions.

Enacting traumatic embodied life-metaphors and solutions.
Remaining in their shared dialectical world, child and therapist enact constellations of actions, images, emotions, and words representing others' traumatic responses the child has internalized; therapist participates in each enactment, experiencing the quandary with the child, and also enacts solutions that the child internalizes.

Testing and modifying aggressive intentions; inventing/ sharing symbolic behaviors

Subjective self and intersubjective relatedness. Child understands motives and intentions of self and therapist and shares with therapist subjective experiences that represent meanings he or she gave to aspects of traumatic events.

Constructing a new psychological landscape/self and matrix of embodied life-metaphors. Child idealizes, internalizes, and integrates behaviors and meanings that therapist enacted to solve quandaries the child expressed; therapist idealizes child's victories; child engages therapist and others in new interactions and negotiations that are growth fostering.

Consolidating embodied meanings of solutions to quandaries child and therapist enacted

Constructing a new psychological landscape/self. Traumatic meanings child and therapist enacted are resolved and transformed, resulting in the child's developing a new self and new relationships with human and nonhuman landscapes.

with little variation. Equipped with these representations, the child is able to anticipate what to expect, determine what is going on, and experience trust in the shared world he or she and the therapist are constructing. As child and therapist enter the dialectical circle more and more frequently, a shared interactive language and trust begin to be reflected, for instance, by the child's explicitly reciprocating the therapist's emotions and body language more often. Once a shared interactive language and trust are established, the child and the therapist coauthor, enact, and reexperience embodied life-metaphors related to the child's traumatic past (addressed in Table 5–1, cycle IV). Ernest and Vera illustrate cycles I, II, and III.

Ernest and I Develop a Shared Interactive Language and Repair the Relationship Between His I-Self and His Me-Self: Examples of Cycles I, II, and III

Because of the severe detachment Ernest initially presented, what happened during our first meetings provides behavioral examples, in slow motion, of how he and I recycled through cycles I, II, and III. During the first session, Ernest remained behind a couch on which I sat. I chatted with mother and held a piece of rope draped over my shoulder, with the hope that he would interact with me by taking hold of the other end. Throughout the hour, however, he remained invisible and silent (cycle I). Engaging as much as possible the dialectical relationship between my I-Self and my Me-Self, I concluded that, given Ernest's silence, my typically animated, nonverbal, interactive language, and my eagerness to establish a connection with Ernest, had spilled into the vigor with which I had interacted with mother. I reminded myself that during the next meeting I would try a more subdued interactive style that might better match Ernest's.

During the second and third sessions, I intentionally remained silent and motionless for minutes at a time, but Ernest did not respond (cycle II). My efforts, however, very likely contributed to Ernest's stepping into a dialectical circle with me for a brief moment when, about five minutes before the third meeting was to end, he took hold of the rope (cycle III). Attempting to express a greeting, I pulled on my end with what I thought was a gentle movement, but I failed to fit Ernest's rhythm of interactive dialogue, for he immediately let go of his end and returned us to cycle I. Later I decided that I had pulled the rope too soon and with too much vigor and reminded myself again to pay closer attention to how I was regulating my interactive language during these initial meetings.

In the fourth meeting, when Ernest again took hold of the rope, this time I waited for several minutes before tugging ever so slightly on my end. Much to my pleasant surprise, he continued holding his end of the rope. During these moments we were contouring our respective interactive vocabularies to each other (cycle III). When, intending to continue interacting, I tugged the rope again, however, Ernest let go of his end and returned us to the first cycle. I tried to subdue my rhythm of interacting with mother even more and sometimes slowly swayed the rope back and forth. Ernest eventually took hold of the rope, and I held on to my end while relating to mother (cycle III). Now I waited at least five minutes before tugging on the rope ever so slightly. This time, Ernest held on to his end for several minutes and remained within a dialectical circle with me (cycle III).

During the next meeting I again felt that Ernest had taken hold of the other end of the rope, and again I waited at least five minutes before tugging slightly on my end. When I did, Ernest continued to hold on to his end. Several minutes later, while I continued to chat with mother, I felt a slight tug. I waited several minutes before responding and then tugged my end. Ernest continued to hold on. For the remainder of this hour we interacted by exchanging slight tugs with the rope (cycle III). By reciprocating, Ernest demonstrated that a shared interactive language and trust were beginning to gel and that I had been sufficiently successful in putting myself on Ernest's schedule of rhythms, much as is required of a mother during interactions with an infant (Nahum, 1994). In the sixth session, after we again exchanged tugs on the rope, Ernest eventually stood up so that we could see each other—an achievement that was an outgrowth of our negotiations.

When I stepped away from the waiting room, at the start of the next meeting, Ernest, holding his end of the rope, walked along with me. During these moments I focused on moving my body very slowly. When sitting in the cave, in an effort to learn what Ernest was experiencing, on occasion I moved a branch to one side and wondered what was out there. Apparently my interactive rhythm at that moment was discordant with Ernest's because he lowered his head and became more detached. Later I had another opportunity to engage Ernest in coordinating our rhythms of nonverbal and verbal behaviors by whispering a long, soft "aaah" when he lowered a branch of the hew over which he had draped our rope. Ernest joined me in repeating this expression and later spontaneously sang "choo" when he released the tension on the rope and the branch snapped up to its original position. Recall that for many sessions we repeated this "aaah-choo" activity as we continued to practice coordinating our interactive language and rhythms.

In the playroom, Ernest engaged in activities that provided us with additional opportunities to negotiate our respective interactive vocabularies and also offered me the opportunity to express that I was registering his unformulated emotional experiences. When he placed a toy truck on the floor and repeatedly rolled it back and forth, for example, I rolled my truck too in an effort to imitate his rhythm. When he stepped into and out of an inflated tire tube a number of times, I imitated his body rhythm and postures as best I could. And when he surveyed the large rug that covered one end of the playroom floor, I registered that he wanted to engage it in some way. Therefore, I stepped from one medallion on the rug to another in slow motion. Soon Ernest imitated me, as I had imitated him, when he engaged the tire tube and toy truck. That Ernest reciprocated suggests that our shared interactive language was continuing to take shape and mutual trust was developing further. Throughout these first meetings, Ernest and I oscillated several times through cycles I, II, and III, while I searched for opportunities to let him know that I was registering his unformulated emotions and body experiences.

Vera and I Develop a Shared Interactive Language and Repair the Relationship Between Her I-Self and Her Me-Self: Examples of Cycles I, II, and III

When Vera began constructing a barricade against the door of the playroom at the start of each evaluation session, I immediately joined her by gesturing, grunting, and moving my body in ways to convey that I knew she was experiencing anxiety and fear and that I would try to prevent anything from entering our room. Since she accepted and responded to my participation, these interactions appeared to indicate that we were constructing a shared interactive language (cycle III).

In the first therapy session, however, after we barricaded the door, she slowly walked about the playroom while ignoring me (cycle I). Minutes later, she examined a number of toy animals and placed them in a line on the floor, sometimes turning an animal toward and then away from the animal immediately behind it. In an effort to express my understanding of what she was experiencing, imitating her rhythm and gesture, I moved one of the animals in the line very slightly several times. About 10 minutes later, she manipulated a toy elephant that asked each animal in line for its name. At one point I spontaneously asked the toy animals if they wanted to know my name. Recall that Vera subsequently assigned my name to one of the animals but continued to ignore me except at the close of the session, when she asked if we could save the toy animals. For most of this meeting, then, each of us remained in our respective subjective worlds (cycle I). When she assigned my name to one of the toy animals, Vera did step into a dialectical circle, but, at that time, I did not know what she had in mind or how I should respond, so I did not step in (cycle II).

In the next sessions, although we examined a book about the offsprings of animals and insects, each of us was still standing outside a dialectical circle, for the most part. I tried, however, to coordinate myself with her rhythm of movements and sounds when we examined each page of the book. It was clear that she was into the issue of "mothers and their babies," but I was not sure what other aspect of her interactive language I should engage. After we looked over the book, she took out pairs of toy animals, designated one "mother" and the other "baby," and placed them in a column of two. On a number of occasions, while on my hands and knees, I took a careful look at the toy animals in the column and edged one about half an inch forward or backward. Vera ignored me, or at least did not respond with a gesture or comment, which still qualified our interactions mostly for cycle I.

At one point, she placed a baby animal next to a mother that was a different animal. With each mismatch, Vera expressed confusion, which I thought she very likely had experienced in the orphanage. In an effort to convey that I understood what she was experiencing, I tied a piece of yarn of one color on a mother animal and a piece of another color on a baby animal, so that they could tell who is who. This time instead of ignoring me, Vera accepted my participation and joined me in tying a piece of the appropriate yarn around each animal, as well as on each of our wrists. This activity facilitated our constructing a shared interactive language and repairing the relationship between Vera's Me-Self, which was experiencing confusion, perceived by her I-Self, which accepted my solution (cycle III). Apparently this activity also clarified for Vera that she was the child and I the parental figure.

In subsequent sessions, Vera invited me to join her in locating pairs of toy animals in a column of two and tying pieces of the appropriately colored yarn around each one. Having identified who was who, on occasion I took a toy baby animal and, moving it across the floor, played that it was desperately trying to be free. Apparently, Vera's Me-Self experienced and her I-Self interpreted what I was experiencing as evidenced in enactments she introduced in the following sessions that enabled her to relive various meanings of the traumatic interactions she had internalized when living in the orphanage.

Cycle IV: Reliving Traumatic Embodied
Life-Metaphors and Enacting Solutions

Once a child repairs the relationship between the I-Self and the Me-Self to a sufficient degree, experiences that a shared, interactive language is being developed, and trusts that the therapist is willing to be recruited to enact roles related to conflicts with which the child is struggling, the child enacts an unconscious embodied life-metaphor. This embodied life-metaphor represents some aspect of internalized traumatic or stressful interactions with others. The child also hopes and expects that the therapist will participate in reliving the meaning and eventually enact a solution. In short, during this cycle, the child enacts some meaning that essentially conveys, "Show me; be who I need you to be; don't just talk"—an issue also discussed by Bacal (1988). This process, projective identification, is determined by the shared interactive language and trust that has been created between child and therapist (Ogden, 1990; Ginot, 1997).

After the first enactment, a child typically introduces over many sessions a series of others, each representing a meaning within the constellation of embodied life-metaphors the child assigned to the total traumatic experience and internalized into his or her matrix of embodied life-metaphors. Each solution that child and therapist enact, and that the child internalizes, builds on previous solutions; thus the child is enabled to resolve all or most of the ways in which the traumatic experiences derailed his or her psychological landscape/self. This process of child and therapist participating in enactments parallels Stern's (1985) concept of "intersubjective relatedness" between infant and caregiver and relates to the concept that mutual understanding between persons leads to the desire to enact what is known (Smith and Franklin, 1979; Ginot, 1997).

Discussing how relational psychoanalysis applies to clinical practice, Aron (1996) asks, "How much does the analyst get caught up with the patient in therapeutic action? How much is the analyst involved in the enactments and interactions?" (p. xii). For the conduct of child psychotherapy and psychoanalysis, the response from my model is, "As much as is indicated by the child and as much as the therapist can handle." In this cycle, then, at issue is the therapist's capacity to accommodate the child's needs and to allow himself or herself to be recruited by the child to enact roles related to experiencing the traumatic meanings the child is expressing and to enact solutions (Holinger, 1999). Since enacting a traumatic embodied life-metaphor is conceived of as reliving a past traumatic experience, it would be appropriate for us to ask if these enactments qualify as memories.

Enacting Traumatic Embodied Life-Metaphors and Memories of Infant Trauma

Paley and Alpert (2003) remind us that professionals, as well as parents, continue to ask questions posed initially by Freud more than a century ago: "Can infants store traumatic experiences in memory? How, if at all, do they emerge later in life?" (p. 329). To address these questions, the authors integrated the findings of nine studies investigating what children remember of trauma that occurred during infancy or early childhood. Paley and Alpert compared these reports with third-party documentation of the events in question (e.g., eye witnesses, police reports). They concluded that these studies indicated four types of memory presentations:

Behavioral memories are spontaneous expressions of trauma in everyday activities. "Usually there is no awareness of the link between the behaviors and the original trauma that gives rise to them" (p. 332). Examples include repetitive play; chronic withdrawal or tantrums;

sadistic or sadomasochistic behaviors; and protest behaviors such as reluctance to eat, speak, or travel.

Somatic-somatosensory memories are physiological arousals closely connected with trauma-specific experiences. "This category of memory presentation is particularly relevant to traumatized newborns or young infants who may perceive trauma predominately as concrete, sensory perceptions" (p. 337). Examples include sensations across one's skin, rashes, pains, or aches; changes in bladder, bowel, or digestive function; and startle reactions.

Visual memories are typically depicted in drawings, or the child identifies photographs as representing figures present at the time of the trauma (e.g., hospital personnel).

Verbal memories are spontaneous verbal statements about a traumatic experience, with or without prompts from others. Some researchers have acknowledged that verbal memory presentations might have been elicited by questions and expectations of parents, police and the researchers themselves (p. 341).

Ernest and I Relive and Solve Traumatic Embodied Life-Metaphors: Cycle IV

Apparently, from Ernest's point of view, we had become sufficiently familiar with each other's interactive language, constructed a good enough, shared interactive vocabulary, and established mutual trust; what followed made clear that he believed I was able and willing to participate in reliving and solving traumatic embodied life-metaphors. Ernest repeatedly rolled a ball out of the cave. Each time, expressing fear, I scrambling out to retrieve it and then crawled back now expressing relief. His emotional expressions and gestures made clear that he identified with my fear and frantic efforts to retrieve the ball and my relief when I returned.

My solution that the ball could be returned to the safety of our relationship helped Ernest to introduce the next enactment, which elaborated the traumatic meaning we were reliving. He repeatedly raced out of the cave, placed the palms of his hands on pine needles, and screamed, representing physical pain he had endured early in life during hospitalizations. Each time, I joined him and placed my hands on pine needles while also screaming. This enactment appears to be an example of behavioral and somatic-somatosensory memories.

The first few times Ernest enacted this activity, I responded by racing back to the safety of our cave. As he continued to repeat the enactment, he spontaneously raced back to the cave, which indicated that he had internalized my solution symbolizing that, if the outer world inflicts pain, we can escape to the safety of our relationship. Ernest elaborated the meaning of danger and pain the outer world could inflict when he enacted the "poison" game and screamed with fear as he ran from the spray of a water sprinkler. Also screaming, I spontaneously enacted another solution. Now I ran to an area under a cluster of large trees and exclaimed with relief that we were safe. We ran to the safety of this area during many repetitions of this enactment. Building on the previous solution that our cave or personal relationship provided safety, this time my solution differentiated the outer world so that it contained safe places as well as danger. The poison game qualifies both as a behavioral memory and as a somatic-somatosensory memory.

Our solutions to representations of danger and the pain Ernest had suffered freed him to enact negotiating developmental issues that had been neglected in his first years of life because of his mother's depression. Negotiating reciprocation, Ernest slowly moved a tower of wooden blocks toward my tower with a bulldozer, while I moved a tower toward his. Then we exchanged bulldozers and moved the towers again. We repeated this enactment many times. Recall that on occasion Ernest brought attention to the fact that, from his point of view, my rhythm of movements sometimes was not coordinated with his—an observation reflecting the importance of coordinating rhythmicity in negotiating issues, also observed in mother–child interactions (Nahum, 1994).

Ernest introduced two other enactments, confirming that I was unconditionally available and capable of healing what had been damaged in his core self. In one, toy vehicles were sick, and I responded by being a "car doctor" capable of healing them. In the other, he rolled on the rug as though he were being attacked by sharks, and I pulled him to safety using our rope. Having internalized my responses and negotiated my unconditional availability and ability to heal, he introduced a new series of enactments indicating that he was ready to cultivate his competence and join me in coping with whatever dangers and demands the outer world presented. He shot arrows and plastic balls as high as he could. He ran about the Therapeutic Garden as a "little train engine," and I as a "big train engine," each of us experiencing and sharing power. One indication that Ernest was internalizing and idealizing my responses of confidence and competence is reflected by his enacting that our shadows held hands as we ran about.

Building on these experiences and achievements, Ernest launched a new and very significant enactment, representing his attempt to conquer the fear that was the source of the detached, autistic-like embodied self he had brought to treatment. Sword in hand, he explored the entire Therapeutic Garden to hunt for and destroy Monstro, who had been terrorizing the outer world. Later he played at frightening the clinic staff by dropping pillows on them from the second floor and kept a record of their endurance and ability to cope. From these interactive experiences Ernest constructed a new psychological landscape/self and matrix of embodied life-metaphors with enactments that are summarized in cycle V.

Vera and I Relive and Solve Traumatic Embodied Life-Metaphors: Cycle IV

Once Vera and I had constructed a shared interactive language and established mutual trust, she enacted a series of embodied life-metaphors, each representing a traumatic meaning from the constellation of meanings she had internalized to signify responses of staff at the orphanage. She located about 10 animals in a column, the space between each exactly the same and moved each an inch at a time so that the column crept across the floor and into a large box. Joining Vera, I imitated her movements and painstakingly moved each toy animal. After many sessions, during which we moved a column of sometimes 30 toy animals, I occasionally initiated responses in an effort to learn if Vera would join me in constructing the beginning of a solution to the severe intrapersonal and interpersonal regimentation we were experiencing. I took one of the animals in the line, for example, turned it around, and exclaimed, "Hey! Who are you?" On other occasions, I expressed frustration, primarily by my emotional tone and gestures, over having to remain in line. When Vera included handcuffing a doll, I protested for the doll. Whenever I initiated one of these responses, however, she did not join me.

Given that Vera ignored my protests, I eventually realized that she needed to relive, for an extended period of time, the embodied

meaning of severely regimented interpersonal and intrapersonal interactions before she could join me in solving her quandary. Accordingly, I decided that my main job at this point was to continue
participating with Vera in reliving the regimentation with as much
authentic involvement as I could muster; I continued to acknowledge her emotional experience by gesture, action, and emotional
tone. The next traumatic embodied life-metaphor Vera enacted
concerned animals, and then ourselves, being fed under conditions of
severe regimentation and our being slapped if we touched food.
Slowly moving a line of toy animals, handcuffing a doll, feeding toy
animals and ourselves exactly the same food, being slapped and
scolded, all qualify as behavioral memories (Paley and Alpert, 2003).

At one point, when Vera and I were enacting regimented eating,
I placed a stick of gum in my mouth and vigorously chewed it, expressing the wish to eat freely. By this time, Vera had apparently
sufficiently relived the meaning of regimentation because she internalized my response and accepted it as our first attempt to escape
into freedom. During this and the next sessions, she requested sticks
of gum and chewed as many as five at one time. This shared activity
eventually led to her asking for food, which I provided and which she
ate with increasing pleasure. My chewing gum also led Vera to enact
our preparing and eating food from our respective cultures of origin.
That enactment reflected the degree to which her matrix of embodied life-metaphors and mine had formed a constellation of shared
meanings. The resolution we achieved to the severe regimentation of
embodied, interpersonal, and intrapersonal interactions also resulted in Vera's eating more freely at home. That Vera internalized
my wish to escape to freedom was dramatically reflected by her asking me to write a story about a girl who "wants to run away." With her
next enactment, however, she made clear that escaping to freedom
was not yet possible. While hiding under bushes in the Therapeutic
Garden, Vera said that we were surrounded by "danger eyes," representing another embodied meaning that derived from interactions
with personnel of the orphanage. For Vera, the outside world was
dangerous, and other traumatic meanings were in need of resolution
before she could gain emotional freedom.

Before Vera could deal with what danger eyes represented, her
psychological landscape/self required that she first continue resolving the embodied meaning of severely regimented interpersonal interactions, but now extended to her first-grade classroom. At the

same time, she also visited my office. She examined and discussed various items—for example, a globe displaying her country of origin and mine and photographs of a village from which my family of origin had emigrated. She asked many questions about my family and my daily activities and commented that I was a "doctor of body parts."

With these interactions, Vera continued to internalize my responses, provide opportunities for each of us to become more familiar with the matrix of embodied life-metaphors of the other, and strengthen her identification with me. Given the content of her next enactment, Vera apparently had relived and resolved to a sufficient degree the embodied meaning of regimentation, and had adequately consolidated a shared matrix of embodied life-metaphors with me, so that she was now ready to relive and solve the major traumatic meaning that had crippled her psychological development.

Vera devoted six months to reliving that traumatic meaning. As we slept in our "village," we were continually attacked by "bad guys" whose arrival Vera announced by thumping her feet against the floor. Each time, I responded by leaping out and vigorously battling the imaginary enemy. First we engaged in this enactment in my office, followed by the hallway outside my office, then the playroom, and finally the Therapeutic Garden. In each location, Vera identified with and internalized my responses. She paid close attention to the vigor with which I physically fought the enemy. This shared enactment represented a meaning that in the past her body-self had always been in danger of being assaulted and qualified as behavioral memories of the trauma she endured.

At one point, Vera introduced an elaboration that could qualify as a related visual memory. She searched through magazines and cut out pictures of faces of male figures that she designated were ID cards carried by men who approached the village. Vera passed these pictures over stones she had gathered from my collection to determine which men had to be beaten away. This activity symbolized that my stones, or my body-self, which she had internalized, could serve her in evaluating dangerous or safe relationships. She and I, finally defeating those evil men, thus were able to obliterate the responses of persons in the orphanage Vera had construed as dangerous and internalized. From this victory Vera engaged in enactments designed to construct and express a new psychological landscape/self and matrix of embodied life-metaphors.

Cycle V: Constructing a New Psychological Landscape/Self and Participating in New Experiences

Once a child sufficiently relives the internalized traumatic meanings that he or she assigned to responses of others, and internalizes solutions the therapist enacts, the child begins to construct a new psychological landscape/self and matrix of embodied life-metaphors. With the availability of this new self, the child, during treatment sessions with the therapist and with others outside treatment, now searches for new experiences with human and nonhuman environments that previously could not be engaged—experiences that gradually reform the child's matrix of embodied life-metaphors and promote the child's development.

Ernest Constructs a New Psychological Landscape/Self and Matrix of Embodied Life-Metaphors: Cycle V

To appreciate the new matrix of embodied life-metaphors and self that Ernest eventually constructed, I remind us that before treatment he was viewed by others as "autistic-like," detached from the outside world. Over the course of treatment, the meanings of my solutions with which Ernest identified and internalized included, for example, that we could enter the outside world (near–far activity); that there were safe places in the outside world in spite of danger and pain that could be inflicted ("ouch" and "poison water" activities); that I was capable of saving him and helping him manage danger (repairing "sick" toy cars and rescuing him from sharks); that we could develop the power to manage that world (e.g., shooting arrows high in the air, running like train engines); and that we could (and did) destroy danger in the outside world (hunting for and destroying Monstro).

Internalizing these and other responses resulted in his constructing a new psychological landscape/self and matrix of embodied life-metaphors that were capable of maintaining flexible, dialectical relationships between his Me-Self, experiencing human and inanimate environments as empathic, trustworthy, and caring, and his I-Self, perceiving and understanding these experiences in ways that served his development. To illustrate: he invited another boy to enter the cave and join him singing our aaah-choo song while I filmed them; he picked flowers for office staff, with whom he chatted; he enacted being Guard of the Garden, feeding and talking to plants in reassuring, affectionate tones; he enacted being Officer Dandelion, ensuring that weeds were removed; he interacted with frogs and established a special friendship with one of them; he removed leaves from the rill so that "clog river" became the River of Life; he sailed a leaf, Champion Sailor, down the River of Life; and he assigned an identity to each part of the Therapeutic Garden. Last, and of special significance, he pressed his hands on the same pine needles that once caused him pain but now provided warm, caring, pleasurable sensations. This new self continued developing years after we concluded treatment, as noted by his parents.

Vera Constructs a New Psychological Landscape/Self and Matrix of Embodied Life-Metaphors: Cycle V

For two years I participated with Vera in reliving meanings and emotions that represented traumatic responses she had internalized while interacting with staff of an orphanage: all interacting, including eating, was severely regimented, and one was always in danger of being attacked. This traumatized psychological landscape/self searched for environments and interactions that would provide opportunities to reexperience repeatedly several traumatic meanings: severe interpersonal regimentation (e.g., not touching food and tilting her head back when being fed); lack of relatedness (e.g., ignoring relatives); fear and the danger of possible physical assault (e.g., barricading the door of her bedroom). I, by my responses, attempted to cope with and solve each quandary she enacted. For example, while joining her in moving a column of toy animals, I, too, moved one, expressing the wish for freedom; and I battled "bad guys" to prevent possible physical assaults. Vera internalized my responses, which, when integrated, made it possible for her to construct a new psychological landscape/self and matrix of embodied life-metaphors, which included flexibility, mutuality, affiliation, and dialectical relationships with available human and inanimate environments.

She used the same material that formed our village to construct what she called "our home," initially located in my office, then in the

playroom, and later in the Therapeutic Garden, a progression signifying that she had dissolved the barriers between herself and human
and inanimate environments. In each location, instead of battling
evil men, we enacted that we were parents, preparing meals, taking
our children to school, receiving mail from friends, and entertaining
visitors. On occasion, Vera actually invited other children and their
therapists into our home.

In dramatic contrast to the constricted matrix of embodied
meanings she had maintained, Vera and I now lived in an environment consisting of persons and places that permitted individuality,
friendships, safety, and mutual affection. One particular enactment
qualifies as a verbal memory. Vera assigned a name to a doll ("our
daughter") that had been her name when she lived in the orphanage.
Her parents indicated that Vera had never used that name before.

Illustrating that her psychological landscape/self and matrix of
embodied life-metaphors had developed a growth-fostering dialectical relationship with available human and nonhuman environments,
Vera designated various areas of the Therapeutic Garden as parts of
our home, the school our children attended, and a park we visited.
Following a response by me that I enjoyed feeling the texture of the
tall grass we were sitting on, Vera frequently passed her hand over
grass and leaves, commenting "nice," reflecting that her sense of
touch, which many view as the foundation of experience (e.g.,
Barnard and Brazelton, 1990; Blackwell, 2000), was free of traumatic
interference.

Vera also enacted being the adoptive mother of frogs. She constructed a collection of stones located in her backyard and the
Therapeutic Garden to "keep her company," representing the integration of our experiences within her matrix of embodied life-metaphors. Another datum supporting that Vera had constructed a
new self comes from her having received the Flexibility Award
given to the second grader who had shown the most progress socially and academically. Finally, the story Vera wrote for a school
assignment reflected that her new psychological landscape/self and
matrix of embodied life-metaphors could consider and articulate,
through the use of verbal metaphor, an awareness of the trauma she
had experienced but that no longer played an active role in her psychological functioning. Aspects of this story also qualify as a verbal
memory.

The Relational-Dynamic Unconscious

According to Bacant, Lynch, and Richards (1995), the concept of a dynamic unconscious, which is pivotal in contemporary classical psychoanalysis, "becomes a mere whisper in relational theory" (p. 75), which focuses on interactions and the new relationship that emerges between patient and therapist. For relationists, that focus distracts a therapist's attention away from the importance of unconscious processes during treatment. These authors also take issue with relational psychoanalysts, who have "offered the unconscious as a static concept—like a file cabinet . . . for old records" (p. 76). Likewise, Modell (1995) argues that relational theory has not provided adequate alternatives for considering the dynamic unconscious. Recently, however, increasing attention is being given to understanding the process of a relational unconscious in treatment (Gerson, 2004; Harris, 2004). In an attempt to maintain the primacy of the concept of a dynamic unconscious within a relational point of view my model addresses the following questions.

What Is the Content of a Child's Unconscious?

As discussed in chapter 1, a child's unconscious consists of a matrix of embodied life-metaphors, a constellation of interrelated meanings constructed during dialectical interactions between the child's psychological landscape/self and other persons, as well as environments in which they were interacting. Three important issues are embedded in this definition of the content of a child's unconscious. One concerns my proposal that embodied life-metaphors represent plans for action for negotiating such core developmental issues as attachment/trust/love, separation-individuation, and reciprocating and asserting.

Piaget's (1973) discussion of the affective unconscious and the cognitive unconscious accords with this view. He proposed that the unconscious does not contain fantasies and ideas that are already formed and that come into view when we "shine a light on them. . . . [Rather,] the unconscious is furnished with sensorimotor or operational schemata, organized into structures . . . expressing what a subject can 'do' and not what he thinks" (p. 257). Along the same lines, Lear (1990) proposes that the unconscious consists of "orientations to the world" (p. 93) that guide actions.

The second issue embedded in my defining the content of the unconscious as embodied life-metaphors has to do with my proposal that unconscious meanings of embodied life-metaphors are constructed during interactions with others. The construction of unconscious meanings, then, is always intersubjective.[4] Recall the anecdote I described in chapter 1 about the toddler who initiated a series of play rituals, each negotiating an embodied life-metaphor: from directing father to button and then unbutton his shirt around the boy's body, following which the boy toddled off with father "searching" for him; to directing that father sit next to him everywhere; to directing that his glass and father's contain the same amount of water; and so on. I emphasized that how another person participates in interactions with a child plays a part in the structure an embodied metaphor achieves in the child's unconscious. This view coincides with that of Gerson (2004), who noted in his discussion of the relational unconscious, "We may describe each individual's life as existing in a continuous relation with the unconscious life of all other persons and groupings in which his or her life is lived" (p. 74).

The third issue embedded in my definition of the unconscious as consisting of embodied life-metaphors is the position elaborated throughout this volume—namely, that meanings representing embodied life-metaphors are enacted in the form of constellations of actions, rhythms of gestures and dialogue, body and touch sensations, facial expressions, and images and emotions. That enactments are manifest expressions of unconscious meanings also is consistent with Gerson's (2004) idea that "enactments may be thought of as a manifest content of the relational unconscious . . . [and] as derivatives in action of the relational unconscious" (p. 85).

How Does the Content of a Child's Unconscious Become a Part of the Child's Conscious Awareness, and What Role Does a Therapist Play in This Process?

Piaget (1973) also proposed that to become conscious requires a "reconstruction on a higher level of something that is already organized

---

[4]Gerson (2004) has a useful discussion and review of the intersubjective creation of meaning.

but differently on a lower level" (p. 256). Along the same lines, while reminding us that Freud tended to treat unconscious thoughts and fantasies as fully formed but hidden, Lear (1990) notes that Freud sometimes suggested that repression is able to contain a wish or meaning within the unconscious by preventing it from developing into a fully fledged form. This position suggested, according to Lear, that Freud recognized that the transition from unconscious to conscious levels is a developmental process. Lear notes that the "orientations" he proposes the unconscious contains become conscious when they are "restructured" during a gradual process of "progressive development" in which the meaning in question is gradually reconstructed simultaneously at unconscious and conscious levels of activity. Likewise, Spezzano (1995) conceptualizes that unconscious meanings are inherently driven to bring their contents into consciousness.

For unconscious meanings to become restructured at a higher (conscious) level requires that a therapist participate in the restructuring. If a meaning is to become conscious, another mind must show that it is "capable of receiving, containing and expressively elaborating one's experiences" (Gerson, 2004, p. 70). That the therapist must show a capability to receive, experience, express, and elaborate unconscious elements of the child's experiences is at the core of the interacting and negotiating I have described that should take place during the treatment cycles outlined earlier. I illustrated how, while negotiating and enacting embodied life-metaphors and solutions to their meanings, child and therapist are registering, expressing, and interrelating each other's bodily experiences and emotions, and summarizing and conserving these shared unconscious representations. Moreover, these representations become integrated within the child's existing matrix of embodied life-metaphors and within that of the therapist in a dialectical process; the unconscious meanings of each influence the unconscious meanings of the other. In addition to child and therapist constructing a shared interactive language, then, the matrix of embodied life-metaphors of each gradually contains shared, dialectically negotiated, unconscious meanings. That the embodied life-metaphors of child and therapist share unconscious meanings meets the requirement proposed by several theorists (e.g., Gerson, 2004).

As shared unconscious meanings are constructed, when the child enacts an embodied life-metaphor, the unconscious meaning is initially expressed in the form of a global plan of action. The child is not conscious of the meaning or of the position of that meaning within his or her matrix of embodied life-metaphors. In order for the meaning of an unconscious embodied metaphor to approach conscious awareness, a continuous dialectical process needs to take place between, on one hand, the child consciously perceiving his or her body experiences and emotions and the actions and emotions of the therapist, and, on the other, the unconscious meaning prescribing the actions in question. During this dialectical exchange, then, the actions and meanings the embodied life-metaphor prescribes are gradually restructured, and, at the same time, the related organization of consciously perceived actions, sensorimotor experiences, thoughts, and emotions is also restructured, each influencing the other.

The case of Vera illustrates this point. She certainly was consciously aware, for example, of tilting her head back at the dinner table, flushing food down the toilet, the distress of her parents when they observed her difficulties eating, the classmate who rhythmically tapped her head on a desk top, the experience of standing alone at the edge of the playground, and the items she used to barricade her bedroom door. The unconscious embodied life metaphors that prescribed these various actions, however, did not influence Vera's conscious thoughts and were not known either to her or to me.

Gradually, over the course of treatment, as Vera consciously perceived and experienced my actions and emotions and her own during our enactments, the meanings of the embodied life-metaphors were gradually restructured in a progressive development. At the conscious level, Vera and I experienced and perceived ourselves engaged in such activities as barricading the door, moving a line of toy animals slowly across the floor, and feeding each toy animal exactly the same food. By my demonstrating that I was willing to perceive, experience, and elaborate these activities, while participating in enactments, the unconscious meaning of interpersonal regimentation and control that prescribed these activities was gradually restructured, reorganized, and differentiated. This restructuring resulted in an unconscious meaning representing that emotional and interactive freedom was permitted and that the world could be engaged in mutual, reciprocal interactions, illustrated by Vera's directing that we prepare meals representing each of our ethnic origins.

After Vera had established interpersonal attachment and trust with me, another meaning in her unconscious drove its expression forward, resulting in her conscious experience of seeing "danger eyes" in bushes, which signified that the world could not yet be entered freely. While we sketched on paper the location of many danger eyes, this unconscious meaning was gradually differentiated and restructured, now prescribing that Vera thump her feet on the floor, experience fear, and exclaim that bad men were attacking our village. As she consciously perceived and experienced me swinging my arms, vigorously battling the attackers in a series of locations (office, hallway, playroom, and Therapeutic Garden), the unconscious meaning of diffuse danger was gradually differentiated and restructured. It reached its final form representing that persons in the outside world who can assault you have been defeated.

As a result of this progressive dialectical interaction between Vera's constellation of traumatic meanings and her consciously perceiving the actions and emotions she and I performed that were prescribed by these meanings, the final conscious organization, linked to a significantly restructured and differentiated unconscious embodied metaphor, was expressed by the story she wrote for third grade. Recall that she "decided to go on a trip to the past . . . when I got spanked with a belt . . . [then] I . . . flew back to when I was older. Now my parents come. I was taken care of."

The Significance of the Location and Sequence of Locations in Which Psychotherapy Takes Place

We have noted that environmental psychology focuses on changes in behaviors associated with changes in physical locations in which a person is interacting. Accordingly, environmental psychology proposes that the unit of study should be the person-in-the-environment. In contrast, the concept of a matrix of embodied life-metaphors defines a person's interactions with human and nonhuman landscapes as guided by unconscious meanings the person gives to experiences not only with physical locations, but also with humans, attributes of nature, and inanimate objects. Of special importance is that these meanings are interrelated so that the meanings a child gives to interactive experiences with humans determine the form and content of meanings the child gives to experiences with physical locations, nature, and inanimate objects. In other words, the environment, both human and nonhuman, is an extension of meanings that form a child's matrix of embodied life-metaphors. Therefore, I propose that the unit of study should be a person-in-his-or-her-matrix of embodied life-metaphors. Accordingly, the locations in which treatment takes place should make available human and nonhuman environments into which the child can extend, experience, and negotiate embodied meanings.

From this viewpoint, the limitations of a playroom and office become very apparent. In addition to the person of a therapist, a playroom provides only a narrow inanimate environment, consisting primarily of toys. It does not include, for example, a hill to climb, providing the opportunity to experience bodily the power of the meaning "up," or a tree trunk to embrace, providing an embodied experience of a loving, animate-nonhuman object, or a pond into which a child can sink her hand and feel the bracelet that the water forms on her wrist, evoking an embodied experience she constructed when, in a play ritual, mother playfully placed her bracelet around the child's wrist. With the outdoors available, then, as well as a playroom, child and therapist have many more opportunities to get to know each other's matrix of embodied life-metaphors. By making indoor and outdoor locations available, the therapist has the opportunity to observe whether a child's psychological landscape/self extends meanings with relative ease into human and nonhuman environments or extends meanings into a very narrow set of attributes in each, or into only one. Ernest and Vera are examples. Initially Ernest limited himself to a rope and cave while outdoors, and Vera limited herself to toy animals and the playroom.

The sequence of person–environment units a child constructs during treatment is connected with my proposal that limiting interactions to a playroom restricts the degree to which a child can resolve traumatic meanings at the embodied level and develop a new self and matrix of embodied life-metaphors. Because the trauma a child experienced is almost always construed by the child as related to responses of people, typically it is difficult for children early in treatment to initiate reliving traumatic meanings while interacting within the human environment of a therapist's body and person. For this reason, whenever indicated, the therapist could begin by helping a child relive traumatic meanings in the most distal environment (inanimate-nonhuman, e.g., with toys) and then animate-nonhuman (e.g., bushes, a trail through trees, a hill), and, finally, during enactments in the human landscape provided by the therapist's body and person where the child's traumatic meanings are finally resolved at the embodied level.

As one example, although I attempted to participate during our sessions, Vera focused her interactions for the most part on toy animals that she moved in a line, and then dolls she placed in chairs to enact the context of a classroom. It was only after many months that she was prepared to include my body-self in a major way, as I battled bad men attacking our village. Then she expanded the environment with which she interacted to include other therapists and children she invited into our "home" and frogs she adopted and fed.

Determining If a Child Is Developing a New Matrix of Embodied Life-Metaphors

That treatment should help a child enter as wide a range of environments as possible provides a therapist with guidelines to determine whether or not growth is taking place within the child's matrix of embodied life-metaphors. If the child's psychological landscape/self projects a meaning representing danger, for example, into some attribute of human or nonhuman environments (as Ernest did when he experienced pine needles as a source of pain) and later projects the meaning of interpersonal affection and reciprocity into that same attribute (as Ernest did when he experienced the same pine needles as giving warmth), this signals that a new matrix of embodied meanings is beginning to develop. Set side by side, these enactments represent that Ernest's matrix of embodied life-metaphors had undergone a transformation, experiencing interpersonal affiliation when interacting with others instead of pain and danger. As another example, Vera repeatedly experienced the embodied enactment of thumping her feet against the floor to announce the arrival of dangerous men. Later in treatment, she experienced and expressed the same embodied enactment to announce the arrival of friendly neighbors.

A positive change in a child's matrix of embodied life-metaphors is also reflected when the child projects a meaning into two or more attributes in his or her environment in order to experience and negotiate a particular meaning. For example, Ernest negotiated the embodied meaning of empowerment by projecting this meaning into climbing to the top of the mount, shooting Styrofoam arrows with a bow as far as possible, jogging along the pathways of the Therapeutic Garden and pretending he was a train, and shouting at the "bad wind" to go away. These examples relate to a concept formulated by Heinz Werner (1948) that defines growth as taking place whenever a person develops multiple behavioral alternatives to express the same meaning with its emotion and to achieve the same goal and also when a person accepts different goals as alternatives satisfying the same meaning with its emotion.

Concluding Comment

I take the position that in relational psychotherapy child and therapist grow together much as infant and caregiver do. This growing together requires that child and therapist communicate primarily in the language of nonverbal interactions and enactments. I have also reminded us that, in the beginning, the child's interactive language of origin is foreign to the therapist and the therapist's is foreign to the child, so that each must participate in dialectical cycles of interaction to learn the other's matrix of embodied life-metaphors. If the child is to overcome traumatic responses by others that the child has internalized, the child must first relive the meanings of these stressful events in his or her interactive language of origin during enactments with the therapist and then identify with and internalize the solutions the therapist enacts. During these interactions, a dialectical process takes place between the child's conscious experiences with the therapist and the child's unconscious meanings that prescribe the behaviors and emotions that were the source of the child's difficulties.

As the child consciously perceives his or her bodily experiences and those of the therapist, and internalizes the therapist's solutions, the unconscious meanings are gradually restructured, resulting in the child's constructing a new psychological landscape/self and matrix of embodied life-metaphors. This new matrix contains meanings that prescribe that the child interact in new ways with a wide range of attributes in human and nonhuman environments, interactions that enable the child to continue negotiating developmental needs and promoting his or her development. I discussed several issues related to achieving this goal: repairing the dialectical relationship between the child's Me-Self and I-Self and between the child's psychological landscape/self and available environments; why conducting psychotherapy in various locations makes a unique contribution; the significance of the sequence of person–environment units a child should construct during treatment; and how a therapist can determine the extent to which a child has developed a new self.

6   Environments, Interactions, and Embodied Meanings
Probing How Three Are One

Sketching my efforts to treat an adolescent girl, which provides another illustration of the goal and techniques of the treatment model described in the previous chapter, I also set the stage for a discussion of a series of interrelated questions that the psychoanalytic-relational model I propose could raise in the mind of a child psychotherapist who has not yet fully embraced the point of view I advocate.

Alice and Her Embodied Meaning of a Belly

Alice was referred for treatment during her sophomore year in high school because she was experiencing difficulty completing schoolwork and interacting with teachers, especially females. Her enactments during treatment, and my participation, illustrate concepts and techniques of my psychoanalytic-relational model, which integrates human and nonhuman environments in which child and therapist interact and the embodied life-metaphors they negotiate and resolve.

197

From the start, I experienced Alice as very bright, verbally articulate, and pleasant. During one of our first meetings, I mentioned to her, as I do to all my patients, that we could go outside anytime she felt like it. Alice did not respond. Instead, at the start of each session, she would lead the way to my office, where, gesticulating with vigor and shifting about in her chair, she rehashed the theme she had launched in our first meeting. With a sarcastic tone, she focused on her teachers. She criticized their style of relating, giving instructions, and announcing homework assignments. Noticing that she "evaluated" only female teachers, I asked about her male teachers, but each time she set that topic to one side.

Throughout these weeks I struggled to negotiate a shared interactive language with her. I tried to imitate her sarcastic, disrespectful tone when reflecting her comments about teachers. I noticed that at times she slowly moved the palm of her hand in a circular motion over her stomach. Although I did not yet have a way of understanding the meaning of this gesture, I did the same to my stomach. At other times, without notice, and with a playful tone, she jumped up from her chair and, stretching out on my analytic couch, held a pillow to her stomach. Commenting only, "This feels good," she continued her diatribe against teachers. In the next few meetings she again playfully flopped on the couch for several minutes, held a pillow on her stomach, and continued her discussions. Because Alice sometimes overate, I wondered to myself if rubbing her stomach, and holding a pillow to it while lying on the couch, were expressions of embodied metaphors related to nurturance. However, I did not comment.

Influenced by Alice's enactment, in addition to rubbing my stomach, on one occasion when we entered the office to start a session, I playfully flopped on the analytic couch. I joked that we were developing a new form of therapy in which the analyst lies on the couch and the patient sits in a chair. Alice burst out laughing. Joining the enactment, she directed that in this new therapy the analyst had to hold a pillow on his stomach while lying on the couch. When I first placed the pillow on my stomach, I exclaimed, "Wow, am I fat!" Alice screamed with laughter. As we continued our discussion of Alice's experiences at school that day, the pillow moved to the side of my stomach without my being aware of it. Alice corrected me several times and reminded me to hold the pillow at the top of my stomach.

Then, at the start of one session, Alice surprised me by asking if we could go outside, and she led us into the Therapeutic Garden. After slowly walking about, she climbed to the top of the mount and sat down (area M, Figure 1, Introduction). I sat next to her. Looking about, she commented, "It's nice out here," and continued discussing her experiences at school that day. During each of the next four sessions, while continuing her discussions, she spontaneously went outside, sometimes sitting on the top of the mount and sometimes stretching out in a prone position with her head propped up on her hands and elbows. I continued to sit next to her and to participate in her discussions.

At one point she suddenly stopped talking, seemed upset, and commented, "I just got a weird feeling." I asked her if she could help me understand what she meant by "weird," but she refused, adding that the feelings were "too embarrassing." She remained silent for several minutes. I stretched out in a prone position a couple of feet from her, in an effort to convey that I was joining her and trying to experience what she was experiencing. While prone, I commented that I hoped Alice could eventually share with me more about the "weird feeling" because I wanted to help her with it. After remaining silent for a number of minutes, she commented, "It feels like I'm lying on the belly of a pregnant mother."

During the next several sessions, continuing to lie prone on the top of the mount while I lay alongside her, Alice gradually shared embodied meanings from a time in her life that her parents had discussed with me before treatment started. Mother became pregnant when Alice reached her second birthday. As the fetus grew larger, Alice and mother evolved play rituals. With one, Alice patted mother's belly and said, "Hi! I want to play." And when mother lay in bed to rest during the afternoon, Alice, laying across mother's belly, played, "I'm the baby." A girl was born a few months before Alice turned three. Two months later, the baby died because of physical complications. Mother became very depressed and left home for four months to be with her parents. A nanny was hired to care for Alice.

After reliving that she was lying on the stomach of her pregnant mother, during the next months Alice enacted several embodied meanings representing various aspects of the emotional trauma she had experienced as she construed it. For example, she introduced a contest in which we hurled rocks from the top of the mount at a large tree trunk and a small tree trunk, and she kept a careful record of our hits and misses. This enactment eventually led to her designating the large tree as her mother and the small tree as her deceased sister; while throwing rocks, she expressed anger at her mother for "deserting me" and "taking away my sister" as well as anger at her sister for "dying." With other enactments she sat on the mount and vigorously gulped down various snacks we had prepared and then gradually regulated her eating.

Toward the last phase of our work, she planted a small evergreen tree in honor of her deceased infant sister and gradually showed that she was in the process of constructing a new self. She completed school assignments on time, and teachers reported to her parents that Alice's insolent, sarcastic attitude had decreased appreciably and that she had actually "made friends" with several of her teachers and chatted with them after school. In my opinion, Alice's occasionally flopping on the analytic couch and then lying on the mount, along with my participating in these enactments, clearly gave rise to embodied meanings representing her experiences with mother's body and having been abandoned by mother. I also believe that had I made use of only talk therapy, the anger Alice felt toward mother, which was being displaced onto schoolteachers, would have remained underground, continuing to affect her school performance and relationships.[1]

Why the Emphasis on a Form of No-Talk Child Psychotherapy?

Rather than focus only on what patient and therapist say to each other, relational psychoanalysis, as noted, attends to how patient and therapist interact and the meanings they give to these interactions.[2]

---

[1] Readers interested in the use of action metaphors in the treatment of adolescents should find discussions by Holinger (1999) and Duhl (1999) useful.

[2] In psychotherapy with adults, for example, "interaction itself is viewed as a factor that may legitimately lead to change" (Aron, 1996, p. 214); nonverbal, expressive techniques have been advocated for the treatment of adults (Wiener, 1999); and the nonverbal behaviors of adult patients and their therapists have been shown to contribute importantly to the treatment process (Knoblauch, 1997).

Mayes and Cohen (1993) argue that the "very process of enactment through fantasy play [without discussions and interpretations] . . . is, in and of itself, developmentally restorative" (p. 1236), a position elaborated by Scott (1998). Slade (1994) notes, "In our attempt to tell children what we think they mean, we sometimes interfere with their playing in ways that are not helpful [because] . . . for some children it is the playing itself that is curative" (pp. 102–103). Slade describes a child who initially engaged in play representing that she felt abandoned by her mother; she then began building an elaborate structure with Legos. Instead of joining the child, Slade confessed, "Going counter to my judgment regarding too much talk in therapy, I began telling her a story about a girl who had worries very much like the patient" (p. 101). The child shouted to the Lego pieces, "You better shut up!" (p. 101). (Notice that this vignette is similar to the one reported by Coppolillo, 1987, and discussed in chapter 1.)

As my participation in the treatment of Ernest and Vera clearly demonstrated, I agree with the growing number of child therapists who recommend that play activity, instead of discussions and interpretations, can itself be restorative. But I must add that enacting embodied life-metaphors, in particular, is most powerful in helping a child overcome difficulties and developing a new self.

Inasmuch as No-Talk Therapy Emphasizes Use of Enactments, How Does My Definition of Enactment Relate to Definitions Offered by Others?

The term enactment has received considerable attention within relational psychoanalysis.[3] In addition, Aron (1996), Ellman and Moskowitz (1998), and Frank (1999) have compared various definitions and provided historical reviews of how the one-person concept of a patient's "acting out" and "acting in," which refers to a patient's behaviors outside and inside treatment that satisfy some urge or fantasy, have been replaced by the concept of enactment; enactment generally refers to the ways in which patient and therapist act on one

---

[3]The following references are useful here: Anchin (2002), Chused (1991), Frank (2002), Hirsch (2000), Maroda (1998), McLaughlin (1991), Renik (1998), and Safran (2002).

another verbally and nonverbally (Aron, 1996, p. 198). A definition of enactment on which all therapists concur, however, has not yet been formulated (e.g., Ellman, 1998). To highlight how I believe the term serves child psychotherapy, we can compare my definition of enactment with selected definitions offered by others.

The Purpose and Content of Enactments

For Maroda (1998) an enactment is a repetition of past events buried in the unconscious. For Chused (1991) an enactment is an attempt by the patient to create an interaction with the therapist that represents some aspect of a relationship that would satisfy what the patient longs for in fantasy. Chused also takes the position that enactments are not therapeutic in themselves but could provide useful information about the patient's inner world and interactional style. Anchin (2002) suggests that the concept of enactment should be limited to "only maladaptive intrapsychic-interpersonal [behaviors] as played out both within treatment and in extratherapy relationships" (p. 312). Altman et al. (2002), authors of a volume describing a relational approach to child psychotherapy, do not appear to have settled on a definition of enactment. They point out that a therapist can embrace a restrictive, traditional view (e.g., a child hits the therapist in a fit of anger) or a broader view (i.e., all interactions during play are enactments). They also imply that a definition depends on the limits that are set for treatment with a given child. For example, if a therapist discourages physical contact, and the child tries to sit on the therapist's lap, this behavior would qualify as an enactment.

Ellman (1998), distinguishing between enactments initiated by the patient and those initiated by the therapist, proposes that those initiated by the patient occur "when analytic trust either has been disrupted or has not yet been firmly established" (p. 187). Ellman adds, "Usually mutual enactments result in or reflect impasses in the treatment situation" (p. 200). In contrast, Theodore Jacobs (1991), who Aron (1996) suggests is probably the person most responsible for cultivating acceptance of the concept of enactment within psychoanalysis, defines the term as conscious and unconscious subtle verbal and nonverbal communications between a patient and therapist that express meanings as they interact. Renik

(1998) defines enactments as interactions between patient and therapist that provide the patient with corrective emotional experiences and opportunities to change meanings of past traumatic experiences that have been internalized by the patient. And Frank (2002) proposes that, when enacting, a patient interacts with the therapist in ways that are similar to those that have created difficulty in the patient's daily life; Frank adds that enactments may be deleterious if they represent old traumas, or they may be beneficial, depending on the therapist's response.

To a layperson, the notion of enacting means representing a role on a stage. The audience is invited to experience the personality and events portrayed as real, although the audience knows those enactments are really pretend. My definition includes this notion of representing a role, except that what is being portrayed by the child and therapist during an enactment is "real." I define an enactment (see chapter 1) as a repetitive constellation of physical actions, gestures, body sensations, rhythms of movements and dialogue, facial expressions, touch perceptions, images, and emotions expressed by a child. That repetitive constellation simultaneously represents at an unconscious level past experiences, both developmentally appropriate and traumatic, construes current interactions, prescribes behaviors and emotions, and anticipates particular actions and emotions from others.

In the treatment situation, when a child is enacting, his or her conscious or unconscious intention is to engage the therapist, much as a caregiver, in an interaction that serves either to negotiate some developmental need in ways that assist the child in developing his or her self or to share a traumatic experience with the therapist in order to receive a response representing a solution the child can internalize. In the treatment situation, all enactments are potentially beneficial. Finally, to respond to Aron's (1996) point that the word enactment may imply a discrete event, whereas the word interaction conveys a sense of continuity, I would like to stress that, as I use the term, enactments are repeated many times within the context of child–therapist interaction. Therefore enactments are relational experiences that "constitute the very essence of treatment" (Aron, 1996 p. 215).

My definition is at odds with those offered by Chused (1991) and Anchin (2002) noted above and with an aspect of McLaughlin's (1991) opinion that responses by a therapist to a patient's enactments come from "blind spots" in the therapist that have been provoked by the patient's behavior. My definition aligns most closely with Jacobs's (1991), Renik's (1998), and Frank's (2000) that, when enacting, a patient attempts to influence interactions with a therapist in particular ways based on emotionally charged experiences from the past, and that enactments can provide lived experiences on the basis of which a person changes meanings of past experiences and engages new experiences. Moreover, my definition of enactment, in sharp contrast to Ellman's (1998) that enactments occur when trust has been disrupted, emphasizes that a child initiates an enactment only when he or she has established sufficient trust and a shared interactive language with the therapist.

Preliminary Negotiations Are Necessary in Order for a Child to Engage in Enactments

I have not yet come across authors who believe that a child and a therapist should negotiate in the service of learning each other's interactive language in order for the child to be able to express an enactment that has therapeutic value. Several discussions about enactments in adult psychotherapy, however, address this issue. Aron (1996) reviewed writings that defined enactments to include all aspects of interactions between patient and therapist that have some influence on each of them, especially gestures, tone of voice, body postures, and facial expressions. In his comprehensive discussion of enactments, Frank (1999) states,

> All patient–therapist interactions must be considered as possible enactments. . . . It can be argued, plausibly, that every single interaction, including the pair's efforts at clarification, might involve levels of enactment encompassing each's attempt to influence the other, consciously or preconsciously, so as to maintain a safe attachment [pp. 61–62].

I view the particular interactions underlined by Aron and Frank as aspects of the negotiating I defined in the previous chapter: negotiating takes place between child and therapist during the first three cycles of my model in the service of developing a shared interactive language with the therapist, an achievement that enables the child to develop trust in the therapist's unconditional availability. A child introduces an enactment only when he or she has had sufficient opportunity to negotiate these issues.

How Can Enacting During Treatment Itself Be Restorative?

My response to this question, also raised by Mayes and Cohen (1993), relies on studies of children my colleagues and I conducted in the laboratory and also on longitudinal observations of children participating with me in psychoanalytic treatment.[4] Taken together, the studies represent my efforts to engage in a process in which therapy, research and practice inform each other (Rigazio-Digilio, Goncalves, and Ivey, 1996).

In the laboratory studies, children were administered psychological procedures designed to evaluate the degree of directness and delay that characterized how they expressed meanings in each of three modalities: action, fantasy, and language. Other procedures were designed to evaluate whether a child preferred to express meanings with one of these modalities more than with the others. To illustrate the latter, with one test item, a plant and a watering can were located behind one screen; a picture of a person watering a plant was behind a second screen; and a microphone was behind a third screen. Each child was asked to water the plant, look over a picture of someone watering a plant, and imagine what is going on and speak into a microphone about watering plants. The child was encouraged to do first what he or she preferred to do most of all, and then to engage the remaining activities in the order preferred.

In one series of studies (e.g., Santostefano, 1970; Eichler, 1971), 6- to 8-year-old public school children expressed themselves significantly more often in the action mode, whereas 10-year-olds showed the beginnings of a shift toward expressing themselves in the fantasy mode as well as action. As another example, in related studies (Blaisdell, 1972; Santostefano, 1977), the manner in which children expressed

---

[4]This program of research is described by Santostefano (1968, 1970, 1977, 1985, 1988, 1991, 1995, 1998a, 1999), Eichler (1971), Blaisdell (1972), Santostefano and Wilson (1968), and Santostefano and Calicchia (1992).

meanings in the action and fantasy modes was evaluated before and after they experienced a treatment condition that involved expressing vigorous actions (e.g., punch a Bobo doll; twist metal coat hangers). After experiencing the treatment condition, the children showed a shift toward expressing actions in more delayed and indirect forms while simultaneously experiencing fantasies that expressed meanings with more directness and less delay.

Examination of the behavior of children participating in psychoanalytic psychotherapy or psychoanalysis (e.g., Santostefano, 1998b) demonstrated that, if the therapist physically participated in the child's play, rather than interpreting its meaning, the child typically organized and expressed an enactment representing some aspect of a stressful or traumatic experience. Moreover, the enactment was initially expressed by the child with macroactions—moving his or her total body in elaborate and differentiated ways throughout the total space available—and repeated many times.

With another observation (Santostefano, 1985, 1998b), as the therapist physically enacted a solution to a quandary, the child internalized the response and initiated another activity expressing a related meaning that also required a solution. When the constellation of meanings the child expressed had been adequately resolved, from the child's point of view, the child constructed a fantasy into which the macroactions were integrated and subordinated, resulting in the child's using microactions. In some cases the child's enactments eventually included linguistic metaphors emerging from the meanings that were negotiated and resolved in the action and fantasy modes.

Ernest provides an illustration. Recall that, as we repeatedly ran away from sharp pine needles and "poisoned" water, once he had internalized my solutions that our body-selves could find safety in our cave (relationship) and within a cluster of trees located in the outside world, Ernest showed that he had sufficiently negotiated with macroactions the embodied metaphor representing that it was possible to be rescued from a dangerous world. He next used microactions integrated within an elaborate fantasy to continue negotiating this same meaning. While sitting on the playroom floor, he moved toy vehicles a few inches and fantasized that they were ill. I responded by playing I was a car doctor, healing each one. It was not until Ernest and I enacted and negotiated a number of other meanings that he returned almost two years later to negotiate in the language mode the same meaning of danger the outer world contained. He spent several sessions discussing how to handle a boy in his class who was teasing him.

Body Action, Fantasy, and Language: Alternative Modalities for Expressing Meanings

On the basis of the results of these laboratory and clinical studies, I have proposed that body action, fantasy, and language are alternative modalities with which a child experiences and expresses meanings while negotiating embodied life-metaphors with others (Eichler, 1971; Santostefano, 1977, 1978, 1985, 1998b). Although the three modalities are available throughout life, a developmental principle defines the interrelationships among them. A meaning is usually experienced and expressed initially in the body-action mode and then extended into the fantasy mode and later into the language mode, if links between these modes have been established and not disrupted in any major way. From the first days of life to about 7 or 8 years, the body-action mode dominates and is, as Frank (1999) puts it, "our original mother tongue" (p. 45). From about 9 to 12 years, the body-action mode is gradually subordinated by and integrated within the fantasy mode, and from about 12 or 13 years and beyond the body-action and fantasy modes are subordinated and integrated within the language mode. Although subordinated, the body-action mode is not replaced by the fantasy and language modes but remains active, influencing the form and content of fantasies and verbal expressions. This developmental principle converges with Harris's (1998) proposing that relational theory commit itself "to a view of body states and processes as inseparatable from fantasy, interaction, and meaning" (p. 43).

The sequence of behaviors that Ernest and Vera displayed throughout treatment illustrates this progression, as does one of Mahl's (1987) clinical anecdotes illustrating this relationship among modalities in an adult. He describes a patient who, while lying on an analytic couch and discussing her thoughts and feelings, repeatedly rubbed the back of her hand against a nearby, roughly plastered wall. From this experience in the body-action mode, a fantasy (childhood memory) eventually emerged of her father's regularly rubbing his beard against her face, leaving her tingling with excitement. This experience, beginning with body perceptions and then including fantasy, led the patient to verbalize meanings connected with her relationships. Stoops (1974) reviewed 55 studies by other investigators who compared two or more modes of expression. Although they employed a wide variety of assessment techniques, he concluded that 35 of the studies supported my developmental model, 9 offered inconclusive support, and 11 reported contradictory results.

The Importance of Repetition in Constructing Links Among the Modes of Body Action, Fantasy, and Language

As an infant or toddler repeats cycles of interactions with humans and objects, mental schemas or representations of these interactions are constructed, the organization of which initially approximate the embodied experience. During many repeated cycles, the paradox between a body action and image or fantasy is gradually negotiated so that it increasingly provides a more adequate representation of the body-action experience. Similarly, the paradox between fantasy or image and verbal statements is gradually negotiated over many interactive cycles so that language expressions increasingly provide a more adequate representation of the fantasy in question. With repeated cycles of interacting, then, experiences in one modality eventually establish representational roots in the others. From this viewpoint, as a corollary to Freud's (1933) statement that "thinking is experimental action" (p. 89), I have proposed (Santostefano, 1998b) that enactments repeated within the body-action mode are forms of experimental thinking.[5]

Perhaps one of the first "studies" of the importance of a child's repeating enactments was reported by Freud, who, when living with an 18-month-old toddler and the boy's parents, observed the boy playing a particular "game." He repeatedly flung into the corner of his room or under his cot "all the little things he could lay his hands on," accompanying each throw with a sound that Freud and the boy's mother understood to mean "gone" (Erikson, 1950). The next enactment was of a wooden reel with a piece of string wound around it. Holding the string, the boy repeatedly threw the reel over the side of

---

[5]Solnit (1998) has put forth a similar view.

his cot. Making a sound that meant "gone" as it disappeared, he drew it back into the cot, the reel reappeared, and he made a joyful sound meaning "there." Freud observed that the toddler made these same sounds whenever mother left the house for hours and then returned. As Erikson noted,

> This was therefore the complete game, disappearance and re-turn. . . . To understand what Freud saw in this game . . . he was interested in . . . the strange behavior of the repetition com-pulsion—i.e., the need to re-enact painful experiences in words or acts . . . [in order] to overcome . . . or master a situa-tion which in its original form had been too much [p. 216].

The importance of a child's repeating some action many times has not been given attention in more recent discussions of play (e.g., Benveniste, 1998; Solnit, 1998; Altman et al., 2002). I described how Ernest and Vera repeated an enactment sometimes hundreds of times, whether it involved running from poisoned water or battling men attacking a village. What is the significance of a child's repeat-ing body actions during play? Decades ago Walder (1933) made use of the classical psychoanalytic concepts that predominated at the time. He pointed out that, if a child has had an experience that was "'too difficult or too large to assimilate,' the id drives the child to reexperi-ence it many times . . . thereby gaining mastery over it" (p. 212). In ad-dition, Walder stated that the vigor and frequency with which a child repeated an activity was related to the child's "relative strength of masculinity or femininity" (p. 214).

I agree that a child repeats an enactment in order to master the traumatic meaning it represents. Rather than relying on the concept of masculinity–femininity, however, my model holds that an enact-ment is repeated many times in the body-action mode because, as observed in studies (e.g., Reckling and Buirski, 1996; van der Kolk, 1996; Paley and Alpert, 2003), when a child is exposed to stressful events, meanings representing these experiences are typically regis-tered at the embodied level and assimilated into bodily activity rather than as images or words. Accordingly, when a child is exposed to extreme stress, his or her fantasy and language modes do not con-tain sufficient representations of the traumatic experience, nor do they yet have adequate access to the embodied meanings associated with the trauma. During treatment, though, if a child is given the opportunity to express meanings associated with traumatic experiences in the modality in which the meanings are most fully represented—namely, in body actions—the child will continually repeat macroactions in an effort to master the stress, especially if the therapist participates physically. Moreover, if a traumatic meaning is repeatedly expressed with body movements, the meaning is extended into, and establishes roots within, the fantasy mode, which then aids rehearsing and mastering the meaning. And with further repetitions of actions and fantasies, the meaning sometimes is extended into the language mode. In the developmental hierarchy that I propose, body action, fantasy, and language are alternative modes for experiencing and expressing meanings.

The Royal Treatment Highway Has Four Lanes

In sharp contrast to the assumption by classical psychoanalysis and cognitive-behavioral therapies that expressing feelings and meanings with spoken language is the "royal treatment highway," in the model I have outlined the royal treatment highway has four lanes. One is the body-action mode, expressing a child's embodied meanings that represent both appropriate and stressful interactions. The second lane is the child's images and fantasies that emerged from and represent body-action experiences. The third is linguistic metaphors derived from the fantasy mode also representing these experiences. And the fourth lane is the child's activities and conversations that do not express, in any significant way, embodied life-metaphors.

On Which Lane of the Treatment Highway Should a Therapist Travel with a Child?

As a relational psychoanalyst, Aron (1996) asks, "How much does the analyst get caught up with the patient in therapeutic action?" (p. xii), a question that is particularly relevant to my model and to child psychotherapy generally. If we accept that the goal of treatment is to resolve the embodied roots of a child's difficulties and help the child develop a new embodied self, my response to Aron's question would be that in child psychotherapy the therapist should travel in the body-action lane as much as possible; the therapist should participate with a child in enacting with macroactions the meanings of traumatic embodied life-metaphors with which the child is struggling, as well as enacting solutions. If the therapist's participation is authentic and empathic, especially through gestures, body movements, and facial, vocal, and emotional expressions, the child typically remains in that lane, as Ernest and Vera did, until the traumatic meaning is mastered. For many children traveling in the body-action lane during play activities is itself sufficient to resolve the meaning of an internalized traumatic event.

Frequently a child may return to reenacting the same meaning in the fantasy lane and subordinate and integrate macroactions into microactions. Recall that Ernest shifted from running throughout the garden and enacting being rescued from danger to sitting on the playroom floor and moving toy vehicles that also needed help. Similarly, after spending many months in the body-action lane and enacting with macroactions that we were being attacked, Vera repeated this same embodied metaphor with microactions integrated within an elaborate fantasy of wooden beads longing to escape from other beads guarding them. Our task was the same as when we physically battled attackers. But now we enacted microactions, moving wooden beads a few inches on a table top.

If a therapist interprets to a child what the child's body actions and play mean, the child can openly refuse to leave the body-action lane, as did the patients of Slade (1994) and Coppolillo (1987). On the other hand, a child could readily join the therapist in the verbal lane, in response to an interpretation, before the child has had sufficient opportunity to negotiate the embodied meaning in question and internalize an action solution. If this occurs often in the treatment process, the child's new self could become dominated by intellectualizations, consisting of balloons filled with "insight" that float without being tied to the embodied level.

Why Do Some Children Prefer to Remain in the Fantasy and Language Lanes?

Some children, choosing to remain in the language lane, discuss thoughts, feelings, relationships, and experiences while engaging in very little or no physical activity. Other children, remaining in the fantasy lane, manipulate human and animal figures or game pieces while sitting on the floor or at a table and imagining elaborate scenarios. In my opinion, one of two possible developmental issues is responsible (assuming we hold to one side that a therapist could be most comfortable with, and prefer to remain in, the language lane). With one, the child has not had sufficient interactive physical experiences with caregivers to cultivate the body-action lane, especially early in development. With the other, a child may have adequately developed the body-action lane but defensively remains in the language or fantasy lane in an effort to avoid experiencing the meaning in question at the embodied level.

As an example, one aspect of the treatment of an adolescent illustrates the therapeutic challenge of helping a child who has not had sufficient interactive experiences in early childhood that involve macroactions. Midway through his junior year in high school, Thomas was referred by his parents (who were college professors) because it seemed to them that he was becoming increasingly depressed and moody. They frequently tried to engage him in discussions to learn what was troubling him, but he typically responded that everything was fine. When Thomas arrived for his first meeting, and for each of the next several meetings, he was holding a piece of paper on which he had written an item or two that he wanted to discuss—for example, "Who really are my friends?" I experienced Thomas as formal and didactic when he started each meeting by announcing his agenda and then launching into an articulate discussion. I did my best to join him while trying to focus on negotiating a shared interactive language. A meeting I held with his parents confirmed my suspicion that the didactic way he interacted had roots in "discussions" they had held with him since early childhood. They were interested in my working with their son because they had learned that I was "very active and open to going outside." I also guessed that, in addition to Thomas's not having had sufficient experience interacting physically during his childhood, he brought an agenda to each meeting in an effort to avoid an especially painful "topic."

To help him be as spontaneous as possible, I handed him a piece of paper, on several occasions, and asked him to write down any topic that jumped into his mind at that moment. I tried several other tactics. When I asked him to tell me what jumped into his mind if he did not bring a list, he grinned and said I sounded like his parents, who had invited him since childhood to select a topic for discussion that concerned him. With another strategy that invited Thomas to use his body, if only in the mode of microaction, I asked him to play a game of pool on the clinic's pool table. He accepted. Over the course of several meetings, while we were playing pool, his interactive style gradually included more spontaneous gestures, body postures, and emotional and facial expressions.

At one point, he reminded me that months before I had mentioned we could go outside whenever he wanted to, and he wondered if "that's still okay." I replied, "Absolutely," and we went outside. After giving the Therapeutic Garden a quick look, he followed the rill and sat on one of the large stones through which the rill passes. I sat on the stone next to him. As we continued talking, I noticed that clumps of grass and leaves were clogging the water running along the rill in that area. I recall having the conscious thought that the leaves and grass clogging the rill were metaphorically the same as the frustration clogging me, because I was having difficulty helping Thomas be spontaneous. I wondered, too, if the leaves and grass were the same as the issues and emotions clogging Thomas from giving spontaneous bodily expression to his concerns. I knelt down and began to remove leaves and clumps of grass from the rill while we conversed. During this activity, I interjected various related linguistic metaphors, such as, "When a river is clogged, it can't get where it wants to go." At one point, much to my surprise and pleasure, Thomas joined me in removing leaves and twigs while continuing his conversation.

At the start of the next several sessions, while continuing to converse, Thomas suggested that we walk along the rill and clear it of twigs, leaves, and grass. Our interacting and laughing increased as, while clearing the rill, we shared linguistic metaphors (e.g., "Hear it! Now the rill is breathing") and related fantasies (e.g., we imagined the running water was a long line of marathon runners, whom we cheered as they jogged along). After repeating this activity for several weeks, he said we should hold our discussions while "hiking" along pathways that meander through the thick trees and bushes in the periphery of the garden. We pretended we were participating in a "walk marathon." Before and after each walk, however, he "inspected" the rill to ensure that the water flowed freely, and he removed any grass or twigs. During these sessions I noticed that sometimes Thomas held his piece of paper but did not read the topic of the day; at other times, he did not bring a piece of paper with him. I also noticed that he spontaneously associated to hiking with his father years ago in the forests of northern New England during family vacations.

In one session, while we hiked through the garden, he said, with tears in his eyes, that he had an "enormous problem." Sobbing quietly, he shared that, when he was in second grade, a teenager who lived nearby and with whom he had frequently played games, had fondled him sexually but eventually stopped when Thomas protested vehemently. Thomas elaborated that, since he liked the teenager very much, he was afraid to tell his parents because the teenager would get in trouble. Thomas's sense that his parents would be devastated if he told them what happened mounted to a level he now found unbearable. From this beginning, Thomas and I successfully resolved the effects of this traumatic experience. In my opinion, the embodied interactive experiences involving shooting pool, clearing the rill of anything that impeded the flow of water, and walking over the pathways served Thomas to cultivate his action lane and share his turmoil.

What Is Required of a Therapist to Participate in the Body-Action Lane?

For a therapist to share his or her psychoanalytic skin, as Aron (1996) puts it, and grow with a child, the therapist must abandon the view that he or she has superior knowledge that has the power to change the child. Instead, the therapist provides the child with interactive experiences analogous to those that take place, especially during the first five or six years of life, when the child's Me-Self can experience a meaning with his or her body and the child's I-Self can perceive and articulate that meaning. To accomplish this goal, a psychotherapist will have to consider several requirements. The therapist must accept participating with a child in authentic ways both physically and emotionally and remain attuned to the meanings of the emotions the child is experiencing. Being an active, authentic participant obligates a therapist to become as familiar as possible with the matrix of embodied life-metaphors he or she introduces into a given treatment situation; notice when and why he or she feels excited, uncomfortable, tired, or bored; and also notice the meanings expressed by his or her postures, gestures, facial expressions, and changes in rhythm of dialogue and how these meanings influence his or her thoughts, feelings, and intentions. The therapist must also be alert to whether his or her matrix, with its unique interactive vocabulary, is being experienced by the child as too passive or too stimulating, for example, and therefore impedes the goal of treatment.

But the therapist is not alone—relational psychoanalysis emphasizes mutuality. Accordingly I have proposed that the matrix of embodied life-metaphors of the therapist and that of the child are engaged in continuous dialectical interactions. As Aron (1996) points out, if treatment follows the assumptions of relational psychoanalysis, "meaning is negotiated and coconstructed. Meaning is arrived at through a meeting of the minds [a child's and therapist's mind]" (p. xii).

Becoming aware of one's body language requires time and effort and is a skill that needs to be practiced (Pruzinsky, 1990; Cash and Pruzinsky, 2002). And while cultivating an awareness of his or her body language, a therapist must determine whether or not his or her matrix of embodied life-metaphors is dancing in the same rhythm as the child's. The issue of rhythmicity between a therapist's matrix and a child's has to do with interpretation. As we discussed in chapter 1, although verbal interpretations are advocated by many child psychotherapists, relational psychoanalysis has introduced a different point of view—that is, that an understanding can be conveyed to a patient through nonverbal actions (Ogden, 1994) and "interaction is in itself interpretive, which is to say it conveys meaning" (Aron, 1996, p. 214). Holinger (1999) has provided an excellent review of discussions concerning the use of "noninterpretive interventions."

Along the same lines, Gaines (1997) encourages child therapists following an interpersonal model to use "indirect interpretations. These include stories, anecdotes, metaphors, visual images and so on" (p. 4). I agree with Gaines but propose that, instead of using these indirect interpretations, a child therapist should, as often as is appropriate and indicated, use what I consider more direct interpretations, namely, physical actions and interactions. My view is similar to Aron's (1996) that an "interpretation is an interpersonal participation. It is an observation from within the interaction rather than from outside of it" (p. 118).

To illustrate, when I silently joined Vera, slowly moving a line of up to 30 toy animals an inch at a time and occasionally anxiously wiggled a toy animal in the line that I was holding, my participation and actions expressed the following interpretation in her language of the moment: "I understand that you must surrender your body-self to this severe regimentation, but you might also want to escape into freedom." And when Ernest rolled the ball out of the cave, and I anxiously scrambled out to retrieve it and return it to him, my actions and participation expressed the following interpretation in his action language of the moment: "You would like to enter the world but it frightens you very much. As you can see, if you do enter, it is possible that you can return safely." Likewise, when I began clearing leaves and twigs from the rill with Thomas, the high school student we discussed earlier, my participation and actions meant: "Something is clogging your mind and emotions. I'm not sure what and why, but we can find a way to clear out what is in your way."

If a therapist is inclined to interpret verbally the meanings the child is experiencing, and the therapist wants to discuss possible connections between these meanings and the child's past and present relationships, I recommend that the therapist make a conscious effort to deemphasize this kind of verbal participation, at least in the early phases of an interaction. Instead, the therapist should express himself or herself in the interactive language the child is using. On the other hand, I also recommend that if a child tends to prefer interacting primarily through verbal discussions, it is useful if initially the therapist joins the child in that mode, as illustrated by the case of Thomas.

From this beginning the therapist attempts to help the child participate in a progression of interrelated interactions: from expressing a linguistic metaphor representing a salient issue with which the child is struggling, to expressing a related fantasy accompanied by microactions, to expressing a fantasy dominated by macroactions, and eventually helping the child move into the body-action lane. The aim of engaging a child in physical enactments, as I noted earlier, is to resolve meanings interfering with the child's development at the embodied level. To the degree that this is accomplished, the child constructs a new embodied self. This new self serves the child throughout the remainder of childhood and during adolescence by continuing to negotiate embodied life-metaphors in human and nonhuman environments in ways that promote development and by recycling developmental issues and needs in the fantasy and language modes. As I have argued, along with other therapists, in many cases it is not necessary to provide a child during treatment with a conceptual understanding of his or her difficulties in order for the child to undergo change.

How Much Time Does It Take for a Child to
Grow a New Self?

In a review of a previous presentation of a model for child psychotherapy (Santostefano, 1998b) in which I attempted to integrate cognitive functioning, behavioral interactions, and fantasy from a psychoanalytic viewpoint, and that I have integrated into the foundation for the model described here, Powell (1999) acknowledges that the model demonstrates theoretical strength and effectiveness as reflected in the treatment cases presented. But he also states, "The biggest problem with the model is the length of time it takes to implement [which is no longer possible because of] managed care" (p. 418). He explains, "[For] the practitioner of today ... four to eight visits is the norm" (p. 415). Powell's point receives support especially from ecopsychotherapists. Burns (1998), for example, describes a patient who was cured by participating in discussing a single fishing trip, and children are reported to have benefited from participating in a wilderness program of several weeks (Williams, 2000). To use the constructivist, organic metaphor of a person as a plant, if a plant cannot grow in 8 to 10 days, then we should not expect a child to grow a new self in 8 to 10 sessions and be able to travel on a new developmental pathway. It would be difficult to imagine that Ernest and Vera, as well as other clinical cases I have sketched, could have overcome their difficulties in 8 to 10 sessions. And I know from experience that there are many other children who need many months to grow a new self.

What Is Your Response to the Claim by
Ecopsychotherapists That Nature Inherently Provides
Pleasure and Heals?

I disagree with ecopsychology's presumption that contact with nature inherently is pleasurable, reduces stress, and promotes well-being. I have proposed that nature forms only one of the four environments implicated in a child's development. Nature becomes a source of pleasure only if it is defined as pleasurable by the landscape at the foundation of all experiences—namely, the child's unique body build, sensory and kinesthetic perceptions, and rhythms of nonverbal, verbal, and emotional dialogues that have been constructing embodied meanings from experiences since the child's first years of life in interactions with the rhythms of dialogue and bodies of others. I have already discussed how these first representations of interactions spiral throughout development and give meaning to the three other landscapes with which the child interacts: persons, attributes of nature, and inanimate objects. Furthermore, the meanings the child constructs from experiences with each of these landscapes become integrated and organized to form the child's matrix of embodied life-metaphors, which influences the meanings the child gives to ongoing interactions and experiences.

Illustrative of the concept of this matrix of metaphors is the anecdote shared by Burns (1998), who, when a child, after being scolded by his mother, felt empowered and reassured whenever he climbed up to a tree house built by his father. In her volume describing a form of no-talk therapy for children, Straus (1999) provides another illustration. She writes, "When I was a kid, restless and in trouble too much of the time, my father took me fishing . . . to a favorite spot . . . and [we would] sit there, rocking in amiable silence . . . we just loved being together. My father didn't know he was the first no-talk therapist in my life" (p. xi). Those early experiences formed the meanings of Straus's matrix of embodied life-metaphors, which, in turn, prompted her to recommend that no-talk therapy involve child and therapist sharing a wide range of pleasurable activities (e.g., growing plants, visiting a nearby park, cooking).

But when a child experiences severe stress while interacting with human and nonhuman environments, the meanings representing these events are also projected into ongoing interactions with persons and nature. Ernest and Vera are convincing examples. How can we understand the sharp difference between my idea that a person can construe nature as dangerous and painful and ecopsychology's notion that nature inherently provides pleasurable experiences and promotes well-being? My thoughts on this question rely on the following piece of history.

When the discipline of human psychology was taking shape, and two years before Freud (1886) wrote that his interests were shifting from neurology to psychology, Sir Francis Galton (1884) surveyed what professionals of the day were doing. He wrote, "There are two sorts of [investigators] . . . those who habitually dwell on pleasanter circumstances . . . and those who have an eye but for the unpleasing ones" (p. 180). One source for his opinion lay in how investigators were using the "free association method" that Galton introduced in Europe (Santostefano, 1976). With this procedure, Galton spoke a word to which the subject responded with the "first word it suggests to you." Reaction times to stimulus words, and the content of associations, were used to study a person's "emotional life."

Galton's free association method was introduced into the United States in 1887 by James McKeen Cattell and immediately captured the interest of behavioral scientists. As it turned out, however, numerous studies supported Galton's opinion that investigators dwell on either pleasant or unpleasant circumstances. Friedrick Lyman Wells (1911, 1912), who was investigating the free association method, reviewed studies by others and observed a trend that disturbed him. In his opinion, too many investigators were avoiding the "unpleasant" task of learning about a person's emotional life by focusing their attention on "more pleasant issues," such as grammatical connections between stimulus words and the words people associated to them. Wells (1912) made clear his frustration:

> Such experiments [of the word association method] lay bare the mental and emotional life in a way that is startling and not always gratifying . . . [so much so that] workers . . . seem to have been effectively blocked from any progress. . . . The psychology of today is very much a science of looking for the truth and hoping you won't find it [p. 346].

When Wells made this statement, Freud (e.g., 1912) was actively pursuing the free association method as applied in treatment sessions. But he was focusing on, rather than avoiding, the "unpleasant" task of learning the "truth" about a person's emotional life, and he was clearly hoping he would find it.

Since the work of Galton, Wells, and Freud, the science of human psychology, according to Ken Wilber (1977, 1979), has been oriented to construe experiences as containing either pleasure or unpleasure. In this regard, it is interesting to note that Jean Piaget acknowledged that he had chosen to focus on the more pleasant topic of cognition. When Decarie (1978) brought to Piaget's attention that, in Piaget's many years of publishing, he seldom referred to emotional processes, Piaget replied, "Freud focused on emotion, I chose intelligence" (p. 183). Piaget gave the reason for his choice in his biography (Campbell, 1977): "I have always detested any departure from reality . . . preferring the study of normalcy and the workings of the intellect over that of the tricks of the unconscious" (p. 116). He also wrote that his choice related to his mother's poor mental health, which had a profound impact on him when he was a child. Ecopsychotherapy, in my opinion, is an example of a school of thought that focuses on pleasurable stimulation while avoiding the "unpleasant" stimulation a person can experience when interacting with nature. Classical psychoanalysis draws the same boundary but represents the other side of the coin; it tends to ignore experiences that bring pleasure while focusing on experiences that cause emotional turmoil.

As I have pointed out, following the assumptions of constructivism, relational psychoanalysis avoids drawing boundaries and embraces a holistic view, integrating a person's representations of past experiences, both pleasurable and stressful, with the meanings the person gives to ongoing interactions and relationships with humans, nature, and inanimate objects. Accordingly, if a child extends traumatic meanings into interactions with the therapist and nature and eventually resolves these meanings, the child can then experience as pleasurable those attributes of nature and people that were originally experienced as unpleasant or frightening. Recall that, at the start of treatment, Ernest experienced pine needles as inflicting intense pain. At the close of treatment, after resolving a constellation of traumatic meanings, he placed his hands and cheeks against the very same pine needles and experienced sensations of warmth and caring.

How Does One Understand Ecopsychology's Assertion That the Alienation Between a Person and Nature Is the More Fundamental Conflict and Must Be Resolved?

Roszack (1995) argues that, whereas conventional psychotherapies seek to heal the alienation within a person or between a person and others, ecopsychology is devoted to healing what he refers to as the "more fundamental alienation" between a person and nature. Similarly, Burns (1998) states that the "disruption of oneness" between a person and nature "leads to illness whether physical or mental" (p. 8). Certainly Ernest, who sat in the cave in silence for many weeks, and

Vera, who barricaded the door to the Therapeutic Garden, are vivid examples of persons alienated from nature. While I agree that treatment should try to heal the alienation between a child's self and nature, I believe it is important that we first define what we mean by this alienation so that we may consider the techniques that are necessary to repair it.

On the basis of my model, I argue that "fundamental" alienation should not be defined as existing between a person and natural environments. Rather, the alienation that is "fundamental" exists within a child's matrix of embodied life-metaphors and among its meanings, representing both traumatic and positive experiences with humans and nature. For example, Ernest was fed, held, and rocked with love by mother and father; consequently he had positive representations of attachment/trust with humans. At the same time, his body-self was assaulted by various painful medical procedures, as well as being disrupted by mother's bouts with depression and lack of responsiveness. Representations of these traumatic experiences within his matrix of embodied life-metaphors collided with and dominated representations of positive interactions, eventually alienating his total psychological landscape/self from humans and nature.

Accordingly, to heal the alienation a child exhibits between himself or herself and human and nonhuman environments, while interacting with the therapist and outdoor environments the child should first be provided opportunities to enact traumatic meanings that are the source of the alienation and to construct solutions. For instance, during the "near–far" enactment, each time Ernest ventured into the world he feared by rolling a ball out of the cave, he internalized my repeatedly returning the ball to the safety of our relationship. And with each desperate escape from the danger of poisoned water, he internalized my guiding us to the safety provided by a cluster of trees. From this initial success, he was able to stand up high on the mount to shoot Styrofoam arrows and run over pathways through bushes and trees pretending he was a train engine, all in the service of developing the assertiveness and competence necessary to cope with the main source of his alienation. He finally penetrated nature and destroyed the danger (Monstro) that he construed the world contained. From this achievement, he projected new interactive meanings into nature. He removed "bad weeds" from the garden, made friends with frogs, sailed leaves down the River of Life, and eventually pressed his cheeks and hands against the same pine needles that had caused him pain but now offered warmth and pleasure. This sequence of behaviors dramatically illustrates that, once Ernest resolved the alienation among traumatic meanings within the landscape of his matrix of embodied life-metaphors, he was able to resolve his alienation from nature.

Discussing therapeutic camping programs for children, Levitt (1991) notes that we still do not understand what is therapeutic about camping and engaging flora and fauna in the wilderness. I have been proposing that a person's relationship with nature is determined by the meanings contained in his or her matrix of embodied life-metaphors that derive from past experiences with significant persons and places and that are metaphorically projected into current experiences. Unlike Searles (1960), who postulated that a kitchen table inherently provides a toddler with a sense of emotional stability, Spitzform (2000), who reports that her patient experienced being attractive when hiking through a national park, and Burns (1998), whose patient overcame anxiety by walking along a river, I argue that these restorative experiences are possible only under certain conditions. Searles's child must have first internalized interactions that occurred at a kitchen table with a caregiver who represented stability during stressful times; Spitzform's and Burns's patients must have walked along a trail or seashore with someone they were attached to and loved. If a child experiences harmony and pleasure when interacting with nature, then the child has already established a sufficient degree of harmony among the embodied meanings within his or her matrix of embodied life-metaphors.

Concluding Comment

On two occasions in this volume I have quoted Erik H. Erikson, a pioneer in psychoanalytic-developmental theory and child psychoanalysis. These particular statements, in my opinion, represent the conceptual transformation that has been taking place within psychoanalysis from a drive-based, one-person model to an intrapsychic-interpersonal, relational, and interactive model. Recall that, discussing his observations of how young children played during psychotherapy sessions, Erikson (1964) stated, "Children . . . need to be induced by systematic interpretation to reconsider, on a more verbal level, the constellations that have overwhelmed them in the past" (p. 265).

Nearly 20 years later, while discussing "infancy and the rest of life" before the first World Congress of Infant Psychiatry held in Cascais, Portugal, in 1980, Erikson revealed that a radical transformation had occurred in his view of the therapeutic process with children. He noted, "As we learned to treat . . . children and their families, we found that [therapeutic] intervention in the widest sense really means involvement [by child and therapist] in the overall dynamic of growing together . . . which alone can heal" (Erikson, 1983, p. 425).

The therapeutic techniques indicated by this conceptual transformation, which defines child and therapist as participating in a relationship and as growing together, are just beginning to be formulated. Only a few years ago, in a discussion of the psychoanalytic-relational point of view, Greenberg (1995) notes, "At this point in our history, technique lags behind conceptualization. The implications of an interactive model of the psychoanalytic process have not yet been fully integrated into our thinking about method" (p. 12). And, discussing relational theory as it applies to technique in child psychotherapy, Altman (1994) has noted, "We need an approach in the psychoanalytic interaction that takes into account both what the child brings and the analyst's input" (p. 393). Altman et al. (2002) state, "With few exceptions the child's psychoanalytic world was, until recently . . . seemly unaffected by the relational turn in the literature" (p. xii).

My intention in this book is to proffer a set of concepts and techniques for child psychotherapy that can guide both child and therapist to grow together to heal the child and enable the child to develop a new self with which the child can interact with human and nonhuman environments in ways that provide a pathway to optimal development. To form a context for my model, and because my focus is conducting therapy in various locations, including a playroom, I have asked you to try on three hats: the hat worn by transactional-environmental psychology, which holds that the unit of study should be the person-in-the-environment; the hat worn by ecopsychology, in which contact with nature heals; and the hat worn by relational psychoanalysis, which emphasizes the dialectical relationship between embodied intrapsychic meanings and interacting and participating in relationships.

Addressing how each of these hats fits the needs of conducting child psychotherapy indoors and outdoors, my model attempts to show how and why relational psychoanalysis is the source of the most heuristic concepts. Diagrammed in Figure 6–1, my model emphasizes

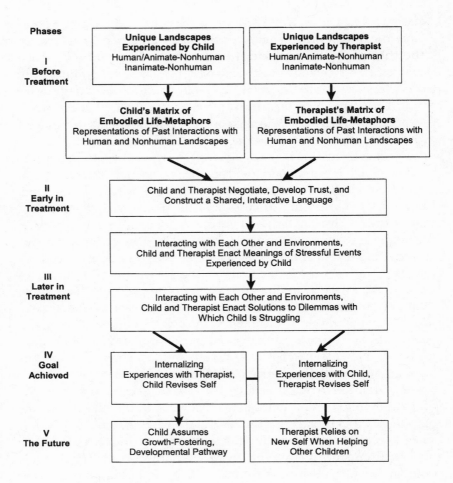

FIGURE 6–1   Summary of a relational model for conducting child psychotherapy.

that interacting with nature and toys does not inherently promote a sense of well-being, but is defined by a child's matrix of embodied life-metaphors, which must be transformed and reorganized. The matrix the child brings to treatment is constructed dialectically during the child's past interactions with human and nonhuman environments and contains traumatic as well as nontraumatic meanings.

Similarly, a therapist brings his or her unique matrix of embodied life-metaphors into the treatment relationship. I have underscored that notion by making the outdoors, offices, and hallways, as well as a playroom, available as locations for treatment. Thus, the child and the therapist have available the widest possible range of environments within which to interact physically and coconstruct a shared interactive language. With the benefit of this shared language, child and therapist can enact traumatic embodied meanings with which the child is struggling as well as solutions to these meanings, which the child can internalize.

One child psychoanalyst has discussed a treatment case to illustrate that adventure outdoors is important in adolescent development (Harrison, 1990). Harrison, however, used the teenager's *description* of an experience as a metaphor to represent obstacles in the way of maturing. The boy described being frightened by a rock he came upon while walking on a path. I have stressed throughout this book that, instead of, or at least in addition to, discussing a child's descriptions of experiences, the child and the therapist should actually walk along a path. By so doing, if the child experiences fear when coming upon a rock, the child is more likely to construct an embodied solution to the meaning of this fear. As the child internalizes the solutions he or she enacts with the therapist, the child's embodied self is revised and a new embodied self emerges. This new self enables the child to interact with human and nonhuman environments in ways that now promote development. The therapist's embodied self is also revised as he or she internalizes enactments experienced during interactions with the child, and the therapist relies on this revised matrix of embodied metaphors in his or her future efforts to help other children.

My model postulates that relational psychoanalysis should consider giving more emphasis in its concepts and techniques to the locations in which child and therapist interact and negotiate. I have defined a relationship not only as between child and therapist (or between child and parents and child and peers) but also in terms of the meaning each person gives to the surrounding location. The partners in these relationships form a unit with the environment in which they are interacting. Accordingly, I have proposed that a relationship should be defined by the matrix of embodied life-metaphors each person introduces into the interaction and relationship, each person giving meaning simultaneously to the other and to the location surrounding them. When integrated, they all form a shared matrix.

Relational psychoanalysis, then, should develop techniques and concepts that address the unit formed by child plus therapist plus location in which they interact. I encourage child psychotherapists to continue wearing the hat of relational psychoanalysis in search of techniques that integrate a child's experiencing-developing self, behaving self, and interpersonal self.

References

Acredolo, L. & Goodwyn, S. (1998), Symbolic gesturing in normal infants. *Child Dev.,* 59:450–466.

Alexander, F. (1950), Analysis of the therapeutic factors in psychoanalytic treatment. *Psychoanal. Quart.,* 19:448–500.

———— (1956), *Psychoanalysis and Psychotherapy: Developments in Theory, Technique and Training.* New York: Norton.

Altman, N. (1994), A perspective in child psychoanalysis 1994: The recognition of relational theory and technique in child treatment. *Psychoanal. Psychol.,* 11:383–395.

———— Briggs, R., Frankel, J., Gensler, D. & Pantone, P. (2002), *Relational Child Psychotherapy.* New York: Other Press.

Anchin, J. C. (2002), Relational psychoanalytic enactments and psychotherapy integration: Dualities, dialectics, and directions: Comment on Frank. *J. Psychother. Integration,* 12:302–346.

Aragno, A. & Schlachet, P. J. (1996), Accessibility of early experience through the language of origin: A theoretical integration. *Psychoanal. Psychol.,* 13:23–24.

Aron, L. (1996), *A Meeting of Minds: Mutuality in Psychoanalysis.* Hillsdale, NJ: The Analytic Press.

———— (1998a), Introduction: The body in drive and relational models. In: *Relational Perspectives on the Body,* ed. L. Aron & F. Anderson. Hillsdale, NJ: The Analytic Press, pp. xxvii–xix.

_____ (1998b), The clinical body and the reflexive mind. In: *Relational Perspectives on the Body,* ed. L. Aron & F. Anderson. Hillsdale, NJ: The Analytic Press, pp. 3–37.

_____ & Anderson, F. S., eds. (1998), *Relational Perspectives on the Body.* Hillsdale, NJ: The Analytic Press.

Bacal, H. A. (1988), Reflections on "optimum frustration." *Learning from Kohut: Progress in Self Psychology,* 4:127–131. Hillsdale, NJ: The Analytic Press.

_____ (1990), The elements of a corrective self-object experience. *Psychoanal. Inq.,* 10:347–372.

Bacant, J. L., Lynch, A. A. & Richards, A. D. (1995), Relational models in psychoanalytic theory. *Psychoanal. Psychol.,* 12:71–87.

Balint, M. (1932), Character analysis and the new beginning. In: *Primary Love and Psycho-Analytic Technique,* enl. ed. London: Tavistock, 1965, pp. 151–164.

_____ (1934), The final goal of psycho-analytic treatment. In: *Primary Love and Psycho-Analytic Technique,* enl. ed. London: Tavistock, 1965, pp. 178–188.

Barnard, R. E. & Brazelton, T. B., eds. (1990), *Touch: The Foundation of Experience.* Madison, CT: International Universities Press.

Beckwith, M. E. & Gilsten, S. D. (1997), The paradise: A model of the garden design for those with Alzheimer's disease. *Activities, Adaptation, Aging,* 22:3–16.

Beebe, B. & Lachmann, F. M. (2002), *Infant Research and Adult Treatment: Co-constructing Interactions.* Hillsdale, NJ: The Analytic Press.

Benveniste, D. (1998), Play and the metaphor of the body. *The Psychoanalytic Study of the Child,* 53:65–83. New Haven, CT: Yale University Press.

Berg, M. & Medrich, E. A. (1980), Children in four neighborhoods. *Environ. & Behav.,* 12:320–348.

Bergman, A. & Lefcourt, I. S. (1994), Self–other action play: A window into the representational world of the infant. In: *Children at Play: Clinical and Developmental Approaches to Meaning and Representation,* ed. A. Slade & D. P. Wolf. New York: Oxford University Press, pp. 133–147.

Bernaldez, F., Gallardo, D. & Abello, R. P. (1987), Children's landscape preferences: From rejection to attraction. *J. Environ. Psychol.,* 7:169–176.

Billow, R. M. (1977), Metaphor: A review of the psychological literature. *Psychol. Bull.,* 84:81–92.

Blackwell, P. L. (2000), The influence of touch on child development: Implications for interventions. *Infants & Young Children,* 13:25–39.

Blaisdell, O. (1972), Developmental changes in action aggression and in fantasy aggression. Unpublished doctoral dissertation, Department of Psychology, Boston University.

Bonaiuto, M. & Bonnes, M. (2000), Social-psychological approaches in environment–behavior studies: Identity theories and the discursive approach. In: *Theoretical Perspectives in Environment–Behavior Research: Underlying Assumptions, Research Problems, and Methodologies,* ed. S. Wapner, J. Demick, T. Yamamoto & H. Minami. New York: Kluwer Academic/ Plenum Press, pp. 67–78.

Burg, J. E. (2000), Adventures in family therapy. *J. Syst. Ther.,* 19:18–30.

Burns, G. W. (1998), *Nature-Guided Therapy: Brief Integrative Strategies for Health and Well-Being*: Philadelphia, PA: Brunner/Mazel.

―――― (2000), When watching a sunset can help a relationship dawn anew: Nature-guided therapy for couples and families. *Austral. & New Zeal. J. Fam. Ther.,* 21:184–190.

Campbell, S. F., ed. (1977), *Piaget Sampler: An Introduction to Jean Piaget Through His Own Work.* New York: Aronson.

Carr, S. C. & Schumaker, J. F., eds. (1996), *Psychology and the Developing Word.* Westport, CT: U.S. Praeges/Greenwood.

Cash, T. F. & Pruzinsky, T., eds. (2002), *Body Image: A Handbook of Therapy, Research and Clinical Practice.* New York: Guilford Press.

Chawla, L. (1992), Childhood place attachments. *Hum. Behav. & Environ.: Adv. Theory & Res.,* 12:63–86.

Chisholm, J. J. (1985), Camping: Serving the total child. *Acad. Ther.,* 21: 205–210.

Chused, J. F. (1991), The evocative power of enactments. *J. Amer. Psychoanal. Assn.,* 19:615–640.

Conn, S. (1998), Living in the Earth: Ecopsychology, health and psychotherapy. *Hum. Psychol.,* 26:179–198.

Coonerty, S. (1993), Integrative child therapy. In: *Comprehensive Handbook of Psychotherapy Integration,* ed. G. Stricker & J. R. Gold. New York: Plenum Press, pp. 413–425.

Coppolillo, H. P. (1987), *Psychodynamic Psychotherapy of Children: An Introduction to the Art and the Techniques.* Madison, CT: International Universities Press.

Davis, D., Ray, J. & Sayles, C. (1995), Ropes course training for youth in a rural setting: "At first I thought it was going to be boring . . . ." *Child & Adolesc. Soc. Work J.,* 12:445–463.

Decarie, T. G. (1978), Affect development and cognition in a Piagetian context. In: *The Development of Affect,* ed. M. Lewis & L. A. Rosenblum. New York: Plenum Press, pp. 183–230.

Demick, J. & Andreoletti, C. (1995), Some relations between clinical and environmental psychology. *Environ. & Behav.,* 27:56–72.

Demos, V. (1992), The early organization of the psyche. In: *Interface of Psychoanalysis and Psychology: Progressing Self Psychology,* ed. J. Barron, M.

Eagle & D. Wolitzky. Washington, DC: American Psychological Association, pp. 200–233.

Drucker, J. (1994), Constructing metaphors: The role of symbolization in the treatment of children. In: *Children at Play: Clinical and Developmental Approaches to Meaning and Representation,* ed. A. Slade & D. P. Wolf. New York: Oxford University Press, pp. 62–80.

Duhl, B. (1999), A personal view of action metaphor: Bringing what's inside outside. In: *Beyond Talk Therapy: Using Movement and Expressive Technique in Clinical Practice,* ed. D. J. Wiener. Washington, DC: American Psychological Association, pp. 79–96.

Dunwell, S. (1997), President's Award of Excellence. *Landscape Arch.,* 87(11):42–47.

Eichler, J. (1971), A developmental study of action, fantasy, and language aggression in latency aged boys. Unpublished doctoral dissertation, Department of Psychology, Boston University.

Ellman, S. J. (1998), Enactment, transference and analytic trust. In: *Enactment: Toward a New Approach to the Therapeutic Relationship,* ed. S. J. Ellman & M. Moskowitz. Northvale, NJ: Aronson, pp. 183–204.

————— & Moskowitz, M., eds. (1998), *Enactment: Toward a New Approach to the Therapeutic Relationship.* Northvale, NJ: Aronson.

Erikson, E. H. (1950), *Childhood and Society,* 2nd ed. New York: Norton.

————— (1964), Clinical observations of play disruption in young children. In: *Child Psychotherapy,* ed. M. Haworth. New York: Basic Books, pp. 246–276.

————— (1983), Concluding remarks: Infancy and the rest of life. In: *Frontiers of Infant Psychiatry,* ed. J. D. Call, E. Galenson & R. L. Tyson. New York: Basic Books, pp. 425–428.

Ewert, A. W., McCormick, B. P. & Voight, A. E. (2001), Outdoor experiential therapies: Implications for TR practice. *Ther. Recreation J.,* 35:107–122.

Fairbairn, W. R. D. (1958), On the nature and aims of psycho-analytic treatment. *Internat. J. Psycho-Anal.,* 39:147–167.

Fast, I. (1992), The embodied mind: Toward a relational perspective. *Psychoanal. Dial.,* 2:389–409.

Fenwick, S. M. (1999), The dreaming Earth: Foundations for a process-oriented approach to ecopsychology. *Dissertation Abstracts International, Section B: The Sciences and Engineering,* 59(10-B), 5565.

Ferenczi, S. (1920), The further development of an active therapy in psycho-analyses. In: *Further Contributions to Theory and Technique of Psycho-Analysis.* London: Hogarth Press, 1969, pp. 198–217.

————— (1931), Child analysis in the analysis of adults. *Internat. J. Psycho-Anal.,* 12:468–471.

————— (1932), *The Clinical Diary of Sándor Ferenczi,* ed. J. Dupont. Cambridge, MA: Harvard University Press, 1985.

Fine, N. M., Coffman, R. & Aubrey, H. (1996), Therapeutic recreation—
What is it all about? In: *Therapeutic Recreation for Exceptional Children: Let
Me In, I Want to Play,* 2nd ed., ed. A. H. Fine & N. M. Fine. Springfield,
IL: Charles Thomas, pp. 3–31.

Flagler, J. & Poincelot, R. P., eds. (1994), *People–Plant Relationships: Setting
Research Priorities.* New York: Food Products Press/Haworth Press.

Flavell, J. H. (1963), *The Developmental Psychology of Jean Piaget.* New York:
Van Nostrand.

Fonagy, P. & Target, M. (2003), *Psychoanalytic Theories: Perspectives from Developmental Psychology.* New York: Brunner-Routledge.

Frank, K. A. (1999), *Psychoanalytic Participation: Action, Interaction, and Integration.* Hillsdale, NJ: The Analytic Press.

———— (2002), The "ins and outs" of enactment: A relational bridge for psychotherapy integration. *J. Psychother. Integration,* 12:267–286.

Freud, A. (1965), *Normality and Pathology in Childhood.* New York: International Universities Press.

Freud, S. (1886), Report on my studies in Paris and Berlin. *Standard Edition,*
1:5–15. London: Hogarth Press, 1966.

———— (1900), The interpretation of dreams. *Standard Edition,* 4 & 5. London: Hogarth Press, 1953.

———— (1912), Recommendations to physicians practising psycho-analysis.
Standard Edition, 12:109–120. London: Hogarth Press, 1958.

———— (1916), Introductory lectures on psycho-analysis. *Standard Edition,*
15:15–239. London: Hogarth Press, 1963.

———— (1923), The ego and the id. *Standard Edition,* 19:12–66. London:
Hogarth Press.

———— (1933), New introductory lectures on psychoanalysis [1932]. *Standard Edition,* 22:5–182. London: Hogarth Press, 1964.

Gaines, R. (1997), Key issues in the interpersonal treatment of children. *Rev.
Interpers. Psychoanal.,* 2:1–5.

Galton, F. (1884), Measurement of character. *Fortnightly Rev.,* 36:179–185.

Gay, P. (1998), *Freud: A Life in Our Time.* New York: Norton.

Gerson, S. (2004), The relational unconscious: A core element of inter-
subjectivity, thirdness, and clinical process. *Psychoanal. Quart.,* 73:63–97.

Gill, M. M. (1984), Psychoanalysis and psychotherapy: A revision. *Internat.
Rev. Psycho-Anal.,* 11:161–179.

———— (1995), Classical and relational psychoanalysis. *Psychoanal. Psychol.,*
12:89–107.

Ginot, E. (1997), The analyst's use of self, self-disclosure, and enhanced integration. *Psychoanal. Psychol.,* 14:365–381.

Goldberg, A. (1987), Psychoanalysis and negotiation. *Psychoanal. Quart.,* 56:
109–129.

Greenberg, J. (1995), Psychoanalytic technique and the interactive matrix. *Psychoanal. Quart.,* 64:1–22.

Harris, A. (1998), Psychic envelopes and senorous baths: Citing the body in relational theory and clinical practice. In: *Relational Perspectives on the Body,* ed. L. Aron & F. S. Anderson. Hillsdale, NJ: The Analytic Press, pp. 39–64.

———— (2004), The relational unconscious: Commentary on papers by Michael Eigen and James Grotstein. *Psychoanal. Dial.,* 14:131–137.

Harris, M. W., Fried, K. L. & Arana, J. (1995), The counter-gang: A program of therapeutic growth for New York City youth. *J. Child & Adolesc. Group Ther.,* 5:201–213.

Harrison, A. M. (1990), Adventure in the outdoors: Its importance in the development of an adolescent boy. *The Psychoanalytic Study of the Child,* 45:317–334. New Haven, CT: Yale University Press.

Harter, S. (1999), *The Construction of the Self: A Developmental Perspective.* New York: Guilford Press.

Hartig, T., Mang, M. & Evans, G. W. (1991), Restorative effects of natural environment experiences. *Environ. & Behav.,* 23:3–26.

Heidegger, M. (1962), *Being and Time.* New York: Harper & Row.

Herzog, T. R., Herbert, E. J., Kaplan, R. & Crooks, C. L. (2000), Cultural and developmental comparisons of landscape perceptions and preferences. *Environ. & Behav.,* 32:323–346.

Hirsch, I. (2000), Observing-participation, mutual enactment, and new classical models. *Rev. Interpers. Psychoanal.,* 4:6–8.

Hoffman, I. Z. (1992), Some practical implications of a social-constructivistic view of the psychoanalytic situation. *Psychoanal. Dial.,* 2:287–304.

Holinger, P. C. (1999), Non-interpretive interventions in psychoanalysis and psychotherapy: A developmental perspective. *Psychoanal. Psychol.,* 16:233–253.

Jacobs, T. J. (1991), *The Use of the Self.* Madison, CT: International Universities Press.

Jaffe, J., Beebe, B., Feldstein, S., Crown, C. L. & Jasnow, M. D. (2001), Rhythms of dialogue in infancy: Coordinated timing and development. *Monographs of the Society for Research in Child Development,* Serial No. 265, Vol. 66, No. 2.

James, W. (1890), *Principles of Psychology.* Chicago: Encyclopedia Britannica.

Jesse, P., Strickland, M. P., Leeper, J. D. & Hudson, C. J. (1986), Nature experiences for hospitalized children. *Children's Healthcare,* 15:55–57.

Johnson, M. (1987), *The Body in the Mind: The Bodily Basis of Meaning, Imagination and Reason.* Chicago: University of Chicago Press.

———— (1993), A culturally sensitive approach to therapy with children. In: *A Comprehensive Guide to Child Psychotherapy,* ed. C. Brems. Boston: Allyn & Bacon, pp. 68–73.

Kaplan, R. & Kaplan, S. (1989), *The Experience of Nature*. Cambridge, England: Cambridge University Press.

Kiewa, J. (1994), Self-control: The key to adventure? Towards a model of the adventure experience. *Women & Ther.*, 15:29–41.

Knell, S. M. (1995), *Cognitive-Behavioral Play Therapy*. Northvale, NJ: Aronson.

Knoblauch, S. H. (1997), Beyond the word in psychoanalysis: The unspoken dialogue. *Psychoanal. Dial.*, 7:491–516.

Kobayashi, N. (1993), Child ecology: A theoretical basis for solving children's problems in the world. *Childhood*, 1:11–25.

Lakoff, G. & Johnson, M. (1999), *Philosophy in the Flesh: The Embodied Mind and Its Challenge to Western Thought*. New York: Basic Books.

Lambie, I., Hickling, L., Seymour, F., Simmonds, L., Robson, M. & Houlahan, C. (2000), Using wilderness therapy in treating adolescent sexual offenders. *J. Sex. Aggress.*, 5:99–117.

Lear, J. (1990), *Love and Its Place in Nature: A Philosophical Interpretation of Freudian Psychoanalysis*. New York: Farrar, Straus & Giroux.

Levine, D. (1994), Breaking through barriers: Wilderness therapy for sexual assault survivors. *Women & Ther.*, 15:175–184.

Levitt, I. (1991), Recreation for the mentally ill. In: *Benefits of Leisure*, ed. B. L. Driver, P. J. Braun & G. L. Peterson. State College, PA: Venture.

Lewis, C. A. (1994), The evolutionary importance of people–plant relationships. In: *People–Plant Relationships: Setting Research Priorities*, ed. J. Flagler & R. P. Poincelot. New York: Food Products Press/Haworth Press, pp. 239–254.

Lichtenberg, J. D. (1989), *Psychoanalysis and Motivation*. Hillsdale, NJ: The Analytic Press.

London, P. (1964), *The Modes and Morals of Psychotherapy*. New York: Holt, Rinehart & Winston.

Mahl, G. F. (1987), *Explorations in Nonverbal and Vocal Behavior*. Hillsdale, NJ: Lawrence Erlbaum Associates.

Maroda, K. J. (1998), Enactments: When the patient's and analyst's pasts converge. *Psychoanal. Psychol.*, 15:517–535.

Mattson, R. H. (1992), Prescribing health benefits through horticulture activities. In: *The Role of Horticulture in Well-Being and Social Development: A Natural Symposium*, ed. D. Relf. Portland, OR: Timber Press, pp. 161–168.

Maurer, R. & Baxter, J. C. (1972), Images of the neighborhood and city among Black-, Anglo-, and Mexican-American children. *Environ. & Behav.*, 4:351–387.

Mayes, L. C. & Cohen, D. J. (1993), Playing and therapeutic action in child analysis. *Internat. J. Psycho-Anal.*, 74:1235–1244.

McLaughlin, J. T. (1991), Clinical and theoretical aspects of enactment. *J. Amer. Psychoanal. Assn.*, 39:595–614.

Merkl, K. (1995), Ecopsychology: Exploring psychological aspects of our relationship to nature. *Dissertation Abstracts International, Section B: The Sciences and Engineering, 56,* 3455.

Mitchell, S. A. (1988), *Relational Concepts in Psychoanalysis: An Integration.* Cambridge, MA: Harvard University Press.

———— (1991), Wishes, needs and interpersonal negotiations. *Psychoanal. Inq.,* 11:147–170.

———— (1994), Recent developments in psychoanalytic theorizing. *J. Psychother. Integration,* 4:93–103.

Modell, A. H. (1995), Discussion of article on relational psychoanalysis. *Psychoanal. Psychol.,* 12:109–114.

Moore, R. C. (1990), *Childhood's Domain: Play and Place in Child Development.* Berkeley, CA: MIG Communications.

Mueller, U. & Overton, W. F. (1998), How to grow a baby: A reevaluation of image-schema and Piagetian action approaches to representation. *Hum. Dev.,* 41:71–111.

Muleski, M. (1974), Play and the hospitalized child. *J. Leisurability,* 1:22–27.

Nahum, J. P. (1994), New theoretical vistas in psychoanalysis: Louis Sander's theory of early child development. *Psychoanal. Psychol.,* 11:1–20.

Ogden, T. H. (1990), *The Matrix of the Mind.* Northvale, NJ: Aronson.

———— (1994), *Subjects of Analysis.* Northvale, NJ: Aronson.

Orians, G. H. & Heerwagen, J. H. (1992), Evolved responses to landscapes. In: *The Adapted Mind: Evolutionary Psychology and the Generation of Culture,* ed. J. H. Barkow & L. Cosmides. New York: Oxford University Press.

Ortony, A., ed. (1979), *Metaphor and Thought.* New York: Cambridge University Press.

———— Reynolds, R. E. & Arter, J. A. (1978), Metaphor: Theoretical and empirical research. *Psychol. Bull.,* 85:919–943.

Ousset, P. J., Nourhashemi, F., Albarede, J. L. & Vellas, P. M. (1998), Therapeutic gardens. *Arch. Gerontol. Geriatr.,* Suppl. 6, pp. 369–372.

Overton, W. F. (1994a), The arrow of time and the cycle of time: Concepts of change, cognition, and embodiment. *Psychoanal. Inq.,* 5:215–237.

———— (1994b), Contexts of meaning: The computational and the embodied mind. In: *The Nature and Ontogenesis of Meaning,* ed. W. F. Overton & D. S. Palermo. Hillsdale, NJ: Lawrence Erlbaum Associates, pp. 1–18.

———— (1997), Beyond dichotomy: An embodied agent for cultural psychology. *Cult. & Psychol.,* 3:315–334.

———— (1998), Relational-developmental theory: A psychology perspective. In: *Children, Cities and Psychological Theories: Developing Relationships,* ed. D. Gorlitz, H. J. Harloff, J. Valsiner & G. Mey. New York: de Gruyer/Mouton, pp. 73–102.

———— (2004), Embodied development: Ending the nativism–empiricism debate. In: *Nature and Nurture: The Complex Interplay of Genetic and*

Environmental Influences on Human Behavior and Development, ed. C. Garcia Coll, E. Beaver & R. Lerner. Mahwah, NJ: Lawrence Erlbaum Associates, pp. 201–223.

Owens, P. E. (1988), Natural landscapes, gathering places, and prospect refuges: Characteristics of outdoor places valued by teens. *Children's Environ. Quart.,* 5:17–24.

Paley, J. P. & Alpert, J. A. (2003), Memory of infant trauma. *Psychoanal. Psychol.,* 20:329–347.

Piaget, J. (1952), *The Origins of Intelligence in Children.* New York: Norton.

———— (1973), The affective unconscious and the cognitive unconscious. *J. Amer. Psychoanal. Assn.,* 21:249–266.

Powell, D. H. (1999), A review of a handbook of integrative therapies for children and adolescents. *J. Psychother. Integration,* 9:415–419.

Pruzinsky, T. (1990), Somatopsychic approaches to psychotherapy and personal growth. In: *Body Images: Development, Deviance and Change,* ed. T. F. Cash & T. Pruzinsky. New York: Guilford Press, pp. 296–315.

Purcell, A. T., Lamb, R. J., Peron, E. M. & Falchero, S. (1994), Preferences for landscape. *J. Environ. Psychol.,* 14:195–209.

Rachman, A. W. (1997), *Sándor Ferenczi: The Psychotherapist of Tenderness and Passion.* Northvale, NJ: Aronson.

Reckling, A. E. & Buirski, P. (1996), Child abuse, self-development and affect regulation. *Psychoanal. Psychol.,* 13:81–89.

Reiser, M. (1990), *Memory in Mind and Brain.* New York: Basic Books.

Relf, D., ed. (1992), *The Role of Horticulture in Human Well-Being and Social Development: A National Symposium.* Portland, OR: Timber Press.

Renik, O. (1993), Analytic interaction: Conceptualizing technique in light of the analyst's irreducible subjectivity. *Psychoanal. Quart.,* 62:466–495.

———— (1998), The role of countertransference: Enactment in a successful clinical psychoanalysis. In: *Enactment: Toward a New Approach to the Therapeutic Relationship,* ed. S. J. Ellman & M. Moskowitz. Northvale, NJ: Aronson.

Rigazio-Diglio, S. A., Goncalves, O. F. & Ivey, A. E. (1996), From cultural to existential diversity: The impossibility of psychotherapy integration within a traditional framework. *Appl. & Prevent. Psychol.,* 5:235–247.

Riordan, R. J. & Williams, C. S. (1998), Gardening therapeutics for the elderly. *Activities, Adaptation, Aging,* 12:103–111.

Roszak, T. (1992), *The Voice of the Earth.* New York: Simon & Schuster.

———— (1995), The greening of psychology: Exploring the ecological unconscious. *Gestalt J.,* 18:9–46.

Rozhdestvenskaya, V. I. & Pavlova, A. I. (1967), *Outdoor Games for the Stuttering Preschool Child.* Moscow: Prosveshchenie.

Safran, J. D. (2002), Relational theory, constructivism, and psychotherapy integration: Commentary on Frank. *J. Psychother. Integration,* 12:294–301.

Sako, T. (1997), Big school, small school revisited: A case study of a large-scale comprehensive high school based on the campus plan. In: *Handbook of Japan–United States Environment–Behavior Research: Toward a Transactional Approach,* ed. S. Wapner, J. Demick, Y. Takiji & T. Takahashi. New York: Plenum Press, pp. 273–282.

Sander, L. W. (1962), Issues in early mother–child interaction. *J. Amer. Acad. Child Psychother.,* 3:141–166.

———— (1964), Adaptive relationships in early mother–child interaction. *J. Amer. Acad. Child Psychiat.,* 3:231–264.

———— (1987), A 25-year follow up: Some reflections on personality development over the long term. *Infant Ment. Health J.,* 8:210–220.

———— (1989), Investigations of the infant and its caregiving environments as a biological system. In: *The Course of Life,* 2nd ed., ed. S. I. Greenspan & G. H. Pollack. Madison, CT: International Universities Press, pp. 359–391.

Santostefano, S. (1965a), Construct validity of the Miniature Situations Test: I. The performance of public school, orphaned, and brain-damaged children. *J. Clin. Psychol.,* 21:418–421.

———— (1965b), Relating self-report and overt behavior: The concepts of levels of modes for expressing motives. *Percept. Motor Skills,* 21:940.

———— (1968), Situational testing in personality assessment. In: *International Encyclopedia of the Social Sciences,* ed. D. L. Sills. New York: Macmillan/Free Press, pp. 48–55.

———— (1970), Assessment of motives in children. *Psychol. Rep.,* 26:639–649.

———— (1976), Tell me the first word that comes to mind: The free association method and the concept of levels of expressing motives. *McLean Hosp. J.,* 1:174–189.

———— (1977), Action, fantasy and language: Developmental levels of ego organization in communicating drives and affects. In: *Communicative Structures and Psychic Structures,* ed. N. Freedman & S. Grand. New York: Plenum Press, pp. 331–356.

———— (1978), *A Biodevelopmental Approach to Clinical Child Psychology, Cognitive Controls and Cognitive Control Therapy.* New York: Wiley.

———— (1985), Metaphor: An integration of action, fantasy, and language in development. *Imagination, Cognition, & Personality,* 4:127–146.

———— (1988), Process and change in child therapy and development: The concept of metaphor. In: *Organizing Early Experience: Imagination and Cognition in Childhood,* ed. D. Morrison. Amityville, NY: Baywood Press, pp. 139–172.

———— (1991), Coordinating outer space and inner self: Reflections on developmental psychopathology. In: *Constructivist Perspectives on Developmental Psychopathology and Atypical Development,* ed. D. P. Keating & H. Rosen. Hillsdale, NJ: Lawrence Erlbaum Associates, pp. 11–40.

_____ (1994), The arrow of time and developmental psychopathology. *Psychol. Inq.,* 5:248–253.

_____ (1995), Embodied meanings, cognition and emotion: Probing how three are one. In: *Rochester Symposium on Developmental Psychopathology, Vol. 6: Emotion, Cognition and Representation,* ed. D. Cicchetti & S. L. Toth. Rochester, NY: University of Rochester Press, pp. 59–132.

_____ (1998a), Cycles in the life of one psychotherapist. In: *Why I Became a Psychotherapist,* ed. J. Reppen. Northvale, NJ: Aronson, pp. 237–248.

_____ (1998b), *A Handbook of Integrative Psychotherapies for Children and Adolescents.* Northvale, NJ: Aronson.

_____ (1999), A psychodynamic approach to treating attention deficit/hyperactivity disorder: Recent developments in theory and technique. In: *Understanding, Diagnosing, and Treating AD/HD in Children and Adolescents: An Integrative Approach,* ed. J. A. Incorvia. Northvale, NJ: Aronson, pp. 319–365.

_____ & Berkowitz, S. (1976), Principles of infant development as a guide in the psychotherapeutic treatment of borderline and psychotic children. *McLean Hosp. J.,* 1:236–261.

_____ & Calicchia, J. (1992), Body image, relational psychoanalysis, and the construction of meaning: Implications for treating aggressive children. *Dev. & Psychopathol.,* 4:655–678.

_____ Rieder, C. & Berk, S. (1984), The structure of fantasized movement in suicidal children and adolescents. *J. Suicide & Life-Threatening Behav.,* 14:3–16.

_____ & Wilson, S. (1968), Construct validity of the Miniature Situations Test: II. The performance of institutionalized delinquents and public school adolescents. *J. Clin. Psychol.,* 24:355–358.

Schiavo, R. S. (1988), Age of differences in assessment and use of a suburban neighborhood among children and adolescents. *Children's Environ. Quart.,* 5:4–9.

Scott, M. E. (1998), Play and therapeutic action. *The Psychoanalytic Study of the Child,* 53:94–101. New Haven, CT: Yale University Press.

Searles, H. F. (1960), *The Nonhuman Environment in Normal Development and in Schizophrenia.* New York: International Universities Press.

Simson, S. P. & Straus, M. C. (1998), *Horticulture as Therapy: Principles and Practice.* New York: Food Products Press/Haworth Press.

Slade, A. (1994), Making meaning and making believe: Their role in clinical process. In: *Children at Play: Clinical and Developmental Approaches to Meaning and Representation,* ed. A. Slade & D. P. Wolf. New York: Oxford University Press, pp. 81–107.

Smith, N. R. (1979), Developmental origins of structural variation in symbol formation. In: *Symbolic Functioning in Children,* ed. N. R. Smith & M. B. Franklin. Hillsdale, NJ: Lawrence Erlbaum Associates, pp. 11–26.

_____ & Franklin, M. B., eds. (1979), *Symbolic Functioning in Children*. Hillsdale, NJ: Lawrence Erlbaum Associates.

Solnit, A. J. (1998), Beyond play and playfulness. *The Psychoanalytic Study of the Child*, 53:102–110. New Haven, CT: Yale University Press.

Spezzano, C. (1995), "Classical" vs. "contemporary" theory: The differences that matter clinically. *Contemp. Psychoanal.*, 31:20–40.

Spiegel, S. (1989), *An Interpersonal Approach to Child Therapy: The Treatment of Children and Adolescents from an Interpersonal Point of View*. New York: Columbia University Press.

Spitzform, M. (2000), The ecological self: Metaphor and developmental experience? *J. Appl. Psychoanal. Stud.*, 2:265–285.

Stamm, I. & Barber, A. L. (1978), The nature of change in horticultural therapy. Directors '78 Proceedings of 6th Annual Conference, National Council for Therapy and Rehabilitation Through Horticulture, pp. 11–16.

Stein, L. K. (1997), Horticultural therapy in residential long-term care: Applications from research on health, aging, and institutional life. *Activities, Adaptation, & Aging*, 22:107–124.

Stern, D. N. (1985), *The Interpersonal World of the Infant: A View from Psychoanalysis and Developmental Psychology*. New York: Basic Books.

_____ Sander, L., Nahum, T., Harrison, A., Lyons-Ruth, K., Morgan, A., Bruschweiler-Stern, N. & Tronick, E. (1998), Non-interpretive mechanisms in psychoanalytic theory. *Internat. J. Psycho-Anal.*, 79: 903–921.

Stern, S. (2002), Identification, repetition, and psychological growth: An expansion of relational theory. *Psychoanal. Psychol.*, 19:722–738.

Stoops, J. W. (1974), The assessment of aggression in children: Arguments for a multimodal approach. Unpublished doctoral dissertation, Department of Psychology, Kent State University, Kent, OH.

Straus, M. B. (1999), *No-Talk Therapy for Children and Adolescents*. New York: Norton.

Summers, F. (2001), What I do with what you give me: Therapeutic action as the creation of meaning. *Psychoanal. Psychol.*, 18:635–655.

Swanson, J. (1995), The call for Gestalt's contribution to ecopsychology: Figuring in the environmental field. *Gestalt J.*, 18:47–85.

Teeple, J. R. (1989), An experiential outdoor family therapy program in the treatment of child and adolescent psychiatric in-patients. *Dissertation Abstracts International, 49*, 3460.

Toronto, E. L. (2001), The human touch: An exploration of the role and meaning of physical touch in psychoanalysis. *Psychoanal. Psychol.*, 18: 37–54.

Ulrich, R. S. & Parsons, R. (1992), Influence of passive experience with plants in individual well-being and health. In: *The Role of Horticulture in*

Human Well-Being and Social Development: A Natural Symposium, ed. D. Relf. Portland, OR: Timber Press, pp. 93–105.

van der Kolk, B. A. (1996), The body keeps the score: Approaches to the psychology of posttraumatic stress disorder. In: *Traumatic Stress: The Overwhelming Experience on Mind, Body, and Society,* ed. B. A. van der Kolk, A. C. McFarlane & L. Weisaeth. New York: Guilford Press, pp. 214–241.

Van Waning, A. (1991), Then be the best or not to be, that is the question: On enactment, play and acting out. *Internat. J. Psycho-Anal.,* 72:539–550.

Verbrugge, R. R. & McCarrel, N. S. (1977), Metaphoric comprehension: Studies in reminding and resembling. *Cogn. Psychol.,* 9:454–533.

Wachtel, P. L. (1987), *Action and Insight.* New York: Guilford Press.

Walder, R. (1933), The psychoanalytic theory of play. *Psychoanal. Quart.,* 2:208–224.

Walzholz, M. (2003), Flower power: How gardens improve your mental health. *The Wall Street Journal,* August 26.

Wapner, S. (1995), Toward integration: Environmental psychology in relation to other subfields of psychology. *Environ. & Behav.,* 27:3–32.

_____ & Demick, J. (2000), Assumptions, methods, and research problems of the holistic, developmental, systems-oriented perspective. In: *Theoretical Perspectives in Environment–Behavior Research: Underlying Assumptions, Research Problems, and Methodologies,* ed. S. Wapner, J. Demick, T. Yamamoto & H. Minami. New York: Kluwer Academic/Plenum Press, pp. 7–19.

_____ _____ Yamamoto, T. & Takahashi, T., eds. (1997), *Handbook of Japan–United States Environment–Behavior Research: Toward a Transactional Approach.* New York: Plenum Press.

Wells, F. L. (1911), Some properties of the free association method. *Psychol. Rev.,* 18:1–23.

_____ (1912), The association experiment. *Psychol. Bull.,* 9:435–438.

Wells, J. A. (1998), A study of people's attitudes toward plants. *Dissertation Abstracts International, Section B: The Sciences and Engineering, 59,* 2.

Werner, C. M. & Altman, I. (2000), Humans and nature: Insights from a transactional view. In: *Theoretical Perspectives in Environment–Behavior Research: Underlying Assumptions, Research Problems, and Methodologies,* ed. S. Wapner, J. Demick, T. Yamamoto & H. Minami. New York: Kluwer Academic/Plenum Press, pp. 21–37.

Werner, H. (1948), *Comparative Psychology of Mental Development.* New York: International Universities Press.

_____ (1957), The concept of development from a comparative and organismic point of view. In: *The Concept of Development: An Issue on the Study of Human Behavior,* ed. D. Harris. Minneapolis: University of Minnesota Press, pp. 125–148.

_____ & Kaplan, B. (1963), *Symbol Formation: An Organismic-Developmental Approach to Language and the Expression of Thought.* New York: Wiley.

White, R. (1998), Psychiatry and ecopsychology. In: *The Environment and Mental Health: A Guide for Clinicians,* ed. A. Lundberg. Mahwah, NJ: Lawrence Erlbaum Associates, pp. 205–212.

Wiener, D. J., ed. (1999), *Beyond Talk Therapy: Using Movement and Expressive Techniques in Clinical Practice.* Washington, DC: American Psychological Association.

Wilber, K. (1977), *The Spectrum of Consciousness.* London: Theosophical Publishing House.

_____ (1979), *No Boundary: Eastern and Western Approaches to Personal Growth.* Boston: Shambhala.

Williams, B. (2000), The treatment of adolescent populations: An institutional vs. a wilderness setting. *J. Child & Adolesc. Group Ther.,* 10:47–56.

Wilson, A. (1995), Mapping the mind in relational psychoanalysis: Some critiques, questions and conjectures. *Psychoanal. Psychol.,* 12:9–29.

Witzum, E., van der Hart, O. & Friedman, B. (1988), The use of metaphors in psychotherapy. *J. Contemp. Psychother.,* 18:270–290.

Wolfe, B. E. (2003), Knowing the self: Building a bridge from basic research to clinical practice. *J. Psychother. Integration,* 13:83–95.

Woodward, A. L. & Sommerville, J. A. (2000), Twelve-month-old infants interpret action in context. *Psychol. Sci.,* 11:73–77.

Woolley, H. & ul Amin, N. (1995), Pakistani children in Sheffield and their perception and use of public open spaces. *Children's Environ. Quart.,* 12:479–488.

Wortham, S. C. & Worthman, M. R. (1989), Infant/toddler development and play: Designing creative play environments. *Childhood Educ.,* 65: 295–299.

Yunt, J. (2001), Jung's contribution to an ecological psychology. *J. Hum. Psychol.,* 41:96–121.

Index

About the Author

After completing training in child and adult psychoanalysis in 1972, Sebastiano Santostefano, Ph.D., ABPP served as Director of the Department of Child and Adolescent Psychology and Psychoeducation, Hall Mercer Center of McLean Hospital, and as Associate Professor of Psychology, Department of Psychiatry, Harvard Medical School. In 1993, he founded the Institute for Child and Adolescent Development, a nonprofit organization that treats children who have endured trauma, trains mental health professionals, and conducts research. Dr. Santostefano is the author of seven previous books, among them *Integrative Psychotherapies for Children and Adolescents with ADHD* (1995) and *A Handbook of Integrative Psychotherapies for Children and Adolescents* (1998).